Women in Management

Women in Management

Laurie Larwood
Claremont Men's College

Marion M. Wood
University of Southern California

Lexington Books
D. C. Heath and Company
Lexington, Massachusetts
Toronto

Library of Congress Cataloging in Publication Data

Larwood, Laurie.
    Women in management.

    Bibliography: p.
    Includes index.
    1. Women executives—United States.   2. Executive ability.
I. Wood, Marion M., joint author.   II. Title.
HF5500.3.U54L37   331.4'81'658400973   76-27033
ISBN 0-669-00973-3

Published simultaneously in Canada

Printed in the United States of America

International Standard Book Number: 0-669-00973-3

Library of Congress Catalog Card Number: 76-27033

Contents

List of Tables

Introduction

Most books are subject only to a narrow range of interpretation. The effect on readers of selecting one interpretation in preference to similar alternatives is generally modest. In consequence, it is rarely, if ever, that an author finds it necessary to suggest that the material must be treated with caution. This book is that exception, however; it is important that the reader understand in advance both the nature of the alternative interpretations and their potential impact.

Women in Management is an unusual book in that it deals with an unsettled and highly explosive political issue—one in which the application of partial information and individual biases is capable of producing highly destructive results. Management—the combined activities of planning, decision making, and directing others—is by tradition and definition a function delegated solely to males in American society. If women are also well-suited for management (a personal belief of the authors), then it becomes important for us to determine why more women are not presently in management, how women can obtain management positions, and how society can prevent the present tragic waste of womanpower from continuing. If the answers can be found and if they are implemented, the entire nature of our society will be altered. If, conversely, women are unsuited for management (a position taken aggressively by many of the author's professional colleagues), then our society must stop arousing women's ambitions for managerial success. Although society has, so far, largely ignored such ambitions, acceptance of the latter position demands that the "revolution of expectations" be stopped before any further personal damage and dissatisfaction occurs.

Those readers who have open minds should weigh the evidence for both positions before taking such actions as seem appropriate. Attempts have been made to facilitate this process by presenting the evidence in a straightforward manner; uncommitted readers will find that much of this material can be interpreted in at least the two ways mentioned. It should be recognized, however, that the authors' personal preferences inevitably have had some effect on the presentation of material, just as the reader's biases influence acceptance of it.

Intentions

One of the purposes of this book, then, is to examine the evidence useful to resolving the question of whether women are suited for management. The statistical basis for a decision often appears neutral, however. Evidence shows, for example, that women having equal education and experience do not earn as much as do men in comparable tasks. Although they are revealing, such findings do not conclusively support either extreme point of view. An individual who believes that women are not adapted to outside employment can reason that women are somehow incapable of performing well and that they are therefore paid less. Opponents can offer the interpretation that women are widely discriminated against in terms of salary.

A review of certain anthropological, sociological, and psychological studies provides the insight needed to correctly interpret the statistical evidence. Continuing the previous example, we may note that a woman's role traditionally has been defined differently from that of a man, with the result that her expectational, experiential, and reward histories differ from his. Few women consider management positions, generally accepting more passive vocations instead. In consequence, society is organized in such a way as to expedite the advancement of male managers while dismissing even the possibility of female managers. Because of the disadvantages with which she must contend, it may be questioned whether the statistically underpaid female manager is in fact worth the same salary as is her unencumbered male counterpart. While the reader need not necessarily come to the same conclusions, a complete analysis of the evidence suggests that women are as capable in management as are men under equal conditions. The conditions are, however, anything but equal.

A second overall question that is addressed is also one for which no ready answer exists: how can a woman best enter and succeed in management? Management makes certain demands of a social and personal nature that may not be as frequently encountered in traditional "feminine" occupations. In response, the woman entering management must decide the extent and the types of demands she is willing to accept. She may then determine the strategy that best applies her particular skills and interests.

This study emphasizes the need for the reader to develop an individualized personal strategy closely fitted to her specific requirements. Although women as a group have special problems in obtaining management positions, every individual woman has her own best solutions for handling her unique situation. The special problems of women should be recognized in the solutions, and the solutions should be tailored to the situation. Nonetheless, the solutions must make personal sense as well. The woman who has entered management but who has found herself uncomfortable in her new position has not succeeded after all.

Organization

Women in Management may be divided conceptually into three major sections. Chapter 1 is concerned with the statistical description of women's employment, salaries, and education. Some international and historical comparisons are provided as well, which demonstrate the extent to which the experience of American women can be considered universal.

Interpretive analysis of the way in which the present situation developed and of what the development means to women is found primarily in the second section. Chapter 2 discusses the system of role norms that stereotype behavior. Masculine and feminine roles are examined to determine their degree of "fit" and "conflict" with the role of manager. The usual definition of a manager is primarily a masculine one. However, the individual tasks involved in management are not strongly associated with either sex unless they are observed operating in the context of the managerial role. It is conformity to sex and work roles, rather than the examination of task abilities and preferences, which largely determines traditional aspirations.

Chapter 3 examines the development of specific traditions more closely. Anthropological data indicate that a sexual division of labor probably developed in response to rational needs, including those of hunting food and bearing children. The recent extension of that division of labor into modern technologically based society, where it may not longer have a discernable rational basis, is open to some criticism.

The psychological effects of this extension are explored in Chapter 4. One of the arguments offered is that the different patterns of training often result in the formation of different concepts of appropriate reward and different types of experience for women in contrast to men. Not only is each sex likely to prefer different work situations, each is also likely to react differently to similar situations. Moreover, the reactions of both men and women are interpreted as being different in socially stereotyped ways as a result of the role training of the observer—even when the reactions are in fact the same.

Together the first two sections should give the reader an understanding of the problems of women in management and an insight into the social forces that produced those problems. The third section is intended to suggest specific means by which ambitious women can enter management and rise in it to the full extent of their capabilities. Chapter 5 examines the personal impact of being a woman manager. The effect of a woman's presence in management may, for example, produce profound changes in the employee-employer relationship. The specific changes depend to a large extent on the personalities and situations involved and on the ways in which the woman chooses to deal with them.

Chapter 6 treats the reader's potential choices in greater detail. Although four major strategies for entering and advancing in management are discussed, emphasis is placed on the development of a personal strategy synthesized from the components of the situation and consistent with the reader's personal goals. Moving beyond the personal perspective, Chapter 7 is concerned with altering the conditions surrounding management's present "masculine bias." No radical new ideas are required to produce revolutionary opportunities for women entering management—but firm application of existing programs is urgently needed. A brief final summary reviews some of the general points discussed in this book and suggests some major trends that may affect the situation of women in management in the near future.

The Question of Discrimination

Despite the lack of intention to do so, any examination of the condition of working women will discover a number of instances of apparent sexual discrimination. Although the term has recently carried the connotation of deliberate political and economic exploitation of one sex for the advantage of the other, the denotative meaning is quite innocent. Sexual discrimination refers to the process of responding differently to the members of each sex.

Rather than necessarily signaling deliberate manipulation, discrimination may be unconscious and a genuine response to real or imagined differences between the sexes. For example, a firm in a highly technical area may discriminate against the hiring of women as managers due to the observation that previous women had been uninterested in the technology and had failed to repay training costs. Such a decision may be viewed as illegal discrimination. It is certainly unfair to the woman who is genuinely interested in the position. Nonetheless, the discrimination in this example has some root in fact and may make good economic sense to the employer.[1]

The problem of discrimination is not one of finding and labeling it—that task is relatively simple. The problem is one of finding the reasons for discrimination and treating those reasons. The employer in the example will attempt to discriminate as a matter of self-interest unless we can make the social changes necessary for potential female managers to be perceived (correctly) as favorably as potential male managers are now. An understanding of the situation and of its causes is prerequisite to the elimination of discrimination and to the advancement of women in management.

Note

1. A complete discussion of the concept of economic discrimination may be found in G. S. Becker, *The Economics of Discrimination*. Chicago: University of Chicago Press, 1971.

Part I: Statistics

In classifying the population, one of the simplest distinctions we can make is between those persons who are working and those who are not. The distinction implies an easy split between persons who are aggressively propelling themselves toward success and others who are unwilling or unable to do so.

When this differentiation is applied to women rather than to men, however, such images disintegrate. Those who do not work are often separated from those who do by differences in their family situations and in their acceptance of traditional cultural values rather than by their willingness to work. Those who do choose to work must overcome serious social barriers to their success. Those differences make it unlikely that the average woman will succeed—despite her best efforts—in reaching the top ranks in her vocation—and particularly unlikely that she will be applauded for the attempt.

The statistics of Part I present only a descriptive portrait of women in the workforce; analysis of the portrait's meaning is left for Part II. The description itself will probably not seem unusual, as all the statistics are available from other published sources. It is the magnitude of the problems faced by women in the labor force that may seem surprising.

Part I was written by Laurie Larwood.

1

Women at Work

As well as we can tell, women have been working, just as men have, from the beginnings of the human race. The extent and type of the contributions made by either sex have varied considerably, however, depending on the nature of the economy and on the cultural traditions of the particular society. Thus the pattern of work done by each sex in present-day America represents only one of the many possibilities. The United States in the 1970s has no more a "natural" division of labor than had Japan in the 1870s.

If there is no single example of the natural division of labor, it is at least possible to compare statistics between sets of working conditions and across various periods of time. Many such comparisons will be made in this chapter. While revealing, the resulting cultural trends must be handled with care. Trends are ephemeral; they may change suddenly with differences in a variety of underlying variables. For instance, women lost many of their recent employment gains in the 1974–1975 business cutback. Yet we would hesitate to project this trend beyond that minidepression or to project it to other nations that do not depend on raw material imports.

This chapter first examines the overall characteristics of the female work force. Marital and family characteristics each profoundly influence the likelihood of a woman's participation in the work force. Other differences between the male and female segments of the workforce are in education, job preference, and quit rates. Later sections of this chapter focus on the characteristics of those jobs that are held by women. Women concentrate in lower-level positions and are generally paid less than men, irrespective of their positions. In both the managerial positions and the professional and technical positions often leading to management, the preferential employment of men is preceeded by differences in education. Not surprisingly, men and women achieve somewhat different patterns of job and life satisfaction as a result of their vocational differences. The final section of this chapter briefly compares the position of working women in the United States with that of their European counterparts.

Characteristics of the Workforce

Women make up over half of the population of working age Americans, but they constitute only 40 percent of the workforce. The lower representation of women in the workforce suggests that different conditions surround the employment of female workers. This section focuses on the reasons why women—for different

3

reasons than men—enter the labor force, while the next section is concerned primarily with the conditions faced by women after they have entered the labor market.

Family Characteristics

In American society, many men unquestionably work because they believe they must do so to support themselves and, if they are married, to support their family. The man who fails to support his family may be seen by his family and himself as a social failure. In fact, evidence shows that many persons of both sexes see men as failures if their wives work outside the home, irrespective of whether or not the women have any pressing economic need to do so.

In consequence, we would expect to find that the highest percentage of male workers is in that group having a family. Similarly, the highest percentage of female workers should be found in that group which is not able to be supported in any way by a family (Jusenius, 1976). The statistics confirm this hypothesis. The woman who does not marry had an average working life in 1970 identical to that of men and seven years longer than that of her sister who marries but who has no children (Fullerton and Byrne, 1976). As of March 1974, differences in likelihood of employment were still strongly correlated with the marital situation. As Table 1–1 shows, a high proportion of married men work outside the home, while a relatively high proportion of married women do not. The long-term trend, however, seems to be in the direction of a flattening of these differences. A comparison of the figures in Table 1–1 between the two years (which are fairly

Table 1–1
Percentage of Persons Employed (16 Years and Older)

Category	March 1973	March 1974
Men		
Average	78.4%	78.2%
Married, Wife Present	84.8	83.9
Married, Wife Absent	79.1	80.1
Widowed[a]	31.5	34.6
Divorced	78.4	80.0
Single	66.1	67.1
Women		
Average	44.1%	45.2%
Married, Husband Present	42.2	43.0
Married, Husband Absent	52.4	55.2
Widowed[a]	25.2	24.8
Divorced	71.4	72.9
Single	55.8	57.2

Source: Data in Hayghe (1975).
[a]Widowed persons are likely to be older than others.

consistent with other recent years) shows that the portion of married men who are working is decreasing relatively, while the similar portion of married women who are working is increasing relatively.

Another important factor influencing the likelihood of a woman joining the labor force is her status as a parent. In general, a woman is most likely to work before she marries (especially before she has children) and again after her children reach adolescence. Twenty-four percent of all employed women in 1970 (both married and single, aged twenty-five years and older) were not employed five years earlier, compared to a 6 percent rate for men. The comparable rates for married persons aged twenty-five to forty-four were 36 percent and 8 percent (Fuchs, 1974). The lifetime working pattern for women thus tends to be "M" shaped, with the M tending to rise and to flatten in recent years as more women have preferred to work irrespective of children and as the size of families has decreased. Some of the differences in womens' employment coincident with children can be clearly seen in Table 1–2.

Quit Rates and Absenteeism

Since many women leave work temporarily in favor of starting a family, it is not surprising that the rates of job quitting are higher for women than for men. In a

Table 1–2
Percentage of Women Employed (by Family Characteristics)

Category	March 1970	March 1974
Average	40.8%	43.0%
Women 16-24 years old		
No children under 18	67.0%	72.3%
Children under 18 (Average)	32.5	36.5
6-17 years old (none under 6)	49.4	60.5
3-5 years old (none under 3)	44.7	43.7
Children under 3	29.6	34.1
Women 25-34 years old		
No children under 18	72.7%	77.7%
Children under 18 (Average)	35.3	40.5
6-17 years old (none under 6)	51.6	56.6
3-5 years old (none under 3)	37.2	40.2
Children under 3	23.9	30.0
Women 35 and older		
No children under 18	36.8%[a]	35.2%[a]
Children under 18 (Average)	44.8	46.8
6-17 years old (none under 6)	48.6	49.8
3-5 years old (none under 3)	34.1	34.5
Children under 3	22.4	25.6

Source: Data in Hayghe (1975).

[a]Many of the women in this group are mothers with grown children

recent study, Barnes and Jones (1973) showed that women do leave their jobs more frequently than men on an *industry* basis. That is, if we ignore the fact that women usually hold different positions from those held by men, the women in most industries are more likely to change jobs or to leave the labor force entirely than are men (Table 1–3). The ratio of men to women becomes more closely balanced during times of economic expansion. Barnes and Jones note that expansion periods allow a male who quits to find a new job—an especially important criterion for someone expecting to remain in the labor force for a long period at a high rate of pay. The quit rate for women is less influenced by economic cycles. This finding is in agreement with the generally higher unemployment rates for women (8.8 percent in November 1976 versus 7.6 percent for males); the result might also be predicted from the lower pay scales for women, which will be discussed later in this chapter. Thus changing jobs is both more difficult and less remunerative for women than for their male counterparts.

In contrast, the rate of womens' absenteeism seems to approximate that for men. The U.S. Department of Labor in 1971 calculated that women lost an average of 5.9 days per year for absenteeism and illness, while men lost 5.2 days (*Women's Bureau Bulletin,* 1971). Other studies indicate that women actually lose somewhat less time than do men (*Issues in Industrial Society,* 1971). The result appears admirable in view of the demands of child care as well as the lower job quality and salaries to which women are differentially subjected.

Education

Large numbers of women are still considered to be transients in the workforce, persons for whom better jobs are relatively unimportant. It may therefore be expected that women will be given less rigorous (and less expensive) preparation for employment. Table 1–4 shows that proportionately fewer women workers completed four years of college than men. The statistics also reveal something

Table 1–3
Ratio of Men's to Women's Quit Rates (1964–1968)

Industry	Ratio
Food	.786
Textiles	1.233
Apparel	.993
Chemicals	.571
Petroleum	.434
Electrical Machinery	.682

Source: Data in Barnes & Jones (1973).

Note: This ratio is between all men and all women working in an industry irrespective of the position held.

Table 1-4
Education of the Workforce (March 1973)

Years of Schooling	less than 8	8	9-11	12	13-15	16 or more
			% of Group			
Women	3.9	5.2	16.7	46.7	14.6	13.0
Men	7.0	7.1	17.8	36.5	15.0	16.7
Women/Men	.56	.73	.94	1.28	.97	.78

Source: Data in Waldman and McEaddy (1974).

more, however. More women (74.3 percent) than men (68.2 percent) completed high school. While the average education of the members of each sex in the work force does not differ remarkably, the education of men is much more variable than that of women. Those males who do complete high school are much more likely than similar females to complete college as well. Following the bachelor's degree, men are still more likely to go on to graduate school for an advanced degree (see Table 1–5).

The importance of an education may be understood when it is recognized that those having a better education are more likely to obtain and keep interesting and high-paying jobs than are those without. Some without education are unable to obtain a satisfactory position, while others who have no interest in a good position probably don't bother with an education. In either event, those having the education find their efforts rewarded. Table 1–6 shows the predictable relationship of education to unemployment and employment participation rates. Both men and women are more likely to be working full time and to be earning more if they have a better education. Although complete figures are slow in coming in, it

Table 1-5
Share of College and University Degrees Earned by Women

Year	All Degrees	Bachelor's	Master's	Doctorate
1900	16.9%	19.7%	19.1%	6.0%
1910	22.7	22.7	26.4	9.9
1920	33.7	34.2	30.2	15.1
1930	39.5	39.9	40.4	15.4
1940	40.5	41.6	38.3	13.0
1950	24.4	23.9	29.2	9.7
1960	34.2	35.3	35.1	10.5
1970	40.4	41.5	39.7	13.3
1975	44.6	45.4	44.8	21.3

Source: Data for 1900-1970 in Blitz (1974); 1975 data are calculated from "Earned degrees conferred 1974-1975," published by the National Center for Education Statistics. Note that the series change may have relatively inflated 1975 figures.

appears that the relative employment value of an education was heightened by the 1974–1975 recession.

A more unusual relationship is also apparent in Table 1–6: men earn nearly twice what women earn at every educational level (actually $11,835 versus $6,772 in 1974). The percentage gap between a man's and a woman's income has been steadily increasing; the difference is still greater for workers over forty-years-old than for younger workers (Sommers, 1974). Although it is tempting to conclude that deliberate pay discrimination exists, such conclusions should be reached with care. A woman leaving the labor force temporarily, as well as career disinterest on her part, may account for some of the remarkable differences in income. Moreover, the differences reported in Table 1–6 are accumulated across educational disciplines, and men and women often study in different areas. A woman who has studied home economics in high school may not be as readily employable as a man who has studied auto mechanics. The importance of these effects in producing differences in income are considered in other sections of this chapter.

Where Women Work—Industries and Unions

Some additional major differences between the female and male segments of the workforce can be seen in terms of the industries in which they work. On the whole, women are more likely to be found in service industries (40.9 percent of working women in March 1973) than are men (18.2 percent) and are less likely to be found in mining and construction (1.2 percent versus 11.2 percent) or in manufacturing (19.4 percent versus 30.3 percent) than are men. Overall, the industries in which women are concentrated (and the firms within those industries— Jaquette, 1976) are those in which the average pay is relatively low. Average weekly pay in the service industries in January 1973 was $111; in the mining, construction, and manufacturing industries respectively, pay was $190, $223, and $159 per week.

Table 1–6
Relationship of Education to Employment (March 1973)

			Income		
Education	*Unemployment Rate*	*% in Workforce*	*Male*	*Female*	*F/M*
11 years or less	8.6%	32%	$ 7,575	$4,305	.57
12 years	5.3	51	10,075	5,770	.54
4 years of college	2.7	61	14,660	8,925	.61

Source: Data in Waldman and McEaddy (1974).
Note: Data represent 1972 median income.

The service industries are among the least unionized; across all industries, men are 2.7 times more likely than women to belong to a union (Raphael, 1974). In general, membership in a union may exert some force in the direction of equal wages for women; however, the impact of union membership bears no simple relationship to wages. Among white-collar workers in 1970, unionized men earned 80 percent more than unionized women, while nonunionized men earned 180 percent more than nonunionized women. For blue-collar workers, unionized men earned 100 percent more, while nonunionized men earned 90 percent above nonunionized blue-collar women.

Job and Employment Characteristics

The statistics suggest questions as to whether women are doing, or are capable of doing, the same types of work as men are. Are male and female white-collar workers in service industries doing the same activity, for example? If the woman works as a secretary, and the man performs as her boss, the normal workings of the economic pyramid dictate that the man earn more. That is, the superior normally earns more than the subordinate. Since a woman is less likely to remain in the workforce for an extended period of time and is less likely to have a college education, her subordination to a male manager seems particularly likely. This section describes some of the characteristics of the positions held (or not held) by women.

Differences in Types of Positions Held

Half of all working women can be found in just twenty-one occupations, while over a quarter of them have one of only five occupations (secretary, retail sales, household worker, bookkeeper, elementary school teacher). In contrast, the Bureau of Labor Statistics reports that only a seventh of male workers are concentrated in the largest five occupations, and half are spread among 65 of 423 possible male occupations (Sommers, 1974).

Although recent years have seen some increase of women in the higher-paid professional and technical employment categories, the proportion seems barely able to keep pace with the overall growth in the number of working women. Thus examination of Table 1–7 shows that an increase of women in the labor force of 38 percent from 1960 to 1970 was accompanied by an increase of 22 percent for woman managers but a rise of 55 percent for clerical workers. The proportionate increase of women in management was outpaced by the increase of women in low-level subordinate positions. It would seem that women's liberation has yet to produce meaningful occupational diversity for working women.

Government grade scales give another indication of the concentration of

Table 1–7

Employment of Women in Major Occupations

	Women as a % of All Workers		
Occupation	1960	1970	% Change in Number
Blue-Collar			
Craft and associated	3.1%	5.0%	+79%
Operatives	28.0	30.5	+21
Nonfarm Laborers	5.2	8.4	+56
White-Collar			
Professional, Technical	38.4	39.8	+61
Managerial, Administrative	14.7	16.5	+22
Sales	35.6	38.0	+21
Clerical	68.0	73.5	+55
Service, Farm Workers			
Private Houshold	96.4	96.6	–37
Other Service	51.5	54.9	+49
Farmers and Managers	4.7	4.6	–47
Laborers	16.7	15.2	–43
Total (with occupations not reported above)	32.8	37.7	+38

Source: Data in Hedges & Bemis (1974).

women in very few, and often low-paying, activities. As shown by Table 1–8, a high proportion of the women employed by government are in low-paying entry level jobs (GS 1 to GS 4). By contrast, the highest-level executive positions (GS 12+) are almost exclusively held by men. As with other areas of employment, the cause of these differences is not readily apparent without more information. The dominance of upper government service levels by men may in part be the result of the interest, effort, and constancy of men, as well as of better educational qualifications.

Pay Scales

The economics of supply and demand specify that an abundant supply of employees will result in competition for positions, thereby keeping wages low. Vocations chosen most frequently by prospective employees, or most easily entered by them, will therefore pay less, other factors being equal. The wages given to unskilled workers will normally be lower than those given to skilled workers (assuming a cost to workers or employers for the acquisition of education and skill). Moreover, as noted previously, lower wages may be given to those workers who expect to be employed only temporarily, while higher wages are required to recruit and retain experienced employees. Fuchs (1974) has calculated in this regard that an 18 percent earnings increment is given to workers of comparable

Table 1-8

Women in Federal Employment (October 31, 1970)

GS Level[a]	Number of Women	% Women of Total
1	2,900	68
2	18,600	36
3	86,300	78
4	139,700	63
5	191,700	32
6	65,100	48
7	54,000	38
8	12,400	26
9	43,400	24
10	3,900	12
11	19,300	12
12	9,900	7
13	4,600	5
14	1,800	4
15	900	3
16+	200	2

Source: Data in Waldman and McEaddy (1974) from "Study of employment of women in the federal government, 1970." U.S. Civil Service Commission, Bureau of Manpower Information Systems.

[a]Higher GS levels carry higher authority and higher salary.

sex, color, age, and education who were at work five years earlier in contrast to the wages of those who were not.

In comparing the wages of part-time receptionists with full-time executives, then, we would have no difficulty in predicting a considerable difference in earnings. In contrast, if a firm were carefully keeping count, it would find that the labor market "should" favor female executives. In the absence of discrimination, the labor market should be concerned only with the aggregate number of qualified persons for a particular type of job. Nonetheless, discrimination against women is often quite blatant, as is shown in this chapter. Under such conditions, the labor market for men may operate somewhat independently of that for women. Similarly, the "Affirmative Action" rulings have in some rare cases been sufficient to place a premium on women. (Affirmative Action will be discussed in the final part of this book.) Women in executive positions are in relatively short supply: less than 17 percent of executives are female (see Table 1–7). Moreover, since the extent of education correlates highly with participation rates of women in the workforce, educated women executives have nearly the same number of years of experience as men in comparable positions do. It "should" therefore be possible to find women in those positions earning at least as much as their male counterparts—and more, if scarcity of executive talent were measured by sex. Table 1–9, however, shows that they do not. Even when experiential and educational factors are the same, as in the construction industry, women are at a salary

Table 1-9

Characteristics of Specific Occupations (1970 Census)

Category	Sex	% of Whole	Median Earnings	% Employed Full Year	Education (Years)
Salaried Managers and Administrators					
Durable goods manufacturing	M	96.5	$14,829	92.5	14.1
	F	3.5	7,989	83.7	12.7
Nondurable goods manufacturing	M	93.8	14,028	91.8	13.9
	F	6.2	6,847	79.1	12.6
Finance, insurance, and real estate	M	85.4	13,322	90.3	15.1
	F	14.6	6,669	82.3	12.7
Construction	M	98.2	12,795	84.8	12.5
	F	1.8	9,344	83.2	12.5
Communication, utilities, and sanitary services	M	89.3	12,741	93.0	13.0
	F	10.7	7,174	83.6	12.7
Wholesale trade	M	95.4	12,464	91.4	12.9
	F	4.6	7,268	78.3	12.7
Maids and Servants	M	3.4	1,631	49.2	8.9
	F	96.6	1,093	45.3	8.8
Busboys	M	85.9	943	20.6	10.8
	F	14.1	925	22.2	10.9

Source: Data in Sommers (1974).

disadvantage. Women in construction management earn only 73 percent of the salary earned by men. In fact, a wage differential between men and women is even apparent for the lowest-paid classifications, which Table 1-9 provides for comparison. Sommers (1974) found that of the 391 comparable occupations examined for men and women, only one, public kindergarten teaching, had a wage differential favoring women rather than men.

National probability samples of 1500 working men and women collected by University of Michigan researchers (Levitin, Quinn and Staines, 1971; Staines, Quinn, and Shepard, 1976) give further weight to these results. The researchers controlled for occupational prestige, supervisory responsibility, length of employment, tenure with employer on present job, and number of hours worked and education. Based on 1969 data, the women surveyed received a mean income $4,372 less than that of men; after removal of the control factors *the difference was still $3,458,* this difference changed only by 1 percent in the period between 1969 and 1973. Using men's wages as the criterion, the women studied "should" have received wages 71 percent higher than they did (Table 1-10).

Table 1-10
Women in Selected Categories Earning \$3500 (or More)
Less than Comparable Men and Discrimination Awareness[a]

Category		1969	1973
Race	White	43.7% (9.4%)	44.3% (16.4%)
	Black	28.2 (2.6)	42.1 (13.8)
Age	16-29	41.7 (9.2)	44.4 (18.7)
	30-44	33.3 (10.5)	35.5 (18.4)
	45-54	40.9 (4.8)	49.5 (12.8)
	55+	65.9 (7.0)	48.5 (12.1)
Skill	White-collar	50.5 (11.7)	46.5 (20.3)
	Blue-collar	25.7 (1.9)	39.6 (10.4)
Occupation	Managerial, professional, and technical	68.4 (13.5)	48.6 (26.9)
	Clerical and sales	40.8 (10.8)	45.4 (16.3)
	Operatives	21.7 (1.7)	38.3 (12.0)
	Service	29.8 (2.2)	37.8 (5.4)
Occupational prestige	High	50.7 (11.5)	46.5 (20.4)
	Medium	23.8 (5.3)	51.3 (16.3)
	Low	29.8 (2.4)	33.8 (8.7)
Industry group	Manufacturing	27.3	
	Wholesale, retail	65.8	
	Finance, insurance, and real estate	63.3	
	Service	57.4	
Union membership	Member	36.9	
	Nonmember	56.1	
Firm employment	49 or less	58.4	
	50-499	55.9	
	500+	34.8	

Source: Industry group, union membership, and firm employment data from Levitin, Quinn, and Staines, based on a 1969 national probability sample. This table from "Sex Discrimination Against the American Working Woman," by Teresa Levitin et al. is reprinted from *American Behavioral Scientist,* (Nov./Dec.) 1971, *15*, (2), 248 by permission of the publisher, Sage Publications, Inc. All other data are from Staines, Quinn and Shepard based on a 1973 sample and a reanalysis of the 1969 data. (Staines, G. L., Quinn, R. P., and Shepard, L. J. "Trends in occupational sex discrimination: 1969–1973." *Industrial Relations*, 1976, *15*, 88–98. Reprinted with permission.) Sample criteria and category definitions differ somewhat between the two surveys; numbers in parentheses are the percent of the category who are aware of discrimination.

[a]Figures in parens represent discrimination awareness.

Significantly, although there was some evidence of financial discrimination against 95 percent of the women surveyed, only 8 percent reported knowing of employment discrimination in 1969; this figure had risen only to 16 percent in a

1973 personal interview. Most women had apparently failed to notice that their wages were lower, had accepted the discrepancy as normal, or were afraid to report it.

Managerial, Professional, and Technical Employment

Clearly, women earn less than men do in managerial positions. Only a part of the earnings gap between men and women is explained by general influences, such as education, which have already been examined. The concentration (and the potential oversupply) of women in a few fields may be one reason for the lower wages paid in those fields, but the "law of supply and demand" can do nothing to explain the low pay of women in such nontraditional areas as the managerial, professional, and technical vocations.

In part, it seems that the very scarcity of women in some fields contributes to the lower incomes of the women who are in them. A shortage of individuals of either sex allows the job to be stereotyped as inappropriate for that sex (Chapters 2–4 will deal with stereotyping in greater detail). In consequence, those men who aspire to be nurses and secretaries, and those women who would like to become college professors and corporation executives, must battle the fact that their doing so is incongruous with the prevailing norm. A nurse or secretary is, by definition, a female, while an executive is a male. When an incongruous stereotype causes employers or others to feel a lack of confidence in an employee, it may greatly impair the employee's ability to handle the necessary tasks and to succeed in a particular field. Thus too few persons of one's own sex in a particular vocation may be as dangerous as too many.[a]

This section examines in some detail the success of women in entering the managerial, professional, and technical vocations—areas in which the number of women has traditionally been very small. It may be speculated that a woman who enters a field in which the overall proportion of women is small enters a field in which women are presently unwelcome. Unfortunately, trend data on the managerial, professional, and technical fields often provide an unsatisfactory test of hypotheses, since information is meager and different investigations have used different definitions of these fields.

Combining across all classifications, Blitz (1974) found that there has been little change in the proportion of women in these fields since the turn of the century (Table 1–11). While women have greatly increased their proportion of the total labor force during the period, they have not made any important headway in

---

[a]Another side to this argument also exists. The lack of women in a profession may sometimes be accompanied by a lack of institutionalized discrimination for women who are able to enter the profession and who are able to demonstrate that they are not stereotypic. In such professions, barriers may be such as to prevent all but the unusual woman from entering, and to thereafter reward the truly exceptional woman with an almost discrimination-free environment.

Table 1-11
Women in Managerial, Professional, and Technical Vocations

| | Womens' Share of Total | |
Year	Labor Force	Managerial, Professional, and Technical Vocations
1870	14.8%	27.5%
1880	15.2	32.1
1890	17.2	35.1
1900	18.3	34.2
1910	19.9	41.2
1920	20.4	44.1
1930	22.1	44.4
1940	24.3	41.3
1950	28.0	39.3
1960	32.7	38.1
1970	37.8	40.8

Source: Data in Blitz (1974), and from private communcation with Dr. Rudolph C. Blitz.

the professions. However, it must be recognized that the share of women in the managerial, professional, and technical vocations was double their proportion in the overall workforce in the early part of this century. Thus further progress would have been extraordinary. In tracking specific professions within the managerial, professional, and technical group (where data were available), Blitz found that those having the lowest initial percentage of women (5 percent or less in 1870) showed the greatest percentage increases, while other vocations generally failed to show overall trends. The lack of apparent improvement in the position of women over a seventy-year period may thus be due in part to the large weights attached to professions, such as elementary teaching, which absorbed 38 percent of all women in 1890 but which decreased in importance thereafter even while remaining an almost exclusively female occupation.

Data for managerial classifications have been disaggregated from other data in Table 1-12 (which applies different class definitions from those of Table 1-11). In substantial agreement with the previous table, the proportion of women engaged specifically in managerial, professional, and technical activities has not improved in half a century.

The Question of Education Revisited

Some observers such as Blitz have suggested that the lack of growth (relatively speaking) of the number of women in the managerial, professional, and technical vocations is a direct reflection of the apparent hesitation of women in obtaining appropriate college degrees. More particularly, women seem to have a statistical

Table 1–12
Proportion of Women Workers to Total in Selected Vocations

| | Vocations | | |
| | Managers, Officials, and | | |
Year	Proprietors	Professional and Technical	Clerical
1900	n.a.[a]	8.2%	n.a.
1910	n.a.	9.9	n.a.
1920	n.a.	11.8	n.a.
1930	n.a.	14.2	n.a.
1940	3.8%	13.2	21.2%
1950	5.5	10.8	26.4
1960	3.5	12.5	29.1
1969	4.2	14.3	34.0

Source: Data in Bernard (1971), pp. 123, 124. Reprinted by permission from Jessie Bernard *Women and the Public Interest* (Chicago, Aldine Publishing Company); copyright © 1971 by Jessie Bernard.
[a]n.a. indicates consistent information is not readily available for this series.

reluctance to enter either undergraduate or advanced programs in areas such as business administration, which would allow them to advance professionally. In choosing between a young man with an MBA (Master of Business Administration degree) and a young woman with a bachelors degree in fine arts, most employers agree that they will enthusiastically endorse the man on the principle of economic self-interest. Some questions are raised by this assertion, however. Do women really tend to obtain different types of college degrees from those awarded to men (nonprofessional as opposed to professional)? If they do, is this the result of a preference on the part of such women? Finally, do women with the same professional credentials as men have equal employment prospects subsequent to graduation? The overall educational pattern has been discussed in the first section to this chapter; it is now necessary to specifically examine the managerial, professional, and technical employment sectors.

Women accounted for 16.4 percent of the bachelor's degrees awarded in Business Administration in 1975 according to the National Center for Education Statistics. This figure is inflated by nearly 10 percent however because many collegiate programs, like those in high schools, still maintain a secretarial program into which women are directed. Worse, the secretarial track prevents many women from obtaining a bachelor's degree at all. For example, a typical two-year community college in New York offers courses in secretarial science and bookkeeping for women but introductory accounting and general business for men. Unless they enter a strong complaint, business students are automatically shunted in these separate directions. The men's courses, however, are later transferrable to four-year college business programs if desired; the women's courses usually are not.

At the graduate level, Robie (1973) found that the Harvard business school graduated 29 women (3.8 percent) in a class of 754 MBA's in 1971, while the University of Chicago graduated just 7 in a class of 280 (2.5 percent). Figures compiled by the National Center for Education Statistics indicate that 8.4 percent of management-related master's degrees went to women in 1975. In the same year, women constituted just 41 (4.0 percent) of those receiving management Ph.D.'s in this country. These figures are considerably below women's share of overall advanced college degrees (see Table 1–5) but are not disproportional with those in other professional and technical fields. However, it should be noted that many business schools have seen a sharp upturn in the enrollment of women in the past few years. For example, the number entering the Stanford Graduate School of Business tripled from 1972 to 1975. The generality and significance of this apparent trend are still uncertain.

Persons with degrees in technical and professional fields are often able to enter management by virtue of their expertise. An examination of the figures for education in these fields shows that the percentage of women obtaining degrees has recently been increasing somewhat (Table 1–13). At the time of writing, women constituted less than 15 percent of overall degree recipients in medicine and law. It appears, however, that these figures can be expected to rise in the late 1970s. By 1974, women made up 23.3 percent of incoming law students, 22.0 percent of beginning medical students, and 6.3 percent of new engineering students (Parrish, 1975).

Of course, managerial, professional, or technical degrees are only necessary when others competing in the labor market already have them. In the absence of such competition, persons without special degrees can still obtain top positions. As the previous statistics (see Table 1–6) have shown, however, competition does exist—the employment market pays a premium for education. A college degree, and preferably an advanced degree, increases the likelihood that the

Table 1-13
Proportion of Women to Total Earning Specialized Degrees

Year	Architecture	Engineering	Law	Medicine
1960	3.3%	.4%	2.7%	5.9%
1962	3.2	.4	3.2	5.8
1964	3.9	.5	3.2	6.3
1966	4.6	.4	3.9	7.2
1968	4.5	.6	4.3	8.6
1970	5.5	.8	5.9	9.3
1975	9.5	1.3	15.1	13.1

Source: Data for 1960–1970 in Parrish (1974) from the U.S. Office of Education; 1975 data are calculated from "Earned degrees conferred 1974–1975," published by the National Center for Education Statistics. Note that the series may have relatively inflated 1975 figures.

holder will enjoy professional success and high earnings. Unfortunately, as may be seen in Table 1–5, the higher the degree, the less likely women are to obtain it. This difference between men and women is exceptionally great for degrees in fields leading to management.

How do men and women use the technical or scientific degrees they possess? The vocational distribution for persons with scientific educations appears in Table 1–14. Men are more likely to apply their training in management, while women are proportionately more likely to teach (primarily in secondary schools). It may be noted parenthetically that of those women who obtain doctorates and teach in universities, only a small number ever reach the highest university rank.

Education and Discrimination

Women do fail to acquire advanced degrees in the managerial, professional, and technical areas, then. There is every reason to assume that this failure partly accounts for the lower positions, lower pay, and limited number of vocations that women generally occupy. In asking why women do not have such degrees and whether additional barriers might stand in the way of the potential success of those who do, we are partly anticipating later chapters of this book. However, some consideration of this topic is useful toward reaching a full understanding of the situation of women anticipating managerial positions.

Table 1-14
Type of Employer and Work Activity of Scientists

	Men	Women
Type of Employer		
Education	27%	48%
Government	17	16
Nonprofit	4	8
Industry, Self-employed	46	20
Other	6	8
	100%	100%
Work Activity		
Research, Development, and Design	35%	37%
Management	24	6
Teaching	15	29
Other	26	28
	100%	100%

Source: Data from 1962 National Register of Scientific and Technical Personnel, in Rossi, A.S. "Barriers to the career choice of engineering, medicine, or science among American women." In J. A. Mattfeld and C. G. Van Aken (eds.), *Women and the scientific professions.* Cambridge, Mass.: M.I.T. Press, 1965. Reprinted with permission.

No doubt, many women feel uncomfortable with nontraditional education and vocations, and many are advised or prefer to become homemakers or to enter the more usual "feminine" professions. For the women who are interested in entering "masculine" fields, however, equality of performance with men turns out to be insufficient to assure success in obtaining admission to schools and to later employment: women must be demonstrably better than competing males. For reasons that will be discussed later, less than superior performance on the part of a woman is often perceived as confirmation of the anticipated stereotyped behavior. The stereotype holds that women are inferior to men in managerial and scientific skills.

There is considerable evidence of the need for women to be superior in order to achieve an average position. Rossi (1965) found that high school grades and admission test scores of women who later became medical doctors were significantly higher than the similar scores of male physicians. Lunneborg and Lillie (1973) found evidence of sexism in college admission recommendations ("I found her acting much more as a very competent secretary than as an independent scholar. Of course this is not entirely unexpected considering the sex and age relationship"). Another study found that all 240 American universities examined discriminated against women applicants of average ability or less, although no difference was found in the admission of members of either sex having high ability (The Spokeswoman, 1970). There is reason to believe that admissions discrimination is slackening in some disciplines (Parrish, 1975), but it no doubt still exists in others.

Once in college, women tend to have higher drop-out rates than do men. A recent study of psychology doctoral students does much to explain some of the reasons for the high rates. Brodsky (1974) found that a large percentage of women (19 percent versus 1 percent for men) selected their program due to their lover's association with it; 12 percent of the women (32 percent of the men) said they were in the field due to its income potential. Thus women's reasons for being in school differ somewhat from those of men, and the drop-out rate may be one result. Other factors are also important, however. Forty percent of the women (12 percent of the men) reported faculty discrimination against them. In critical areas of preparation, the women found themselves deserted by the faculty: 19 percent were invited on consulting or convention trips (35 percent of the men), 41 percent were offered paper authorship (52 percent of the men), 19 percent were introduced to outside scholars (34 percent for men), and 23 percent were given the opportunity to teach (36 percent for men). These results are not necessarily the product of deliberate discrimination. There is every likelihood that the opportunities for interaction with predominantly male faculty members differ as a result of the relatively low number of mutual interests between female students and male faculty. Nonetheless, such wide and consistent differences are gravely suspect of at least unconscious faculty discrimination. What is worse, they cannot help but alter the quality of the education received.

After the Education

Can a woman find employment after obtaining her degree? It has already been noted that women are likely to be paid less than men even after accounting for educational differences. The actual probability of finding a position differs similarly. Fidell (1970) surveyed 228 American colleges and universities with regard to the suitability for employment of 10 hypothetical psychologists. The bogus candidates were randomly identified by either a masculine or feminine first name. Results clearly showed that women were more often selected for the lower rank of assistant professor, while men were more often selected for the higher rank of associate professor.

In a similar study, Rosen and Jerdee (1974) asked male undergraduate business students to take the role of a consultant to a firm that was attempting to fill four managerial positions having varying requirements. After evaluating identical candidates randomly identified by name as either male or female, the students accepted 59 percent of the "female" candidates and 71 percent of the "male" candidates. The degree of discrimination was more extensive when the job was described as demanding (females: 46 percent acceptance; males: 65 percent) than when it was described as routine (females: 72 percent; males: 76 percent). In general, the female candidates were described as having significantly lower technical expertise, lower likelihood of long service, and a smaller potential for "fitting-in" than were males.[b]

In summary, the studies reported here show that the managerially, scientifically, and technically trained woman is exceptional. She is not only rare, but she probably possesses somewhat greater ability than a male of equal education and training. Nonetheless, the woman is likely to encounter some difficulty in obtaining appropriate education if she desires it and considerable difficulty in finding a challenging position thereafter. With the exception of those professions dominated by women (such as elementary school teaching), it may be concluded that success is extraordinarily difficult for most women to obtain in the areas leading potentially to high-management positions.

Job and Life Satisfaction

In general, studies have found that the job and life satisfaction of workers are positively correlated with one another despite a wide variety of vocations and life situations (Levitin and Quinn, 1974). Employees who are more satisfied with their lives are also generally those who are more satisfied with their jobs. How-

---

[b]The reader may note that these studies show, beyond a shadow of a doubt, that much discrimination does exist that is in no way connected with the behavior of individual women. In general, real-life situations are not as pure and simple to assess as are experimental situations, however.

ever, channeling a woman into a position different from her preferences and beneath her capabilities might be expected to result in a lower degree of job satisfaction. A woman who occupies a dead-end job cannot be expected to find satisfaction with her position unless she has no ambition for advancing beyond it. Since only the ambitious can be stifled, it follows that the more educated women in higher positions would be least able to relate their jobs to their total life satisfaction.

In a confirming study discussed earlier, Levitin, Quinn, and Staines (1971) found that women who were more discriminated against (vis-à-vis men) in terms of either wages or working conditions were also more dissatisfied with their jobs. Kavanagh and Halpern's (1977) investigation of the relationship between job and life satisfaction among university employees found a generally positive correlation for both men and women. However, at the highest job level (supervision of faculty), the relationship vanished for women, but not for men. The pattern supports the notion that the most capable women may find their ambitions stifled by discrimination. The women apparently reacted by disconnecting job from life satisfaction; that is, refusing to allow their jobs to greatly influence their life-styles. Thus when the quality of employment is poor relative to expectation and ability, women are less likely to associate job and life satisfaction.

The goals men have for their lives are often more closely linked to their jobs than are those of women. In Table 1–15 nearly 10 percent more of the men than of the women felt that their jobs were instrumental in obtaining various life goals for themselves. In summary, then, the research suggests that women can be as interested and as involved in their jobs as men are. However, conditions that prevent a woman from enjoying equal advantages may, to the extent that the woman is aware of them, serve either to make her dissatisfied with her job or to make her look elsewhere for life satisfaction. In general, women place less emphasis on their jobs as a vehicle for obtaining life goals—a finding consistent not only with discrimination but with the role of the woman as homemaker as well as worker.

Table 1–15
Proportion Agreeing That Life Goals Are Strongly Contingent on How Well They Do Present Jobs

Goal	Men	Women
Happy home life	57.0%	49.1%
Spending old age as you please	53.9	44.4
Being able to do what you like	49.8	39.3
Happy social life	31.4	23.0

Source: Data in Levitin, T. E., and Quinn, R. P. "Changes in sex roles and attitudes toward work." Paper presented at 1974 conference of the American Association for Public Opinion Research, Lake George, N.Y. Reprinted with permission.

Note: sample size was 1011 men and 479 women from a national probability sample of persons living in a household, working more than 20 hours per week, and at least 16-years-old.

Comparisons with Other Countries

Figures for the participation of women in managerial and other work positions in most industrialized nations approximate those for the United States (cf. Cook, 1975). Like the United States, other Western nations also employ higher percentages of men than of women. The relative number of men rises where the status of the position rises, the extent of independent decision authority increases, or the involvement of technology is greater. As well, in most positions and in all countries, women are paid less than men for approximately the same work.

In Table 1–16, it may be seen that British women, like their American sisters, tend to place less emphasis on their jobs than do men, with the degree of emphasis depending strongly on their marital status. The data from Table 1–16 were gathered from a group of university graduates eight years after graduation (in 1960); they thus constitute a sample that is relatively unbiased for age effects. Table 1–17 shows the same group's responses to a second question related to aspirations. Although all respondents grew up in the same cultural environment, the data point to a successive reinforcement of the ambitions of British men and a stifling of those held by British women. Fogarty, Rapoport, and Rapoport (1971), who conducted this study, also found relatively higher aspirations on the part of men with more family obligations in conjunction with lower aspirations on the part of women with family obligations.

Despite many similarities, most countries have a somewhat different share of women working in various professions from that found in the United States. Aside from differences in tradition, a prominent cause of such differences was the occurrence of two major European wars in this century. The availability of a skilled male workforce was temporarily interrupted with the result that women were encouraged to learn skills that many still practice. Nonetheless, inequality

Table 1–16
Source of Greatest Life Satisfaction

	Males			Females		
Source	Single	Married, No Children	Married, Children	Single	Married, No Children	Married, Children
Career	53%	42%	29%	42%	19%	4%
Family	11	42	59	14	58	82
All Other	36	15	13	43	24	13
	100	99	101	99	101	99
Sample Size	58	79	245	112	73	298

Percent Indicating Source

Source: Study of United Kingdom 1960 university graduates 8 years later (1968): Fogarty, M. P., Rapoport, R., and Rapoport, R. N. *Sex, Career, & Family*. Beverly Hills: Sage Publications; London: George Allen & Unwin, 1971. Reprinted with permission.

Table 1-17
Recalled Aspirations — Percent Wanting to "Get to the Top"

Time	Males	Females
Now (1968)	66	21
When in University	57	21
When in Secondary School	34	28

Source: Data in study of United Kingdom 1960 university graduates 8 years later (1968): Fogarty, M. P., Rapoport, R., and Rapoport, R. N. *Sex, Career, & Family.* Beverly Hills: Sage Publications; London: George Allen & Unwin, 1971. Reprinted with permission.

of opportunity is still the rule in spite of wars and despite recent attempts at major social change in regions such as Scandanavia.

Although most developed western nations incorporate the economic and social traditions associated with capitalism, some do not. Those countries with a communist philosophy generally voice their faith in the total economic equality of the sexes. Consequently, it might be thought that the communist countries pose an alternative system with which Western noncommunist nations may be compared. In making comparisons, however, one must recognize that communist doctrine is a late entrant, having been imposed over the prior noncommunist economic and social systems only in this century. The conversion occurred erratically from the 1920s through the 1940s in the Soviet Union.

Fogarty et al. (1971) cite statistics showing that the percentage of Soviet women in vocations traditionally reserved for men in the West is higher than in noncommunist Western countries. In 1964, for example, 31 percent of engineers and geologists, 32 percent of legal workers, and 41 percent of agronomists and veterinarians were women. Women also comprised 63 percent of the economists and statisticians and 74 percent of the physicians.

Although the figures indicate some degree of advance on the part of women, Fogarty et al. note that both men and women in the Soviet Union face conflicts between traditional roles, which have not markedly changed, and the demands of the new system. Evidence of the conflict is not difficult to find. Although 49 percent (1959–1962) of Soviet trade union members are women, women constitute only 13 percent (1963) of chief engineers, 6 percent (1963) of plant managers, and 3 percent (1961) of party central committee members. It appears that women in the Soviet Union have quite successfully penetrated masculine occupations, but they have not found any commensurate degree of success in obtaining visible power within them.

Current Position of Women in Management

In general, the position of women up to this time may be fairly described as "invisible." Women represent only a small portion of managers, managerial-level personnel, or well-educated technical and professional personnel from which managers may be drawn. Across all vocations, male managers earn 85 percent more money than female managers, and female managers are less likely to advance to better positions. The situation does show some signs of change, however. In recent years a larger number of women have been seeking the prerequisite training for management positions; larger numbers have been entering management.

Some of the reasons for the shortage of women in management appear to center about a conflict between the role of a woman as domestic homemaker—wife, mother, and housekeeper—and as an employee external to the home environment. Thus women have a lower probability of being employed if they are more heavily involved in the home environment. Preparation for the homemaker role is substantially different from that for managers, and, in consequence, it is not surprising that relatively more women are found in unskilled and nontechnical employment.

Two major questions are raised but unexplained by the data. Why are women who do have equal preparation and ability usually paid less and given fewer advantages than men? This thread ran through much of the data that have been examined: almost irrespective of the position considered, women were at a disadvantage in the job market. A second major question is, why don't women behave like men in the labor market, working, entering technical professions, and studying management for the purpose of improving their positions?

References

Barnes, W. F., and Jones, E. B. "Manufacturing quit rates revisited: A cyclical view of women's quits." *Monthly Labor Review,* 1973, *96* (12), 53–56.

Bernard, J. *Women and the public interest.* Chicago: Aldine-Atherton, pp. 123–124.

Blitz, R. C. "Women in the professions, 1870–1970." *Monthly Labor Review,* 1974, *97* (5), 34–39.

Brodsky, A. "Women as graduate students." *American Psychologist,* 1974, *29,* 523–526.

Cook, A. H. *The working mother.* Ithaca, N.Y.: New York School of Industrial and Labor Relations, Cornell University, 1975.

"Earned degrees conferred 1974–1975." National Center for Education Statistics. Reported in *The Chronicle of Higher Education,* November 29, 1976, p. 8.

Fidell, L. S. "Empirical verification of sex discrimination in hiring practices in psychology." *American Psychologist,* 1970, *25,* 1094–1098.

Fogarty, M. P., Rapoport, R., and Rapoport, R. N. *Sex, career, and family*. London: George Allen & Unwin, 1971.

Fuchs, V. R. "Women's earnings: Recent trends and long-run prospects." *Monthly Labor Review*, 1974, *97* (5), 23–26.

Fullerton, H. N., Jr., and Byrne, J. J. "Length of working life for men and women, 1970." *Monthly Labor Review*, 1976, *99* (2), 31–35.

Hayghe, H. "Marital and family characteristics of workers, March 1974." *Monthly Labor Review*, 1975, *98* (1), 61.

Hedges, J. N., and Bemis, S. E. "Sex stereotyping: Its decline in skilled trades." *Monthly Labor Review*, 1974, *97* (5), 15.

Issues in Industrial Society, staff introduction, 1971, *2*, 2–20.

Jaquette, J. S. "Political science." *Signs*, 1976, *2*, 147–164.

Jusenius, C. L. "Economics." *Signs*, 1976, *2*, 177–189.

Kavanagh, M. J., and Halpern, M. "The impact of job level and sex differences on the relationship between life and job satisfaction." *Academy of Management Journal*, 1977, *20*, 66–73.

Levitin, T. E., and Quinn, R. P. "Changes in sex roles and attitudes toward work." Paper presented at 1974 conference of the American Association for Public Opinion Research, Lake George, N. Y.

———,———, and Staines, G. L. "Sex discrimination against the American working woman." *American Behavioral Scientist*, 1971, *15*, 237–254.

Lunneborg, P. W., and Lillie, C. "Sexism in graduate admissions: The letter of recommendation." *American Psychologist*, 1973, *28*, 187–189.

Parrish, J. B. "Women in professional training—an update." *Monthly Labor Review*, 1975, *98* (11), 49–51.

———. "Women in professional training." *Monthly Labor Review*, 1974, *97* (5), 43.

Raphael, E. E. "Working women and their membership in unions." *Monthly Labor Review*, 1974, *97* (5), 27–33.

Robie, E. A. "Challenge to management." In E. Ginzberg and A. M. Yohalem (eds.), *Corporate lib: Woman's challenge to management*. Baltimore: Johns Hopkins University Press, 1973.

Rosen, B., and Jerdee, T. H. "Effects of applicant's sex and difficulty of job on evaluation of candidates for managerial positions." *Journal of Applied Psychology*, 1974, *59*, 511–512.

Rossi, A. S. "Barriers to the career choice of engineering, medicine, or science among American women." In J. A. Mattfeld and C. G. Van Aken (eds.), *Women and the scientific professions*. Cambridge, Mass.: M.I.T. Press, 1965.

Sommers, D. "Occupational rankings for men and women by earnings." *Monthly Labor Review*, 1974, *97* (8), 34–51.

The Spokeswoman, 1970, *1,* 1.

Staines, G. L., Quinn, R. P. and Shepard, L. J. "Trends in occupational sex discrimination: 1969–1973." *Industrial Relations,* 1976, *15,* 88–98.

Waldman, E., and McEaddy, B. J. "Where women work—An analysis by industry and occupation." *Monthly Labor Review,* 1974, *97* (5), 12.

Women's Bureau Bulletin, April 1971, 1.

Part II: Analysis

The questions posed in the first chapter are investigated in the Part II of this book. The purpose of the three chapters constituting Part II is to show how the situation of women, described in the first chapter, occurred. A second focus will be on the manner in which some of the factors contributing to discrimination against women operate currently—and on changes in the position of women.

Chapter 2 treats these topics by examining the behaviors and values that comprise the prevailing American sex stereotypes. Overall, the stereotypes describe women who are socially adept but managerially and technically incompetent; for men, the pattern is reversed. The stereotype of the manager closely parallels that for men. The stereotypes are often relevant in describing average self-concept and in predicting the limitation of opportunities offered to women. Nonetheless, they have the effect of ignoring individual characteristics and of specifying an inadequate mix of managerial talents. The discussion concludes that when the stereotypes are ignored most women are as well-suited for management as are most men. Moreover, the act of managing need not affect either the feeling or appearance of femininity for women managers.

The findings of Chapter 2 help to explain the data seen in the first part of this book. However, the conclusions raise the question of how the stereotype came to be at variance with the abilities of women. The traditions underlying our present definition of sex roles are examined in Chapter 3. Anthropological studies have shown that the division of labor is determined in part by physical sex differences that make certain types of work assignments more efficient than others. If the same relationships are needed by our society now, then physical sex differences may provide a basis for maintaining our present roles. The barriers to the managerial success of women would then appear natural—perhaps even desirable. In fact, the conditions that initiated our present role relationships are unique in that they allowed institutionalized inefficiency to replace the earlier division of labor.

Chapter 4 considers individual psychological differences and whether women who enter management are likely to perform differently from their male predecessors. While there are no innate mental or physical differences relevant to a managerial position, those resulting from average differential learning experiences may be quite real. Learned sex differences in self-concept, aspiration level, and anticipated economic and role exchanges are particularly important. Psychological differences may result in men and women behaving, on the average, somewhat differently in identical managerial situations; women may sometimes be placed at a relative disadvantage.

This part completes the description and explanation of the position of women in management. Since women clearly have difficulties in entering and function-

---

Part II was written by Laurie Larwood.

27

ing in management, the section may at first seem unencouraging. However, if one is to walk in alien territory, a map is the most important requirement. The underlying assumption of these chapters is that by knowing the sources and the impact of the problems facing women, the problems may be avoided. If women merely obey the status quo, after all, they will not even attempt to enter management. If a woman understands what is required of her, however, her advancement may be greatly facilitated.

2

Women and Management: Culturally Biased Perspectives

Depending on the observer's perspective, experience, and degree of cynicism, Polk (1974) suggests that any of four different conceptual frameworks may be used to analyze the patterns of employment described in the first chapter. One may view the patterns as being the result of a conflict between two parallel and competing cultures; the masculine culture currently dominates the feminine one. If men and women are believed driven by different underlying psychological processes, the differences in their employment may be ascribed to a specific masculine drive for power. Contemporary political philosophy may be adapted to explain the differences in employment as the result of exploitative political-economic processes. This chapter employs Polk's fourth possibility, a role theoretic approach, which views men and women as behaving according to certain well-defined cultural and psychological processes. The processes involved are similar for each sex; any conflict or exploitation is viewed as coincidental. Role theory appears to be unique, as it has now been sufficiently refined to offer both explanations for sex differences in work patterns and antidotes for those differences.

The role concepts introduced here are applied in an examination of masculinity, femininity, and management. Masculinity and femininity are seen to imply different values and behaviors relative to one another. Because the masculine stereotype is similar to the common image of a manager, persons with feminine values and behaviors may be excluded from management. Nonetheless, good management is neither masculine nor feminine, and there is little reason to suggest that one sex should manage while the other should not.

Categorization Processes[1]

Each of us is constantly bombarded by far more stimuli than we can react to. For example, this passage consists not only of the words, but also of the spaces between the words and the page margins. Although attention to the spaces and margins is possible, it is not usually very valuable. Consequently, you have probably devised an unconscious decision scheme for partitioning the category "book" into component "words" and "nonwords." You can then concentrate almost entirely on the words and discard nonwords without formal examination, unless they are so unusual as to defy immediate categorization. You are often rewarded

29

for correct categorization (by being able to read more rapidly, in this case) and are often punished for being incorrect. In general, we develop categories and the decision schemes to separate the categories such that they allow us to give our attention to important stimuli, rather than spreading it among all of them.

The development of categories often proceeds hierarchically; categories with the most distinctive, general, and important features are learned first. Thus an infant distinguishes itself from its environment before later learning to distinguish between environmental features. Similarly, when language is being learned, both parents (and bystanders) are often first labeled with the name having the greatest utility (frequently "mama"). When the infant is able to distinguish between the parents correctly, it may still apply the same name to a parent as to other same-sex adults.

Both the differentiation and the application of categories are normal processes without which it would be difficult to imagine carrying on intelligent thought and conversation. These processes allow us to simplify our own thinking and to free it from attention to trivial detail. They also provide a partial basis for logical thought in that the features defining one member of a category are likely to be generalizeable to others in the same category. Finally, general agreement on the definition of a category makes possible the rapid transfer of information between people.

Stereotypes and Roles

Stereotypes and roles may be thought of as forms of categorization that are applied in general use by some group of people. The term "stereotype" refers to a consistent pattern of values and behaviors that describes the most remembered set of beliefs or actions of members of the category being referenced. Because the stereotype often contains the most striking values and behaviors, it may accurately describe only a very visible minor segment of the persons in a category. If Henry Kissinger is accepted as the stereotypic diplomat (because he was a member of the category "diplomat" and was extremely visible) the limitations of the stereotype become more obvious. No other diplomat actually behaves or believes quite as does Mr. Kissinger. The stereotype has a great deal of value in providing a simplistic category definition, but it often has little practical utility for describing most individual cases. In fact, a stereotype theoretically can persist even after most of or all the individuals from which it was derived have disappeared.

While a stereotype provides a sharply focused set of points within a category, a *role* may be defined in terms of rather flexible category boundaries. Thus a role may be considered to contain within its boundaries certain important behaviors and values that most people can agree are usually exhibited by those occupying a specific social or organizational position (consensual prescriptive norms). Performance in a role may also require that certain behaviors and values beyond the boundaries not occur (consensual proscriptive norms). At the option of the individual role participant, other behaviors and values may be indulged providing they are consistent with the prescriptive and proscriptive norms. As an example, individuals other than Mr. Kissinger might be said to perform in the role of diplomat when they carefully negotiate between conflicting parties. At their own option, those diplomats may enjoy press coverage or, on the other hand, keep their silence; however, they may not divulge the confidences given them by either party to the conflict.

Few people expect a role player to behave exactly according to the stereotype for that role. However, a great deal of experimental and sociological evidence demonstrates that social pressure (ridicule, ostracism, loss of position, etc.) is sometimes applied to role occupants to ensure that they do not break the proscriptive norms. In part, the reaction may be thought of as a defense against threats to the predictive and logical value of the categorization structure shared by members of a society (Kiesler, 1973). For example, if a diplomat breaks faith with us then we may want to punish the diplomat in an effort to restore the previous arrangement. If we conclude that we cannot trust diplomats, then we may need to go through the involved process of adjusting the definitions (the norms and values) that we apply to that and related categories until they were again useful to us. The people in a society presumably recognize the possibility of punishment for breaking proscriptive norms. Since they share the same category definitions for roles and have some freedom in choosing to play a particular role, they tend to avoid proscribed activities while engaging in role play.

Of course, a third alternative (to either altering role concepts or punishing the offender) for those confronting a disorderly role player is determination that the individual is unrepresentative of others in the role. Since we may assume that the role player shares our knowledge of how the role is usually performed, a unique behavior can then be safely attributed to some personal preference or constraint. In contrast, a person's accurate performance in a role yields no such personal information. Accepting the individual as an eccentric requires no cognitive restructuring on our part—but it does require personal attention and time.

As the foregoing implies, roles are not identical with role players. A person may participate in several roles at once—or in none. In general, people require an evaluator (someone who is cognizant of the role to be played, critical of it, and potentially important to the role player) to be present before they will engage in a role. Moreover, the evaluator must engage in some form of reciprocal relationship by carrying out a different but related role in order for the first role player to continue the performance (Larwood, O'Carroll, and Logan, 1977; Larwood, Zalkind, and Legault, 1975). The roles of employee/employer and husband/wife are examples of such reciprocal role pairs. Without the evaluator's presence, or in the absence of some indication from the evaluator that the role play is appreciated, the original participant may switch roles or terminate the performance.

Thus an employee at a cocktail party would be unlikely to behave deferentially toward an employer who is uninterested in the day's work.

As discussed above, a stereotype is a sort of shorthand for a role—or even for a group of associated roles. The stereotype allows a simplification of categorical thought processes beyond that afforded by a consideration of roles but does so at the further expense of individualization and accuracy. Perhaps as a result, the people who are most likely to use stereotypes are those who have the least experience with the roles or the individuals to whom they apply them. The author would be happy to offer a stereotype of an Uzbekistani goat herder, but would hesitate to stereotype college professors. Nonetheless, the stereotype, like the role, is recognized societywide and may be used for rapid prediction even by members of the group to which it is applied. Because the stereotype is recognized as a caricature, however, social sanctions are not so likely to be applied for violation of a stereotype as for violation of the underlying role.

Sex Roles

The nature of sex roles differs from that of work roles only in that appropriate participants for sex roles can be readily identified by apparent physical characteristics. In the jargon of the role theorist, sex, race, and age roles are "ascribed" in advance, while employment, education, and status roles are usually "achieved." Nonetheless, a person may choose when, and whether, to play a particular sex role. Moreover, the normative definitions of sex roles, like others, are subject to change over time.

While the appropriateness of various sex roles "comes with the territory," then, every woman may decide for herself the way in which she will respond to situations that usually elicit one of the feminine roles. In making a conscious choice, however, she must be aware of the potential for punishment of role deviants as well as the potential loss of anonymity that would have been afforded by in-role behavior. Moreover, friendship and power groupings may be altered by the choice of proscribed behaviors or by refusing to play certain roles.

Femininity

In agreement with the preceding discussion, the consideration of a single "feminine role" is a gross oversimplification. There are hundreds, if not thousands, of consensual feminine roles in contemporary American society alone. As it turns out, however, an overall feminine stereotype is often applied as a summary, however inaccurate, of women's behaviors and values. The stereotype is normative in the sense that each of us (of either sex) can recognize it immediately. Whether or not we accept the feminine stereotype personally, we recognize that "others" believe it exists and act accordingly.

To define the stereotype for yourself, try the following exercise before you read further. In your mind, put together a mental picture of the "typical" woman; then try to imagine an image of the typical woman that a large part of the population would compose and agree on. Next, provide five adjectives or phrases that complete these two sentences: (1) I think the typical woman should be . . .; and (2) Most other people think the typical woman should be . . .

Now examine your responses. As a reader of this book, you probably felt that most people would answer differently from you—probably that they would answer in a less "liberated" manner. In order to check, you may wish to turn to Table 2–1 a little further on in this chapter. If your opinion differed from the way you felt most people would reply, you probably differed in the direction of neutrality by adding traits to your description that most people consider stereotypically masculine. The fact, of course, is that a woman is very much like a man. The exercise misleads one into contrasting women with men when the most important finding should be one of generous overlap and similarity of the sexes (cf. Constantinople, 1973).

One of the best known studies of sex stereotypes was performed in a manner similar to the exercise above (Broverman, Vogel, Broverman, Clarkson, and Rosenkrantz, 1972). The researchers first asked a hundred college students to list characteristics, attributes, and behaviors on which they believed men and women to differ. Examining only those items that appeared at least twice on the initial list, a second group rated the extent to which they also agreed that the items were typical of an adult man or an adult woman.

Analysis of the Broverman et al. results yielded forty-one items (Table 2–1), each stereotypically differentiating men from women beyond any reasonable doubt. As is usual for persons in the same basic social groups, the men and women who responded to the survey were in almost perfect agreement on the items. Further analysis showed that the stereotypic differences divided into two groupings. Men were seen as being more competent than women but as having less warmth and expressiveness. Both competence and warmth/expressiveness were rated as desirable characteristics. Since twenty-nine of the forty-one differentiating items were favorable to the masculine, rather than the feminine, stereotype, investigators concluded that contemporary American society more highly values masculinity than femininity.

The Broverman et al. results should not be interpreted either as an ideal or as the actual way in which any man or woman should be described. A more accurate interpretation would suggest that we simply carry subconscious images of a typical man and woman. The images differ according to the traits of Table 2–1 (although they are probably not as extreme). At times, when we are required to make decisions regarding others based on generalities, we may call on the stereotypes and apply them, however grudgingly. It is then that the small or imaginary differences responsible for creating the stereotypes can have very real social consequences.

How realistic are these particular stereotypes and how important are their

Table 2–1
Characteristics of the Masculine and Feminine Stereotypes

Feminine Stereotype	Masculine Stereotype
Incompetence	*Competence*
Not at all agressive	Very agressive
Not at all independent	Very independent
Very emotional	Not at all emotional
Does not hide emotions at all	Almost always hides emotions
Very subjective	Very objective
Very easily influenced	Not at all easily influenced
Very submissive	Very dominant
Dislikes math and science very much	Likes math and science very much
Very excitable in a minor crisis	Not at all excitable in a minor crisis
Very passive	Very active
Not at all competitive	Very competitive
Very illogical	Very logical
Very home oriented	Very worldly
Not at all skilled in business	Very skilled in business
Very sneaky	Very direct
Does not know the way of the world	Knows the way of the world
Feelings easily hurt	Feelings not easily hurt
Not at all adventurous	Very adventurous
Has difficulty making decisions	Can make decisions easily
Cries very easily	Never cries
Almost never acts as a leader	Almost always acts as a leader
Not at all self-confident	Very self-confident
Very uncomfortable about being agressive	Not at all uncomfortable about being agressive
Not at all ambitious	Very ambitious
Unable to separate fellings from ideas	Easily able to separate feelings from ideas
Very dependent	Not at all dependent
Very conceited about appearance	Never conceited about appearance
Thinks women are always superior to men	Thinks men are always superior to women
Does not talk freely about sex with men	Talks freely about sex with men
Warmth/Expressiveness	*Distance/Inexpressiveness*
Doesn't use harsh language at all	Uses very harsh language
Very talkative	Not at all talkative
Very tactful	Very blunt
Very gentle	Very rough
Very aware of feelings of others	Not at all aware of feelings of others
Very religious	Not at all religious
Very interested in own appearance	Not at all interested in own appearance
Very neat in habits	Very sloppy in habits
Very quiet	Very loud
Very strong need for security	Very little need for security
Enjoys art and literature	Does not enjoy art and literature at all
Easily expresses tender feelings	Does not express tender feelings at all easily

Source: Broverman, I. K., Vogel, S. R., Broverman, D. M., Clarkson, F. E., and Rosenkrantz, P. S. "Sex-role stereotypes: A current appraisal." *Journal of Social Issues*, 1972, *28*, 59–78. Reprinted with permission.

Note: Competence and warmth/expressiveness are socially valued characteristics. For each item, the polls were rated significantly masculine and feminine, as indicated, at $p < .001$ or better by the responses of 74 college men and 80 college women.

consequences? No direct relationship exists between the sexual stereotypes and any individual's concept of self. Each person's self-concept is unique and may be realistic or unrealistic, and similar or dissimilar, to the self-concepts of others. Nonetheless, working with different samples of college students, the Broverman team found that individuals (taken as an average) describe themselves along the lines of the stereotype for their sex—although in a slightly more neutral manner. For example, women describe themselves as religious, sneaky, emotional, dependent, quiet, and illogical. The self-concept of a man is likely to be irreligious, direct, unemotional, independent, loud, and logical. Why is it that our self-concepts tend to parallel the stereotype rather than the roles played? Not all the requisite research has been completed, but educated conjecture is possible. Self-concept may change suddenly but is usually a relatively stable entity, whereas roles can change almost instantly. When asked to answer the question, "Who are you," subjects readily respond with both role ("a student") and stable concepts ("a woman"). In response to a more searching question, "Now, who are you *really?*," however, the role responses tend to drop out. We may speculate that the stable self-concepts remaining represent a sort of long-term average that has survived repeated such prunings and that has proven most useful to its owner. Insofar as the stereotype of femininity or of masculinity is indicative of the average role played by a woman or man and embodies constructs that have proven useful and reinforcing to the individual, it seems reasonable that the person would develop a self-concept net paralleling (but not identical with) the stereotype. It is argued in the next chapter that stable societies must provide reinforcing roles for their citizens. It must be recognized, however, that no one tries to internalize the stereotype; the process is much more involved, nondeliberate, and random.

People tend to behave in accord with their self-concepts. The way in which a person defines herself or himself in part delimits the types of roles that person prefers to undertake (Backman and Secord, 1968). More important, when an individual is not performing in role (when an appropriate evaluator is not present), any difference between behavior and self-concept may result in self-concept change in the direction of the behavior (Bem, 1972). As with other forms of categorization, a stable, accurate self-concept structure provides the highest utility for dealing with the environment. For example, the individual must "know" what abilities he or she possesses in order to achieve the greatest productivity. For that reason, sudden changes in the basic concept net are resisted and, when possible, avoided (Epstein, 1973; Schrauger, 1975). In order to avoid risking self-concept changes, it follows that an individual will tend to prefer behaviors that agree with the established self-concept structure (cf. Maracek and Mettee, 1972). The sad truth is that women whose self-concepts parallel the feminine stereotype often select common feminine roles [which traditionally place them in a position inferior to men (cf. Ireson, 1976)] and tend to behave as though they are relatively incompetent (in accord with their self-concept) even when not playing a role.

In the absence of solid information that the stereotypes are incorrect, both men and women also tend to apply them to each other. A study by Goldberg

(1968) found that the mere labeling of passages from professional journals with the name of a female author was sufficient for the raters (college women) to infer low competence to the articles. Since the result appeared even for passages concerning fields employing large numbers of women, such as dietetics and education, it seems that the stereotype of feminine incompetence was being used indiscriminately. Other studies have shown that subjects appear surprised when it is demonstrated that a woman does well; their reaction is often either that the woman is an exception (indicated in the results of Pheterson, Kiesler, and Goldberg, 1971) or that she was merely lucky (Deaux and Emswiller, 1973).

In summary, self-concepts of men and women tend to parallel the masculine and feminine stereotypes. We prefer to behave in agreement with our self-concepts, and we often base judgments of others on the stereotypes. In consequence, important differences may occur in the behavior of men and women and in our attribution of the causes for behavior.

Masculinity and Management

Since there are few sanctions applied for breaking a stereotype, women whose self-concepts conflict with the feminine stereotype might be expected to freely behave differently from it. Misdirected stereotyping has some far-reaching effects, however, that together serve to limit the range of options open to women.

The second exercise, below, is similar to the one that you completed earlier. Before you read further, try finishing each of the sentences with five traits or phrases that you feel are most applicable: (1) Most people feel that the typical man should be . . .; and (2) Most people feel that the typical manager or executive should be . . .

Many people experience a tendency toward using the same adjectives or phrases to describe a typical business executive as are used in describing a typical man. Perhaps you were aware of the trend and resisted it. If you successfully resisted, you might try a third exercise. Check to see whether those responses describing either the man or the executive could be equally well applied to the other description. Finally, you might compare your results for the second with those of the first exercise.

The second exercise highlights the fact that the contemporary stereotype of the successful manager is nearly identical to that of the ideal man (O'Leary, 1974). Managerial texts have traditionally assumed that the would-be manager is a man, that "he" exhibits only masculine traits, and that the alternative traits are signs of counterproductive "feminine weakness" (cf. McGregor, 1967, p. 23). The extent to which particular men and women believe that masculinity and management are synonomous may differ greatly; nonetheless, there is little dispute that the identity exists. Moreover, the identification is sufficiently general that any work outside the home is somewhat identified with masculinity (Prather, 1971). As will be discussed in another chapter, many women have apparently come to fear and avoid success itself because of its apparent inappropriateness for them (Horner, 1972).

The identification of management, employment, and success with masculinity is much more than an academic nicety. A *Harvard Business Review* national survey of 2000 active executives found that 51 percent of male executives felt that women are "temperamentally unfit for management" (Bowman, Worthy, and Greyser, 1965). While managers have become progressively more cautious about expressing such opinions in the past decade, related attitudes persist (cf. Bass, Krusall, and Alexander, 1971) and have been demonstrated consistently in experiments dealing with personnel policies.

For example, studies of managerial personnel decisions using both students and executives as subjects (Rosen and Jerdee, 1974a, 1974b; Terborg and Ilgen, 1975) found that males are preferred over *identical* female job candidates for challenging managerial or technical positions (only the first name of the candidate indicates sex in these studies). On the other hand, men and women are equally acceptable for routine positions. Male candidates are awarded higher starting salaries and are more often selected for promotion and for advanced professional training. Males are also considered more capable of handling human relations problems and are more likely to be believed and taken seriously when they recommend a solution to a problem. The likelihood of discrimination in these studies has been found to be higher when the subjects voice stereotypic attitudes toward having women in business.

An Examination of Conflicting Values—Are Femininity and Management Really Exclusive?

If the managerial stereotype is identical with the masculine image, there is similarly no question that the feminine image is antithetical to management. It is difficult to imagine a manager who conforms to the feminine archetype listed in Table 2–1 actually succeeding in a competitive environment. A similar difficulty is experienced, however, in visualizing the success of executives who are fundamentally competent but devoid of human warmth and expressiveness. In fact, a good deal of managerial, psychological, and sociological research seems to have converged recently on the concept that the best leaders are often those who are both competent (masculine) and expressive (feminine) as the situation may require (cf. House, Filley, and Kerr, 1971).

Neither sex can successfully enter management (except in unusual circumstances) through total adherence to the social stereotype supposedly appropriate to that sex. Like those of most men, however, the self-concepts of most women only parallel the stereotype for their sex. Since the self-concepts are usually less extreme, their preference in behavior is also less extreme than the stereotype suggests. Most women should experience little discomfort with the moderate behavior (neither stereotypically masculine nor feminine) most useful in management. This is not to suggest that men and women will solve management problems in the same manner. Women might be expected to apply more warmth, and men may apply more technical expertise. Neither sex has an overall advantage or a general handicap, and neither sex should be more or less comfortable than the other in trying to arrive at the optimal mix of managerial strategies.

Both self-concept and the image projected to others may change somewhat depending on experience. It may be asked, therefore, whether the act of managing detracts from actual or apparent femininity. When a woman increases in managerial competence as a result of experience or training, she gains a group of attributes that are traditionally masculine. Although the increase in competence may, at the first glance, appear to detract from the female executive's femininity, for practical purposes that does not happen. Since competence is viewed as a positive trait whether exhibited by men or women, the increase in competence makes the woman more attractive both socially and occupationally (Spence and Helmreich, 1972). As well, a woman can, at her option, project and cognize her vocational and nonvocational interests separately (Berman, 1976). She may appear somewhat masculinely competent at her work, but traditionally feminine outside the work role (Kristal, Sanders, Spence, and Helmreich, 1975). Thus a woman's femininity is not normally a hindrance to her exercise of managerial expertise, and her being in management need not threaten her femininity in any way.

The reaction of coworkers and potential employers to the stereotype rather than to the reality of a woman's abilities or occupational role presents a difficulty that cannot be so easily dismissed. When managers react to the stereotype as though it is fairly representative of the role an incoming woman will play in their organization, they will be almost uniformly negative toward the woman. If the woman behaves according to the stereotype, she is of little value to the organization. If she is not incompetent, however, she is assaulting the concept structure that many managers hold. In the first event, the reaction is to avoid hiring or promoting the woman, as the studies cited in the previous section of this chapter show. If the woman is hired, the reaction to competent vocational role behavior may vary considerably. Angry reprisal and attempted enforcement of the assumed (but mistaken) role norms may occur such as firing the woman because she is "unfeminine." In the Bowman et al. study discussed earlier, 86 percent of the men and 77 percent of the women said that men are uncomfortable working for women; presumably they would act on their discomfort, if possible.

Alternatively, the woman may be accepted as unique and therefore unrepresentative of women in general, or the stereotype might be abandoned in favor of an examination of the woman's occupational role performance. These are occasions when the woman is seen as competent and when her competence enhances her attractiveness. The difference between this reaction and that of reprisal and norm enforcement depends entirely on whether the woman is perceived as playing a sex role incorrectly or an occupational role correctly. It is not surprising that Bowman et al. found that 41 percent of male executives admitted to an "unfavorable" attitude toward women in management, while 59 percent felt pessimistic regarding women's opportunities in management. The same study found that 42 percent of male executives felt the risk too great to ever promote any woman to the position of corporate president.

The problem of winning individual treatment and avoiding the problem of stereotyping by actual or potential employers will be considered in the final section of this book. A variety of possibilities, generally sharing the commonality of partially reidentifying the aspiring woman with her occupational role, are open in most situations. In the reidentification process, sex roles of any type are usually de-emphasized. Ideally the process decreases the likelihood that the woman will be evaluated in stereotypic terms and directs attention toward the skills and needs she may have with respect to the position (cf. Rosen and Jerdee, 1975).

Other Barriers to Women

In practice, the importance of stereotyping in any management decision is often difficult to pinpoint. Attacks on discrimination in recent years have forced the most blatant stereotyping to move "underground"—requiring those who would engage in it to become progressively more sophisticated.

Role processes quite different from those specific only to sex role and stereotyping also complicate any analysis. The members of formal and informal groups routinely defend their groups against incursions by the members of other important groups (cf. Gerard and Hoyt, 1974; Moriarty, 1974). Similarly, adults tend to show a covert preference for the members of their own sex (Larwood, 1974). Some researchers have reasoned that such favoritism may result in a systematic bias by male managers, who are in control of most institutions, toward the unconscious selective grooming for rank advancement of male subordinates with whom the managers are more likely to share close friendships (Terborg and Ilgen, 1975). Others have suggested that the same forces may lead men who are in positions potentially fillable by women to adopt a battlefield mentality through unconsciously devaluing threatening achievements by women (Bass, Krusell, and Alexander, 1971). There is some likelihood that this type of institutionalized discrimination will end when the presence of women in management is more common. With sufficient numbers of women visible in all areas of management, their roles in the organization may overshadow their sex roles (O'Leary, 1974).

Note

1. The introductory paragraphs of this section represent a much-abbreviated view of the general cognitive processes supporting role learning and use. A more detailed account would combine cognitive-developmental, associative, reinforcement, and selective attention theories. Those who demand additional references might examine work by Mackintosh, Kohlberg, Gergen, Piaget, W. Mischel, and K. W. Spence. Although a working paper by the author (Larwood, 1975) does partly integrate the cognitive theories, references have been omitted in this part of the text in the service of simplicity and to the probable relief of readers who are not psychologists.

References

Backman, C. W., and Secord, P. F. "The self and role selection." In C. Gordon and K. J. Gergen (eds.), *The self in role interaction.* New York: John Wiley, 1968.

Bass, B. M., Krusell, J., and Alexander, R. A. "Male manager's attitudes toward working women." *American Behavioral Scientist,* 1971, *15,* 221–236.

Bem, D. J. "Self-perception theory." In L. Berkowtiz (ed.), *Advances in experimental social psychology,* vol. 6. New York: Academic Press, 1972.

Berman, V. A. "Effects of success and failure on perceptions of gender identity." *Sex Roles,* 1976, *2,* 367–374.

Bowman, G. W., Worthy, N. B., and Greyser, S. A. "Are women executives people?" *Harvard Business Review,* 1965, *43.*

Broverman, I. K., Vogel, S. R., Broverman, D. M., Clarkson, F. E., and Rosenkrantz, P. S. Sex-role stereotypes: A current appraisal. *Journal of Social Issues,* 1972, *28,* 59–78.

Constantinople, A. "Masculinity-femininity: An exception to a famous dictum?" *Psychological Bulletin,* 1973, *80,* 389–407.

Deaux, K., and Emswiller, T. "Explanations of successful performance on sex-linked tasks: What's skill for the male is luck for the female." *Journal of Personality and Social Psychology,* 1973, *29,* 80–85.

Epstein, S. "The self-concept revisited." *American Psychologist,* 1973, *28,* 404–416.

Gerard, H. B., and Hoyt, M. F. "Distinctiveness of social categorization and attitude toward ingroup members." *Journal of Personality and Social Psychology,* 1974, *29,* 836–842.

Goldberg, P. "Are women prejudiced against women?" *Trans-action,* 1968, *5,* 28–30.

Horner, M. S. "Toward an understanding of achievement-related conflicts in women." *Journal of Social Issues,* 1972, *28,* 157–176.

House, R. J., Filley, A. C., and Kerr, S. "Relation of leader consideration and initiating structure to R and D subordinates' satisfaction." *Administrative Science Quarterly,* 1971, *16,* 19–30.

Ireson, C. J. "Effects of sex role socialization on adolescent female achievement." Paper presented at 1976 meeting of the Pacific Sociological Association, San Diego.

Kiesler, S. B. "Preference for predictability or unpredictability as a mediator of reactions to norm violations." *Journal of Personality and Social Psychology,* 1973, *27,* 354–359.

Kristal, J., Sanders, D., Spence, J. T., and Helmreich, R. "Inferences about the femininity of competent women and their implications for likability." *Sex Roles,* 1975, *1,* 33–40.

Larwood, L. "The limits of equity: A developmental extension of the Just World Hypothesis to sex roles." (Doctoral dissertation, Tulane University, 1974). *Dissertation Abstracts International,* 1975, *35.* (University Microfilms No. 75-2938).

————. "Who's controlled? Some suggestions for a general theory of social exchange." Working paper #75-09. School of Management, State University of New York, Binghamton, NY 13901, 1975.

————, O'Carroll, M., and Logan, J. "Sex role as a mediator of achievement in task performance." *Sex Roles,* 1977, *3,* 109–114.

————, Zalkind, D., and Legault, J., "The bank job: A field study of sexually discriminatory performance on a neutral role task." *Journal of Applied Social Psychology,* 1975, *5,* 68–74.

Maracek, J., and Mettee, D. R. "Avoidance of continued success as a function of self-esteem, level of esteem certainty, and responsibility for success." *Journal of Personality and Social Psychology,* 1972, *22,* 98–107.

McGregor, D. *The professional manager.* New York: McGraw-Hill, 1967.

Moriarty, T. "Role of stigma in the experience of deviance." *Journal of Personality and Social Psychology,* 1974, *29,* 849–855.

O'Leary, V. E. "Some attitudinal barriers to occupational aspirations in women." *Psychological Bulletin,* 1974, *81,* 809–826.

Pheterson, G. I., Kiesler, S. B., and Goldberg, P. A. "Evaluation of the performance of women as a function of their sex, achievement, and personal history." *Journal of Personality and Social Psychology,* 1971, *19,* 114–118.

Polk, B. B. "Male power and the women's movement." *Journal of Applied Behavioral Science,* 1974, *10,* 415–431.

Prather, J. "Why can't women be more like men." *American Behavioral Scientist,* 1971, *15,* 172–182.

Rosen, B., and Jerdee, T. H. "Effects of employee's sex and threatening versus pleading appeals on managerial evaluations of grievances." *Journal of Applied Psychology,* 1975, *60,* 442–445.

—— and ——. "Effects of applicant's sex and difficulty of job on evaluations of candidates for managerial positions. *Journal of Applied Psychology,* 1974a, *59,* 511–512.

—— and ———. "Influence of sex role stereotypes on personnel decisions." *Journal of Applied Psychology,* 1974b, *59,* 9–14.

Shrauger, J. S. "Responses to evaluation as a function of initial self-perceptions." *Psychological Bulletin,* 1975, *82,* 581–596.

Spence, J. T., and Helmreich, R. "Who likes competent women? Competence, sex-role congruence of interests, and subjects' attitudes toward women as determinants of interpersonal attraction." *Journal of Applied Social Psychology,* 1972, *2,* 197–213.

Terborg, J. R., and Ilgen, D. R. "A theoretical approach to sex discrimination in traditionally masculine occupations." *Organizational Behavior and Human Performance,* 1975, *13,* 352–376.

3

A Question of Tradition

The previous chapter showed that two general sex stereotypes exist—one feminine and the other masculine. The stereotypic man is essentially identical with the stereotypic manager, a person who, while highly competent, may be deficient in warmth and expressivity. In fact, however, it was asserted that the most effective manager is one who conforms to neither the masculine nor the feminine stereotype.

The argument that effective managers should not have exclusively masculine characteristics turns on the potential benefits to management of a flexible mix of resources. Emotional warmth and expressivity are prized by our society, and the individual who is without them is unnecessarily constrained. Although there are unique situations in which a calculative unemotional competence or an unalloyed expressivity is ideal, most situations fall somewhere between those poles.

The assertion of the need for managerial flexibility seems intuitively reasonable. Nonetheless, the assertion does not explain how masculinity and the managerial stereotype first came to be identified with one another. Nor can it explain how men managed to capture the overwhelming majority of managerial positions. If warmth and expressivity are valuable to managers, why are those traits not included in the managerial stereotype? If the people who exhibit warmth and expressivity are not excluded from management, why are there not more women in management? These questions have led a number of careful researchers to suggest that there is some inborn physiological or psychological predisposition favoring male domination of human society (see the analyses of McGuire, 1968; Shields, 1975). Inborn or natural dominance, if it were to exist, could have led to the formation of our sexual stereotypes and roles as well as to male-controlled management. The alternative view to innate predispositions suggests instead that the dilemma posed by the contrast of male management with the androgynous requirements of the managerial role is more apparent than real. Managerial and sex stereotypes can be learned from a variety of sources, including experience, historic traditions, and early childhood observation; they need have no particular relationship to the optimization of managerial ability. The original observations on which a stereotype is based need not be generalizable to the stereotype's eventual application and may be antiquated or irrelevant.

The purpose of this chapter is to continue the role analysis begun in Chapter 2 by examining the primary forces responsible for the evolution of our present division of labor. Any society that is experiencing competitive pressures from others must fulfill the conditions of economic efficiency and transmission of cul-

43

ture. After meeting those conditions, or in the absence of competition, the structure of the society may vary somewhat. As with the others, the structure of our society first evolved in response to physical (not psychological) sex differences so as to meet the needs of a preindustrial economy. Changes arising from growth of the distribution and industrial systems were superimposed on that structure. The chapter concludes that the resulting division of labor is largely an historic artifact, sustained by traditional stereotypes and accepted cultural values, and that it no longer has any survival value for our society. Finally, the results of our present division of labor, in terms of learned dependency and low feminine self-esteem, are found to operate so as to reinforce the present social structure.

Physical and Social Evolution[1]

Since there are obvious physical differences between the sexes, one explanation for our present division of labor holds that there are likely to be inborn psychological differences as well. The hypothesized differences are such that they complement the physical differences; taken together, the two might be expected to have important social consequences. For example, a woman is smaller in stature than a man: a man is both physically and psychologically dominant over her. It is therefore "natural" that the man assume a dominant position of leader or manager and that the woman accept the subordinate position.

The argument just advanced is usually part of a series of self-justifying notions mistakenly based on evolutionary theory: differences exist, the differences evolved as our species developed, because they have some function in ensuring our survival. Therefore our division of labor is natural and must not be altered. As shown with respect to self-concept in the last chapter, psychological differences do exist between the average man and woman. However, the differences are readily explained as the result of our division of labor, rather than a cause of it. Nonetheless, if an argument based on evolutionary theory (the above is a somewhat simplified example) is a poor explanation for our psychological sex differences, it is still extremely useful in explaining the development of our society. This section examines evolutionary theory and its implications for both physical/psychological and social development.

Evolutionary Theory

Organisms that are best able to adapt to their environment have the best chance of survival. To the extent that the parent owes its survival to inborn genetic characteristics, those of the organism's offspring that inherit the characteristics may also be better able to survive. Genetically based characteristics having a "high survival value" are thus the ones most likely to appear in successive generations.

As it is presently used, the expression "survival of the fittest" applies not to the organism itself, but to its genes, which carry the hereditary codes determining an organism's makeup. Competitive pressures (for food, etc.) continually select for superior gene patterns, which better enable the parent to survive and produce viable offspring at the expense of inferior ones. As a result of the selection process, a species may gradually change in appearance and behavior and may become better suited for its particular environmental niche.

Through the process of natural selection, characteristics having negative survival value gradually disappear—or the species itself may disappear if all members have some unfortunate trait. Thus it has been found that the frequency of people with red-green color blindness is exceptionally low in primitive cultures in which survival requires that predators and game be distinguished quickly from foliage (Child, 1968). But what of essentially neutral characteristics, such as long toes? Presumably large feet might have had an evolutionary advantage at one point, but they merely dictate shoe size today. Neutral characteristics are subjected to no evolutionary pressure and may vary freely within certain limits. Thus the average foot size will probably remain stable (unless it is related to a changing characteristic such as overall body size), but the variation from the mean size may increase gradually in successive generations.

Intelligence and Intellectual Differences

It seems clear from most research that intelligence is related to genetic heredity, learning, and the interaction of the two (cf. Ekehammar, 1974; Erlenmeyer-Kimling and Jarvik, 1963), although the exact nature of the relationship is still debated. There is similarly little question that, up to a point, intelligence is selected for in humans. Persons in the lowest IQ levels are less likely than others to successfully reproduce themselves (Reed and Reed, 1965).

Despite the influence of heredity on intelligence, an extensive analysis of research on the subject has found no evidence that any important inherited genetic differences exist in intellectual abilities or predispositions of the sexes (Shields, 1975). Only a single minor difference (spatial reasoning ability discussed in the next chapter) has ever been established. While selection has favored differences in body appearance and function, the premium in the development of human intelligence seems to be on the ability to flexibly adapt to new conditions and to learn quickly from experience and observation. This intelligence is of a general, rather than specific, nature, and it seems most unlikely that the traditional differences in the behavior of the sexes described later in this chapter would be reflected in the evolution of mental ability in any important way.[2]

Nonetheless, the lack of concrete evidence either favoring or disproving the existence of sexual differences in intellectual functioning is disquieting. It is possible that the differences exist, but that they have not yet been found. If that were true, the evidence would be of potentially great importance in showing that some of the social differences we commonly label as needless and callous discrimination are realistic reactions to actual abilities. The burden of proof would then be on an individual woman (or man) to demonstrate that she (he) is not like the others and should not be discriminated against. Fortunately, evidence of a different kind is available. The next two sections show that societal divisions of labor across a large number of cultures occur along the lines dictated by obvious physical differences rather than in agreement with our stereotypes. It is difficult to believe that other cultures could survive in their sometimes flagrant disregard of "innate" sexual differences in intellectual functioning; the appropriate conclusion is that the differences do not exist.

Social Evolution

In a very real sense, any cohesive group or society is a living organism. Social changes follow much the same progression as does the development of an animal species. In a manner analogous to the functioning of the gene pool with a species, it may be said that the success of any society lies in its ability to transmit its culture, albeit a changing one, to successive generations. Consequently the development of a society can be readily described through suitably modified evolutionary notions (Campbell, 1966; LeVine, 1969).

Social evolutionary theory makes the observation that most human societies have long since disappeared. By definition, only the "fittest" societies have survived—those that for some reason have been able to transmit their cultures to succeeding generations. The members of an unsuccessful society, unlike those of an unsuccessful species, have not necessarily died or been the subject of predation. In many cases the initial members have survived, but they have seen their offspring develop as members of a different society as a result of failure to successfully transmit the culture. For example, European civilization destroyed many aboriginal societies by killing their members. More often, however, the younger members were enslaved or otherwise conscripted in such a way that they adopted the culture of the Europeans and abandoned their own.

Short of natural disaster, there are two ways in which a society may be unsuccessful. It may absorb the culture of its neighbors and thereby become indistinguishable from them. For example, telecommunications exert a homogenizing influence on regional accents in the United States. Alternatively, a society may shrink or eventually disappear because of its failure to anticipate and deal with the aggressiveness of other societies, even though the society's culture remains intact. The English language is spoken in most of North America partly because the Spanish and French did not take adequate countermeasures against the English.

Culture also changes from within in response to internal pressures (changing clothing styles) or to meet actual and imagined external pressures (raising a military force). All societies are constantly in a flux with the most desirable and powerful elements of the culture increasing their strength at the expense of others. Such internal changes do not necessarily enhance the society's viability vis-a-vis others or strengthen its long-term likelihood of success. Rather, the internal changes are in response to intracultural requirements; the changes may occur freely providing that they do not reduce the long-term viability of the society.

How does a society ensure competitive success and the transfer of its culture to succeeding generations? Each society in existence today has, de facto, established reasonably correct procedures; the others did not. It should be recognized that the particular solutions that may have been necessary in the past need not be necessary at this time—and may not be sufficient in the future. As in the evolution of an organism, a solution may remain vestigially in the society after the problem for which it was developed has vanished; moreover, random changes may occur in a society that neither help nor hinder it.

Competitive success requires that a society divide the work among its members in a way sufficient to maintain at least a balance with potentially interactive societies. The requirements for achieving some measure of efficiency depend in part on the organization of the society in relation to its environment, including whether the society is based on agriculture, hunting, gathering, or trade, and the family size needed to compensate for famine, war, labor, and procreation. Although this discussion is most concerned with efficiency in the economic sphere, other facets of the society must be similarly developed.

The second requirement is that of the transmission of the culture to succeeding generations. Children appear to have the considerable ability to absorb and reproduce their cultures under an unusual variety of conditions (Whiting and Edwards, 1973). In fact, one view holds that all stable societies (those not undergoing major structural change) as a condition for their stabilization, have to possess means for transmitting their cultures such that each individual internalizes an appropriate role. The young adult fills a fixed position in later playing the role and contributes to the continued steady functioning of the society (cf. Le Vine, 1969). It seems likely that a poor fit between training and available positions would result in the production of individuals who cannot readily participate in the culture without provoking long-term unpredictable changes in it. Any such changes would, of course, continue to occur in succeeding generations until the culture again transmits itself faithfully and absorbs the adults it produces. Perhaps the three most important limits on upbringing are the requirements that the individual must somehow be trained for the roles available (i.e. for those needed by the society when it is functioning in a more or less steady state), the individual's expectations must agree with those roles, and some opportunities for at least minimal physical and intellectual satisfaction must be made available.

To summarize, social evolutionary theory assumes that the society functions similarly to a species. Thus the minimum conditions ensuring long-term survival of a society in a competitive environment may be specified. Those conditions must include both a degree of economic efficiency and a means to transmit the culture to succeeding generations. Societies that survive have developed ways in which to satisfy these two needs, although many other features of the society may, of course, vary freely. It seems likely that if there is a genuinely appropriate division of labor, its importance will be manifested in either a lower efficiency of, or decreased ability to transmit, cultures that do not have that division. Such cultures should fail competitively and will not generally be observed in a crosscultural census made at one period in time.

Crosscultural comparisons

Since the conditions under which societies survive are diverse, the resulting division of labor might be expected to vary widely in the interests of efficiency. Nonetheless, the need for efficiency also imposes some constraints. If men alone have executive abilities, an examination across a wide number of societies should discover few, if any, in which women manage. If only men are capable of labor outside the home, then only men should engage in the external work of each society. Similarly, if it were true that women are incompetent while men are competent, only men would be found in positions requiring competence. A rare exception might exist for a society that has no immediate competitive pressure from others; with no need for efficiency, it might vary somewhat on a particular dimension.

If stereotypic uniformities of the type discussed in Chapter 2 are found in comparison across a wide variety of societies, a fair interpretation of social evolutionary theory would suggest that only such societies are viable—that deviant societies are either impossible for humans to create or are inefficient and therefore unlikely to remain for more than a brief period of time. The "fittest" societies could then be defined as those organized along the lines of sex stereotypes, and it could be extrapolated that the human condition leads naturally and usefully toward masculine control.

A realistic recognition of physical sex differences suggests, however, that instead of occupational uniformity, a different type of result will be found. The fact that women are physically unable to reproduce and simultaneously engage in 100 percent of all possible activities leaves some occupations particularly open to male control. More specifically, the abandoned activities involve travel and high levels of unexpected physical force. They may include hunting and fishing expeditions, exploration, and aggression.[a] Consequently women should be more frequently found than men in alternative occupations demanding a somewhat

---

[a]Some evidence indicates that aggressiveness in humans may be related to serum levels of testosterone and adrenaline. The relationship may be mediated by arousal, instigation, and the direction of causation. Implications for sex differences in behavior are not clear.

lower level of ruggedness and physical activity. The placement of women in the territory of a dwelling may lend itself to child care, agriculture, and a variety of trades, depending on conditions. Males might also participate in those activities to the extent that is advantageous for them to remain in one locale (for example, when hunting or aggression are unprofitable) and to the extent that their other pursuits develop applicable skills.

The first possible explanation for social organization mentioned above predicts that irreducible stereotypic limits exist on the manner of sexual specialization in any culture. These limits are based on physical and intellectual differences between the sexes. In contrast, the second alternative states that complete flexibility is limited only by needs related to childbearing. This latter hypothesis suggests that physical sex differences only, rather than both physical and psychological specialization, are responsible for observable differences between male and female behavior in any society.

The examination of less developed societies provides a test for these two hypotheses. Because of their level of development, such societies are less likely to be "contaminated" by the "Western" cultures with which we are already familiar. One of the most comprehensive studies concerning crosscultural occupational differences is that of Murdock (1937). The data from 224 representative, but mostly subsistence-level, societies investigated by Murdock and his students (Table 3–1) show only three activities—preparing and planting the soil, crafting leather goods, and making ornaments—as equally likely to be given to men or women.

Other occupations might be labeled as masculine or feminine on the basis of the frequency distribution of Table 3–1. As both hypotheses predict, masculine roles include hunting and trapping, while cooking and gathering herbs are feminine. Nonetheless, only a few occupations are nearly always relegated to one sex or another. Only hunting and the pursuit of sea mammals, both of which would present problems for a pregnant woman, are given to men with absolute certainty. The extent of an otherwise neutral activity's association with notably masculine occupations is strongly related to the likelihood that the neutral occupation will also be performed by a man; an association with cooking or the home increases the likelihood that a woman will perform the function. While a particular society may be quite rigid in task delegation, few activities seem exclusively the province of men, and none are exclusively relegated to women.

As noted earlier, in order to remain stable, a society must train its children successfully for the roles that the society will later make available to them. In consequence, it may be anticipated that boys will be trained in the direction best suiting them for the activities of men, while girls will learn those activities most helpful to them as women. Thus it is no surprise to find that an extensive study of 110 societies (Barry, Bacon, and Child, 1957) found none in which boys could be rated more nurturant than girls and none in which girls were more self-reliant than boys.

Rather than rigidly sex-typing nurturance and self-reliance, however, the

Barry et al. study lends further support to the concept that social activity is not fixed but springs from the interaction of physical differences with the needs and organization of society. Of the ratable cultures, boys and girls were found equally nurturant in 18 percent and equally self-reliant in 15 percent. These results are comparable with those of Table 3–1, which shows that many societies allow either sex to perform a variety of functions. A review by Whiting and Edwards (1973) of six diverse cultures (including that of a New England town) similarly confirmed that abilities and preferences are shaped by social needs. The authors found good evidence that societies that treat boys and girls alike because of universal public education or because women are needed in agriculture (thereby forcing older children of both sexes to care for infants) produce boys with traits we might label as stereotypically feminine and girls with traits that are considered masculine. Additional evidence reviewed by D'Andrade (1966) indicates, moreover, that feminine self-concept development occurs in young boys in cultures in which all children live exclusively with the mother.

Table 3-1
Occupational Specialization by Sex

Activity	M	M-	=	F-	F	%M
Metal working	78	0	0	0	0	100.0
Weapon making	121	1	0	0	0	99.8
Pursuit of sea mammals	34	1	0	0	0	99.3
Hunting	166	13	0	0	0	98.2
Manufacture of musical instruments	45	2	0	0	1	96.9
Boat building	91	4	4	0	1	96.0
Mining and quarrying	35	1	1	0	1	95.4
Work in wood and bark	113	9	5	1	1	95.0
Work in stone	68	3	2	0	2	95.0
Trapping, catching small animals	128	13	4	1	2	94.9
Work in bone, horn, shell	67	4	3	0	3	93.0
Lumbering	104	4	3	1	6	92.2
Fishing	98	34	19	3	4	85.6
Ceremonial object manufacture	37	1	13	0	1	85.1
Herding	38	8	4	0	5	83.6
House building	86	32	25	3	14	77.0
Clearing of land	73	22	17	5	13	76.3
Net making	44	6	4	2	11	74.1
Trade	51	28	20	8	7	73.7
Dairy operations	17	4	3	1	13	57.1
Manufacture of ornaments	24	3	40	6	18	52.5
Soil preparation and planting	31	23	33	20	37	48.4
Manufacture of leather products	29	3	9	3	32	48.0
Tattooing, etc.	16	14	44	22	20	46.6
Erection, dismantling of shelter	14	2	5	6	22	39.8
Hide preparation	31	2	4	4	39	39.4
Tending fowl, small animals	21	4	8	1	39	38.7
Crop tending and harvesting	10	15	35	39	44	33.9
Gathering of shellfish	9	4	8	7	25	33.5
Nontextile fabric manufacture	14	0	9	2	32	33.3
Fire making and tending	18	6	25	22	62	30.5

Table 3-1 (Continued)

Activity	M	M−	=	F−	F	%M
Burden bearing	12	6	33	20	57	29.9
Preparation of drinks, narcotics	20	1	13	8	57	29.5
Manufacture of thread, cordage	23	2	11	10	73	27.3
Basket making	25	3	10	6	82	24.4
Mat making	16	2	6	4	61	24.2
Weaving	19	2	2	6	67	23.9
Gathering fruits, berries, nuts	12	3	15	13	63	23.6
Fuel gathering	22	1	10	19	89	23.0
Pottery making	13	2	6	8	77	18.4
Preservation of meat and fish	8	2	10	14	74	16.7
Manufacture, repair of clothing	12	3	8	9	95	16.1
Gathering herbs, roots, seeds	8	1	11	7	74	15.8
Cooking	5	1	9	28	158	8.6
Water carrying	7	0	5	7	119	8.2
Grain grinding	2	4	5	13	114	7.8

Source: Reprinted from *Social Forces*. 15 (May 1937). "Comparative data on the division of labor by sex," by George P. Murdock. Copyright ©The University of North Carolina Press.

Note: Activities centering on child care were not included in this survey. Data are based on 224 representative cultures; horizontal totals less than 224 indicate lacking information or activity not performed in some cultures. Code: M (number of cultures in which activity is always performed by a male); M− (usually performed by a male); = (not differentiated by sex); F− (usually performed by a female); F (always performed by a female); %M (percent of cultures in which the activity was examined having the activity always performed by a male).

These studies each testify to a great deal of flexibility in the appearance of sex roles and related behaviors. The single common factor across all societies is the avoidance by women of activities entirely inimical to childbearing. Thus while there appear to be no differences between the sexes in the performance of intellectual tasks, basic physical sex differences have some importance in determining roles. Each of the cultures examined in this section can be said to have been relatively successful according to the precepts of social evolutionary theory—that is, there is no reason to suppose that the cultural patterns found are in some measure unnatural, transient, or inefficient. On the contrary, their survival indicates their efficiency. The health of cultures different from our own can be interpreted as an indication that our present stereotypes have no basis in innate intellectual differences.

Historical Development[3]

The potential flexibility in the division of labor between the sexes raises the question of why we do not allow that flexibility in our society now. Traditions are not absolute fixtures; they arise in part as solutions to problems related to inter-societal competition and the need to transfer culture to successive generations. As new problems occur, the successful society finds new solutions that may, or may not, alter or destroy older traditions. This section traces the general development of sex roles in Western societies. The scenario suggests that roles were first organized for efficiency, as predicted by social evolutionary theory, and allowed women considerable latitude in behavior. However, the onset of the industrial revolution removed much of the pressure for continued efficiency in the division of labor. Simultaneous rigidification of the legal system then fixed sex roles in the inefficient and stereotypic pattern we now experience.

Until the seventeenth century, over 90 percent of European women could be classified as "rural cultivators" or workers in agriculture in one way or another. The labor of women was necessary in order to produce sufficient food for the family as well as for trading for other necessities. In their homes, women also manufactured clothing for family use. Women who lived in towns managed their kitchen gardens and handled most of the household planning. In contrast to the day-to-day planning possible today, planning in the subsistence, nonmarket economy was seasonal or annual; careful advance planning was crucial to the well-being of the family.

There is little question that women of the Middle Ages had an essential part in their family's welfare. In some major activities, moreover, women dominated. Brewing, tavern keeping, food preparation, and clothing manufacture were often considered the exclusive province of women. Lasch (1973) notes that the guild records for the city of Frankfurt in the Middle Ages listed 201 occupations open to women. Of those, sixty-five were open only to women, and fifty-five were predominantly or equally open to women. Since women often managed their husband's businesses, they frequently became skilled in masculine trades as well as in the more commonly feminine ones. In consequence, even guilds that officially excluded women (such as sword making) in practice admitted the wife as a master on the death of her husband.

Women not only labored in the Middle Ages; they also occupied positions of more or less equal authority, responsibility, and competence with men. Contrary to much current popular belief, many women either did not marry (marriage was not considered necessary among some classes), or married late.[b] Since women were productive, late marriage was of no difficulty or embarrassment to their families. In any event, women who were not otherwise engaged could freely create and join religious orders (which they usually administered) as an alternative to marriage.

Throughout the Middle Ages, guild, religious, and social regulations obviating the equality of women were observed in the breach. The culture recognized, for example, the Roman tradition that a woman should not appear in a public forum, but the requirement of economic efficiency was such that traditions sup-

---

[b]Interestingly, the current trend toward women retaining their original family names after marriage was anticipated during the Middle Ages. When the mother's family had sufficiently high social status, children were also likely to acquire her family name.

porting discrimination went unenforced. Throughout the 1300s (and before), not even wage discrimination existed.

The slow rise of the market economy and the later industrial revolution altered the relationship between the sexes remarkably. Better production and distribution methods began to allow the production and sale in the market place of some farm produce and crafted goods not needed by the family. Families would, of course, not buy what they could readily produce themselves. As a consequence of the type of activities that women had previously performed, the products they made were less likely to enter the market place than were those traditionally produced by men. For example, milk, wheat, and wool (produced by men or by both men and women) could be sold to townspeople without a farm; butter, bread, and cloth (produced by women) could then be readily manufactured within most of those families. Thus men, more often than women, received and thereby controlled the money coming to the family; their control was legitimized by the religious and social doctrines that had previously been known but had also been effectively dormant.

During the same period as the rise of the market economy, the legal system was refined and tightened, and the previously unwritten laws were largely codified. The cultural doctrines supporting male superiority, which had previously all but escaped notice, were formalized in law compatible with the newly arisen societal organization in which men actually did dominate economic life. Thus women were formally reduced to the level of serving the wishes of their husbands, and husbands were formally elevated to the position of total dominance and responsibility. Social positions concerned with the law, such as judge, lawyer, official, etc., were generally in the exclusive hands of men during the period described.

Women's labor was still valuable after the advent of the market economy, but it could not so readily be sold; the value of women's labor depended on the use the family could make of it. As piecework manufacturing methods developed a short while later, women who worked in their homes were also able to sell their labor. Thereafter, women's labor was needed in factories. Nonetheless, by the time the labor of women was capable of earning cash for the family, the laws and traditions formalizing women's subordinate position were being enforced. Had the laws been codified earlier, they would probably have given some recognition to the de facto equality then in existence. Had they been codified later, it is possible that women would then also have been accorded equal status. The system, however, was set by the time the industrial revolution was well under way.

Despite its apparent rigidity, the legal and social system would normally be required to continue changing in order to allow for the efficient division of labor in competitive societies. However the industrial revolution temporarily relieved the need for such efficiency by allowing economic superiority to be achieved through the superior organization of other means of production. In fact, with the advent of sufficient surplus production, it became possible for more affluent men to keep their wives at home, rather than to allow them outside work. Men who did so achieved a measure of status. The new division of labor outwardly copied the earlier fashion of life among European nobility (when the wife actually managed the servants, planning, food preparation, and the kitchen garden), allowed the conspicuous demonstration of affluence, and reaffirmed the legally defined superior/subordinate relationship of the husband to the wife. Growing general affluence allowed the practice to spread gradually until it became institutionalized.

This sequence, although supported in all its elements, is but one possible interpretation of the events surrounding the development of our present society. This interpretation views codification of law, the growth of the market system, and the subsequent industrial revolution as mere chance events that combined to structure our society as it is now. The impact of similar historical forces appears to have produced comparable results in other cultures as well (Boserup, 1970; Fogel and Engerman, 1974). However, it is also possible to view the Middle Ages as a period unlike any other in Western history; thus the sexual equality of that period might be considered coincidental. Probably neither interpretation is entirely correct. Nonetheless, the historic view presented here, when combined with the crosscultural data examined earlier, supports the conclusion established in the prior section of this chapter; that is, there is little absolute limitation on the capacities of either men or women.

A Natural Division of Labor?

Although one sex may not be intrinsically better qualified than another across all conditions, it remains to be considered whether one sex is better qualified for certain occupations under the conditions in which we now live. To return to the ideas of social evolutionary theory, perhaps the continued health of our society requires that we maintain the present division of labor. The survival of our society may be based on the particular fitness of our culture; working men and housewives, or at least male executives and female subordinates, may be needed to preserve our culture. There are good reasons for dismissing these views.

As shown in the last section, our present division of labor arose during an historical period having a particular conjunction of events. The pressure for improvement of living standards, which prompted men to enter the money economy, was quite real; had men not done so, the industrial revolution would have been greatly impeded if not prevented. While the impact of a man's earnings is generally beneficial for the entire family, the impact of preventing a woman from adding to the family's income clearly is not. Women who do not function as efficiently as they might are of less than optimal benefit to their families, their society, and themselves. The economy (and the culture) is made less, rather than more, likely to survive as a result. In fact, it is only lack of pressure from competing societies that has allowed our society to use women in nonoptimal ways.

The most obvious proof of these assertions is our wartime experience. Although surplus value temporarily lifts the pressure for efficiency and allows women to be sent home in normal times, periods of war, in which production efficiency is essential, have inevitably brought women back to work. It must be admitted that our culture has also survived relatively well having women in factories during wartime rather than caring for their children. Child care is no longer an important function for most women. Not only are there fewer children to consider, but they are soon sent to school. While family management is still cumbersome, children do not seriously eliminate the ability of most women to work. Thus the sexual segregation of functions in our society has ornamental, rather than real, value. In fact, it has negative survival value for the culture as a whole in competitive situations.

The division of labor in primitive societies roughly follows actual physical abilities or disabilities. The women in those societies often stay in the area of their homes. In primitive societies, women are also valued, rather than devalued, when they make a net contribution to their families. The conditions for contribution are different in our society. For better or worse, the primary medium of value is money; the work for which it is received is outside the home and primarily involves those functions now controlled by men. In the roles which they often occupy, women do not, and are not expected to, contribute to society to the same extent as do men. So long as their work is considered (or is) unnecessary, surplus, or inferior, it seems reasonable to expect that women will continue to be paid less than men and placed in subordinate positions. The concept of a natural division of labor is thus a mistaken one at this point in history. Natural divisions do exist, but the need for them has been almost entirely eroded in our society. If the concept still persists, it is only because sex stereotypes have been learned too well and, in addition, have been legitimized by rigid laws and traditions. Those laws and traditions are now irrelevant, if not unfortunate, to the most efficient operation of our society.

An Examination of Worth and Trust
in Relation to Sex Roles

Since our society largely prohibits the presence of women in dominant roles, it must also train them for the alternative roles they are expected to play. Women who are not so trained constitute a two-fold "danger" to social stability. In the first place, they do not serve in the capacities expected of them. Although these capacities are poorly regarded and are largely expendable, the lack of a fit between individual abilities and social needs would reduce societal efficiency still further. Additionally, women who do not willingly and readily take their expected places may constitute a sort of fifth column provoking social change. Consequently the women produced by our society must be brought up generally to accept their status in the division of labor. This section considers some of the implications of that acceptance. Readers who personally reject the notion of society's endangerment by changes in the status of women may find the implications of acceptance discussed below to be somewhat painful.

The stereotype of women as incompetent, the fact that women's labor is typically subordinate to that of men, and the lower pay received by women all bear evidence that the positions women hold are less and powerful. Not surprisingly, status usually accrues with actual and imagined power—men have status as a result of their ascribed roles (that is, they are born to it) while, barring exceptional achievement, women do not. Two studies, in which subjects rated the desirability of occupations identified falsely as having either an increasing number of men or an increasing number of women, found that the prestige and desirability of an occupation is diminished simply by the entrance of large numbers of women (Touhey, 1974a, 1974b). Additional data, reported by Bartol and Bartol (1975) indicate that occupational prestige is somewhat linked with fields having a preponderance of men even in the Soviet Union.

A personality counterpart to prestige is self-esteem, the extent to which a person values herself or himself and feels self-assured. People whose capabilities and behaviors are restricted, or are defined as being less important than those of others, might be expected to manifest a lower evaluation of themselves. That expectation is often borne out when men and women rate overall feelings of self-esteem; men give themselves significantly higher ratings than do women. Although that effect is consistent with the pattern of male domination and prestige, a recent study by Spence, Helmreich, and Stapp (1975) carried the analysis one step further.

Spence et al. first obtained self-concept ratings for a set of stereotypic characteristics (See Chapter 2, Table 2–1). Consistent with the discussion above, the researchers found that *both* men and women had higher self-esteem if they had more of the masculine traits in their self-concept. The self-esteem for both sexes was still higher, however, if their self-concepts contained the positively valued components of both the masculine and feminine stereotypes. Thus if, as this chapter has shown, women are not naturally predisposed toward certain occupations, then the social restriction of women to less important positions has probably had the result of artificially lowering their self-esteem and limiting their abilities. The results also support the notion that the flexible adoption of both masculine and feminine traits and activities allows greater freedom of self-development (Bem, 1975; Maccoby, 1966).

The prophecy contained in sex stereotypes is thus self-fulfilling. By adopting the behaviors that are role-appropriate in our society, a woman does not develop the ability to perform the full range of vocational activities. Because women are less apt to have wide experience and are relegated to low status positions, they have relatively low self-esteem. Since they correctly observe that men are more experienced, women are realistically dependent on men even when they are free to behave as they like. The woman who is trained not to assert herself, and for whom competence training is omitted or unavailable, is also trained to trust and use the efforts of men on her behalf rather than to directly control her own life. Although it is probably also true that men are equally trained out of social skills, the impact of some loss of social skills is not so likely to be felt in terms of prestige, self-esteem, job mobility, self-reliance, and power.

As discussed in the last chapter, both competence and social skills are needed to work with people in an ideal manner. However, men and women face the labor market from opposing directions. The assumption is made that a man's "natural" competence and training allow him to perform a superior job in a dominant position. The assumption is also made that a woman should not be in such a position and could not effectively operate in it if she were. The man starts with a presumed advantage and the woman with a presumed disadvantage. While the basis for the presumptions is false, it results circularly in differential opportunities, training, dependence, and self-esteem. Those differences are real in any employment situation and may result in apparent discrimination even by employers who are not predisposed toward bias. The tradition of feminine inferiority thus sustains itself (cf. Block, 1973; Jackaway, 1975).

Notes

1. The concepts of Darwinism and Social Darwinism are most deeply frowned on by intellectuals in a variety of disciplines. There is no intention of resurrecting either of them in their original forms here. Genetic evolutionary theory as it now stands is considerably more enlightened than Darwin's proposals originally allowed. Since this book is primarily concerned with only a few aspects of that theory, and since simplified forms of the theory still resemble the original in many ways, the distinctions between modern evolutionary theory and its predecessor are of little consequence here.

Social Darwinism (actually modern evolutionary theory applied to a society rather than to a species) is often considered to be based on a circular argument that existing societies are best. The part of the argument extracted here is not circular, however. It is to be hoped that those who disagree with Darwinism and Social Darwinism will examine the logic of the arguments presented rather than being concerned with antiquated or unnecessary parts of those theories (which are not used here). Readers who are familiar with utility theory (economics) or reinforcement theory (psychology) will be able to use those concepts to develop the same conclusions as are here arrived at through evolutionary theory (cf. Larwood and Duffy, 1975).

2. Research on this point is arguable admittedly. Broverman, Klaiber,

Kobayashi, and Vogel (1968) have asserted that estrogen, primarily a female ovarian hormone, is associated with a higher activation level of the central adrenergic (sympathetic) nervous system than is testosterone, primarily a male testicular hormone. The higher level of activation, and comparatively lower operating level of the opposing parasympathetic nervous system, supposedly results in a relatively lower ability in females to accomplish complex problem solving but an increased ability to handle overlearned repetitive tasks such as typing.

The study is based in large part on extrapolation from research with other animal species. Broverman et al. (1968) ignore the fact that primates, especially humans, are more likely than other species to be controlled by learned or cognitive abilities instead of hormones or other innate factors. The researchers also bypass the extent to which hormone release may be controlled by physical activity and stress. We are not, in other words, simply more likely to attempt what we are capable of doing; through learning and physical change, we become more capable of doing what we attempt Broverman et al. (1968) may therefore in part be mistaking a cause (sex differences in activities) for a result. A number of other questions also arise in connection with their analysis (see Singer and Montgomery, 1969, and Broverman, Klaiber, Kobayashi, and Vogel, 1969).

3. Appreciation is due to Professor Kathleen Casey for her help in integrating some of this material. The author takes full responsibility for any inadequacies of interpretation.

References

Barry, H., Bacon, M. K., and Child, I. I. "A cross-cultural survey of some sex differences in socialization." *Journal of Abnormal and Social Psychology,* 1957, *55,* 327–332.

Bartol, K. M., and Bartol, R. A. "Women in managerial and technical positions: The United States and the Soviet Union." *Industrial and Labor Relations Review,* 1975, *28,* 524–534.

Bem, S. L. "Androgyny vs. the tight little lives of fluffy women and chesty men." *Psychology Today,* 1975, *9,* 58–62.

Block, J. H. "Conceptions of sex role." *American Psychologist,* 1973, *28,* 512–526.

Boserup, E. *Women's role in economic development.* London: George Allen and Unwin, 1970.

Broverman, D. M., Klaiber, E. L., Kobayashi, Y., and Vogel, W. "Reply to the 'Comment' by Singer and Montgomery on 'Roles of activation and inhibition in sex differences in cognitive abilities.'" *Psychological Review,* 1969, *76,* 328–331.

——, ——, ——, and ——. "Roles of activation and inhibition in sex differences in cognitive abilities." *Psychological Review,* 1968, *75,* 23–50.

Campbell, D. T. "Variation and selective-retention in sociocultural evolution." In H. R. Barringer, G. I. Blanksten, and R. W. Mack (eds.), *Social change in developing areas: A reinterpretation of evolutionary theory.* Cambridge, Mass.: Schenkman, 1966.

Child, I. L. "Personality in culture." In E. F. Borgatta, and W. W. Lambert (eds.), *Handbook of personality theory and research.* Chicago: Rand McNally, 1968.

D'Andrade, R. G. "Sex differences and cultural institutions." In E. Maccoby (ed.), *The development of sex differences.* Stanford, Calif.: Stanford University Press, 1966.

Ekehammar, B. "Interactionism in personality from a historical perspective." *Psychological Bulletin,* 1974, *81,* 1026–1048.

Erlenmeyer-Kimling, L., and Jarvik, L. F. "Genetics and intelligence: A review." *Science,* 1963, *142,* 1477–1479.

Fogel, R. W., and Engerman, S. L. *Time on the cross.* Boston: Little, Brown & Co., 1974.

Jackaway, R. "Achievement attributions and the low expectation cycle in females." Paper read at the Annual Convention of the American Psychological Association, Chicago, 1975.

Larwood, L., and Duffy, J. F. "The price escalator: A behaviorist alternative for dealing with inflation." *Upstate Forum* collection, 1975.

Lasch, C. "Marriage in the middle ages." *The Columbia Forum,* 1973, *11* (Fall).

Le Vine, R. A. "Culture, personality and socialization: An evolutionary view." In D. A. Goslin (ed.), *Handbook of socialization theory and research.* Chicago: Rand McNally, 1969.

Maccoby, E. "Sex differences in intellectual functioning." In E. Maccoby (ed.), *The development of sex differences.* Stanford, Calif.: Stanford University Press, 1966.

McGuire, W. J. "Personality and susceptibility to social influence." In E. F. Borgatta and W. W. Lambert (eds.), *Handbook of personality theory and research.* Chicago: Rand McNally, 1968.

Murdock, G. P. "Comparative data on the division of labor by sex." *Social Forces,* 1937, *15,* 551–553.

Reed, E. W., and Reed, S. C. *Mental retardation: A family study.* Philadelphia: Saunders, 1965.

Shields, S. A. "Functionalism, Darwinism, and the psychology of women." *American Psychologist,* 1975, *30,* 739–754.

Singer, G., and Montgomery, R. B. "Comment on roles of activation and inhibition in sex differences in cognitive abilities." *Psychological Review*, 1969, *76*, 325–327.

Spence, J. T., Helmreich, R., and Stapp, J. "Ratings of self and peers on sex role attributes and their relation to self-esteem and conceptions of masculinity and femininity." *Journal of Personality and Social Psychology*, 1975, *32*, 29–39.

Touhey, J. C. "Effects of additional men on prestige and desirability of occupations typically performed by women." *Journal of Applied Social Psychology*, 1974a, *4*, 330–335.

————. "Effects of additional women professionals on ratings of occupational prestige and desirability." *Journal of Personality and Social Psychology*, 1974b, *29*, 86–89.

Whiting, B., and Edwards, C. P. "A cross-cultural analysis of sex differences in the behavior of children aged three through eleven." *Journal of Social Psychology*, 1973, *91*, 171–188.

4 Why Can't Women Manage?

The title of this chapter is misleading. Women *can* manage. In fact, as Chapter 1 noted, a small proportion already do. The second chapter stated that women are not really expected to manage organizations, but that the average woman's self-concept is not opposed to managing. In taking note of historical trends, Chapter 3 found that women have had major managerial roles in the recent past. Nonetheless, the fact remains that few women manage in major organizations at this time.

The absence of women in key positions results from a wide variety of causes, some of which, such as tradition, have already been examined. Equally important, the absence of women in key positions is itself a cause, leading many people to believe that women need not prepare for the occupations leading to top administration. The expectation has often proven to be justified but for what reason? As evidence in the previous chapters has begun to show, self-concepts and abilities are for the most part neither inborn nor accidental. What we do and what we are capable of doing are both limited by our experiences and by what we and others believe we are capable of doing. The expectation that women will not enter management affects the training given to girls (in comparison to boys), the experiences they seek, and ultimately the ways in which they are able and prefer to cope with their world.

The present chapter traces some of the personality and behavioral differences arising from sex-differentiated expectations held by parents and society at large. Some of the processes leading to self and role concepts will be examined first. These processes will be used as a basis to examine some of the sex differences in adults that sometimes affect managerial interest and behavior. Finally, this chapter assays the importance of those differences in terms of the development of "feminine" strategies of exchange and bargaining.

Some care should be exercised in interpreting the discussions in this chapter. No attempt has been made to summarize all the supposed or known sex differences. Instead, this chapter is deliberately one-sided in that it concentrates only on those differences that seem most closely related to management. Since personality and behavior are undoubtedly multidetermined, additional factors might easily be added. It seems questionable, however, whether the information that could be added is justified in terms of its overall importance to management.

Readers should also be aware that the psychological differences discussed are differences between an average person of each sex—they do not imply that either the reader or anyone else actually fits a particular description. While some research has indicated that women are more dependent than men in certain in-

61

stances, a particular woman may, in fact, be more independent than any man in those same conditions. The discussion is based on statistical generalization. Finally, many of the interpretations are tentative, arguable, and open to the insights of new research information.

Development of Self and Role Concepts

To determine why few women seem to develop a taste for management as we define the term today, it is useful to examine the roots of our experiential and conceptual systems. As it relates to role and self-concept, developmental psychology currently has two major competing streams of theory. Social learning theorists (Bandura, 1969, 1973; Mischel, 1966) feel that individuals learn most readily that which it is actually or potentially reinforcing for them to learn. Hence, if we watch other people being rewarded, we learn how to behave in order to be rewarded ourselves; emphasis is thus on the power of observation and reward. Cognitive-developmental theory (Kohlberg, 1966, 1969) insists that individuals strive to identify themselves and, having done so, to learn those behaviors appropriate to an individual having that identification. Cognitive-developmental theory thus places emphasis on the process of identification and sees the individual as thereafter seeking knowledge relevant to that identity. As Maccoby and Jacklin (1974) have pointed out, there is excellent evidence supporting both theories—but neither is able, without considerable strain, to explain some of the processes predicted by the other. Children do apparently go through an identification process and thereafter appear to learn and behave in ways conforming to their identification. However, they also learn—but are not so likely to repeat unless rewarded for doing so—behaviors that are not appropriate to their identity.

Most evidence indicates that infants under the age of fifteen months are unaware of themselves as entities fully distinct from their environment (Amsterdam, 1972; Gallup, 1973). For example, younger infants react to their own mirror images as though they signal the presence of another infant. The functional relationship linking their movements to those of their mirror twin is not comprehended. Beyond fifteen months, however, children start to react to their own images differently from those of others. Their recognition of themselves indicates that the development of self-awareness has begun. It appears that the concept of sexual identity begins to evolve shortly thereafter. Work reviewed by Money and Ehrhardt (1972) indicates that infants under eighteen months can be arbitrarily assigned or reassigned to either gender without respecting either genital or chromosomal sex. However, beyond that age, successful sex reassignment becomes increasingly difficult (all but impossible by the age of three) as the individual accommodates to his or her sexual identity.

A considerable body of research has investigated for sex differences in children younger than eighteen months; differences have actually been found in a large number of behaviors and abilities. However, while some of these findings may ultimately hold up as further research becomes known, the evidence supporting sex differences at this age is generally contradictory; studies that have instituted adequate controls for differences in parental expectation and physiological requirements (e.g. sleep) have often found that the controls wash out most of the dispositionally related behavior differences previously discovered (cf. Moss, 1967). What seems so far "known" is that major sex differences do not exist in the inborn behavior of infants; we are not able to successfully discriminate between males and females on the basis of behavior during the first 1.5 years in any socially important manner. Thereafter, however, some important sex differences do develop. Differential learning appears to be the most important factor governing these differences, although there may be physiological predisposing factors that enhance the learning of some behaviors.

To best understand the process of sex role learning, we might imagine an infant who is reactive to patterns of reinforcement; it behaves in such a way as to maximize its perceived advantage by repeating rewarded behaviors and avoiding those that are punished. At some point, the child finds (perhaps unconsciously) that reinforcement is given for a particular set of behaviors, a set that clusters together in the meaningful way that adults term sex role. Since parents differentially reward appropriate role behavior (Fling and Manosevitz, 1972), the child is more likely to learn to behave in a manner appropriate to sex role than in one that is not.

The child's identification of his or her sex results in a number of changes in learning, behavioral, and cognitive patterns. Children are not only interested in correct behavior but in finding correct rationales for it and in assuring others that the behavior is satisfactory. Researchers have found that children are more likely to observe and imitate behaviors when modeled by someone of their own sex (Bandura, 1965). Presumably others of the same sex demonstrate the activities that are appropriate and hence more likely to lead to reward for the child imitating them.

A moral code is directly associated with the learning of sex role. Inappropriate activities are subjectively "bad" and may be, perhaps will be, punished. The activities appropriate to the opposite sex are acceptable for those persons, but their performance allows the opposite sex to be stigmatized as subjectively inferior. Consequently, the members of each sex tend to perceive themselves as superior to those of the other. Members of the opposite sex may consequently be readily derogated relative to one's own (Stevenson, Hale, Hill, and Moely, 1967). The same phenomenon, stigmatization of members of the other group as inferior, occurs as a normal consequence of other types of role differences as well (e.g. employee-employer, black-white, etc.). It is interesting to note that not only girls and boys, but men and women as well, discriminate against one another in favor of their own sex (Larwood, 1974, Larwood and Blackmore, in press).

Despite self-identification, children are still cognizant of which circumstances are in fact individually most rewarding. As one result, individuals who control power (for example, by having or dispensing resources in a game) are differentially responded to and imitated (cf. Bandura, Ross, & Ross, 1963). We noted earlier that men's occupations have higher status than those of women. That finding is readily explained by noting that in Western society men and men's occupations control the greater amount of power and are more highly paid. While girls also enjoy and aspire to power, they are placed in the ambiguous position of being reinforced for learning a role that will not lead to it. The identification of boys, and the general enjoyment of the benefits of power and resources, both impel boys in the "appropriate" direction.

Substantial sex role learning has taken place by the time the child is four-to-five-years-old (cf. Fauls & Smith, 1956). By that point, for instance, children of both sexes have a substantial preference for toys that are stereotypically appropriate for their sex (Fling and Manosevitz, 1972). They have been successfully socialized not only by parents, but by playmates, playthings, and observed models as well (McArthur and Eisen, 1976; Sternglanz & Serbin, 1974; Weitzman, Eifler, Hokada, and Ross, 1972). Although self and role concepts do continue to crystalize thereafter, the pattern is remarkably stable (Jorgensen and Howell, 1969; Katz and Zigler, 1967; Stein, 1971; Stein and Smithells, 1969).

If the sex differences in behavior and preferences were confined merely to play activities, we might dismiss them as irrelevant. In fact, of course, they extend well beyond. Stein and Smithells (1969) found that second-grade children were well aware of the sex appropriateness of different types of school achievement. In a later study (Stein, Pohly, and Mueller, 1971), sixth graders were informed that an objectively sex-neutral test was either masculine or feminine. Boys preferred the test when it was labeled as masculine and felt they would do better on the masculine test. For girls, the results were reversed: they predicted better performance on, and preferred, the same test when it seemed feminine. The implications of this study and others like it are that we are influenced by labeling to enjoy and participate in those activities that seem to fit our designated roles. Since sex roles are well-established early in life, they have the potential of substantially limiting that which we seek to do and experience.

The next sections consider some of the ways in which the identification process affects achievement, assertiveness, and dependence. Preferences for activities among children do not translate directly to later managerial performance. Along with their underlying role processes, the preferences may predict the development of perceptual and behavioral patterns that can alter managerial effectiveness, however—at least under certain circumstances.[1] The last topic examined is the manner in which the perceptual and behavioral patterns affect strategy selection in bargaining and pay-performance evaluations.

Achievement

If one is to achieve success, at least beyond that conferred by blind luck, three characteristics are needed. Any task requires some level of ability to complete it. Beyond mere ability, however, the individual should believe that his or her ability is sufficient to proceed. If there is insufficient ability, or if the task requires too much effort, the individual may not care to make an attempt. Finally, of course, there is the question of motivation. Even if we know how to do some task, and find that it is not too difficult, do we care to bother? Researchers in each of these three component areas of achievement have, at one time or another, asserted that women are different from men—that women do not have the same type of abilities as men, do not feel in control of events, and are not motivated to achieve success when they do. It is as a result of these differences, they have maintained, that women have not made the historic achievements that men have accomplished. Research data can be used to support those assertions since there are readily observable differences in the measured ability, expectation of control, and motivation between the sexes. The interpretation of those results is easily challenged, however.

Ability

Although a wide range of aptitudes may be tested for, most intelligence tests are primarily concerned with mathematical and verbal abilities. Tradition has it that men are mathematically more competent while women are more verbal. If research can lend substance to the tradition, then we would have one explanation for the predominance of men in fields requiring mathematical and technical abilities.

On the surface, at least, the stereotypic ability differences do seem to exist. A review of relevant research by Maccoby and Jacklin (1974, pp. 78–90) indicates that while a large number of studies find no sex differences along either ability dimension, many also do. In general, after the age of ten, males seem more likely to score well on mathematical aptitude tests. Conversely, females seem more verbally skilled across a wide range of ages. As Maccoby and Jacklin point out, however, a close examination of the testing methodology and the underlying assumptions throws these results into question. For example, many tests of mathematical ability include elements of spatial reasoning despite the fact that mathematical and spatial concepts require quite different mental processes. Innate aptitude for spatial reasoning appears to be partly linked to an inherited recessive X (sex) chromosome characteristic (Block and Kolakowski, 1973; Vandenberg, 1968). The result is that an unusually high spatial reasoning ability is less likely to occur in women than in men. Many "mathematics" tests are therefore intrinsically biased against women. The inheritance of other intellectual characteristics, however, is not sex-linked in any respect (cf. Wittig, 1976).

Perhaps more important, measures of supposed native aptitudes are influenced by trained differences in ability—that is, IQ can vary. Children spend more time on those activities that they enjoy and feel are meaningful to their future. This effect draws girls toward artistic, social, and reading skills, and boys toward mathematical, athletic, and spatial-mechanical skills according to the stereotypes measured by Stein and Smithells. To that extent, the intelligence differences between the sexes reflect differences in the knowledge acquired rather than underlying aptitude.

A large part of measured "ability" differences also results from interpersonal sex role effects that are purely situational and have nothing to do with actual ability. In Chapter 2, we saw that an evaluator is partly responsible for the behavior of a role player; in fact, sex role behavior can often be elicited by the mere presence of a member of the opposite sex. Most university and high school instructors are, of course, male. On this basis, we can predict that women behave in a role appropriate manner with their male instructors—inhibiting mathematical and similarly masculine skills while striving to do better at more feminine pursuits. Only the substitution of a female instructor would allow women to express their true mathematical capabilities.

Studies working with this and similar hypotheses have confirmed that women perform better at a mechanical task under the supervision of a woman (Larwood, O'Carroll, and Logan, 1977), that girls perform better on a standard mathematical test administered by a female than by a male instructor (Pedersen, Shinedling, and Johnson, 1968), and that women are better able to solve mathematical word problems administered by another woman than by a man (Hoffman and Maier, 1966). Using a related approach, Milton (1959) found that men and women perform better on mathematical problems that are worded to appeal to their sex roles. In the latter case, individuals calculated either the manner in which Snuffy the tramp stretched his supply of cigarette butts, or the way Sally the cook planned her cookie batter. Although the correct response was the same in each form of question, men performed better in answer to "Snuffy"; for women, the results were nonsignificantly reversed.

Taken together, these studies suggest that there is no real difference between the sexes in conventional intelligence. There probably are differences, caused by the different training experiences of men and women, in some highly specialized abilities. However, the experimental procedures applied so far have not been sufficiently balanced for sex role to allow an exact determination to be made. In general, it is safe to say that differential ability is not a factor in achievement differences in the sexes.

Difficulty

Individuals who feel that their abilities are unequal to the requirements of a task, irrespective of the actual relationship, may predict a low likelihood of success for themselves (Weiner, Nierenberg, and Goldstein, 1976). The prediction of success, of course, influences interest in taking up any particular task. If women perceive that they are less capable than men, whatever the truth of the matter, we might expect to find that women are less interested in attempting particular achievements.

In fact, males do appear to have more confidence in their abilities across a wide range of activities, including grade performance, manual dexterity, puzzle solutions, and capacity in emergency situations (cf. Maccoby and Jacklin, 1974). While some men may be more capable than some women in each case, it is inconceivable that the average man is more capable than the average woman in most of these situations.

Although the results concerning differences in reported confidence are clear-cut and have been repeatedly substantiated, the reasons for them are only now becoming clear. Expressed expectations for success seem to follow the logic of sex role learning. Females are taught not to express high expectations for themselves. For example, Crandall, Katkovsky, and Preston (1962) found that while more intelligent grade school boys predicted higher test performances for themselves, more intelligent girls predicted lower performances. Similarly, evidence in another study (Vaught, 1965) indicates that many women take deliberate steps toward the presentation of a feminine image of dependency and incompetence. It seems likely that, while many women harbor some doubts concerning their abilities, their predictions of lower performance relative to men are based largely on the desire to project femininity in situations where sex role is important (Ireson, 1976). When they are unconcerned with sex role, their expectations seem commensurate with their abilities.

Motivation

If we do believe that we are capable of success with some reasonable degree of effort, then we weigh the effort in terms of the probable rewards before deciding to attempt the undertaking. Traditional achievement motivation theory (Atkinson, 1957) proposes two opposing achievement-related motives, one to avoid failure and the other to attain success. Those who prefer to achieve success will do so, according to the theory, by most strongly attempting tasks on which they predict a 50 percent likelihood of success. If women who desire success underestimate their abilities relative to the tasks considered, they probably attempt easier tasks than others who correctly estimate their abilities; the easier tasks would have both less stringent requirements for success and a lower value (or payoff) on reaching success.

Normally, of course, an overly qualified individual of either sex would soon attain success. At that point, the person might decide that she or he is more qualified than anticipated, raise expectations, and attempt more worthwhile activities in the future. Recent modifications of achievement motivation theory (Frieze, 1975; Weiner and Sierad, 1975) have suggested, however, that the path for raising expectations is more open to those already possessing high expectations (men) than to those without them (women—at least for activities generally important to management). We can attribute success on a task either to ourselves (effort or ability) or to the environment (task difficulty or luck). Those believing they have high ability can confirm that supposition by attributing success to ability, thereby raising expectations; failure can be put down to chance. Those believing they have little ability can also confirm their predictions by attributing success to luck or task choice, and failure to lack of ability (see also Crandall, Katkovsky, and Crandall, 1965; Jackaway, 1975).

Of course, anyone with low self-confidence can also eliminate possible embarrassment by avoiding the contest (technically speaking, their fear of failure dominates their desire to succeed). In one example, it was shown that women, more than men, preferred a game of chance and were more likely to persist at it than at an alternative game of skill (Deaux, White, and Farris, 1975). It seems that people who acquire a low expectation of success, for whatever reason, have little likelihood of breaking from it spontaneously. They avoid risks that, if taken successfully, could boost expectation; when they take the risks, they may engage in misattribution for the outcome. Women are more likely than men to be caught in the "low expectation trap" at least when they are concerned with sex roles such as when performing a masculine-stereotyped task or when working with men. Sex role is probably not as important a determinant of expectation among men, since general competence is an acceptable part of a man's role.

The underlying assumption of achievement motivation is that success is valued while failure is punishing. However, if women are not "supposed" to have high expectations for their abilities, we might anticipate that their achievements, which are manifestations of their abilities, are often socially unacceptable. As noted in previous chapters, the work of women is normally considered second-rate to that of men, and indisputable achievements by women are thought unusual. Horner (1970) has attempted to tie these factors together by introducing the concept of "fear of success." According to her theory, women who recognize that they do have ability must purposely avoid seeming successful in order to behave in a socially approved manner. The brightest women would be most affected: as success appears within their reach, the conflict resulting from fear of success (and social disapproval contingent on success) acts to inhibit further effort.

The fear of success motive has now been measured in samples of men as well as women. While the theory was intended to suggest why women are conflicted regarding success, the empirical results often indicate that men are equally affected by the motive to avoid success (Feather and Raphelson, 1974; Heilbrun, Kleemeier, and Piccola, 1974; Wood & Greenfeld, 1976). The concept underlying the theory, however, appears to be sound: anyone should be most interested in achieving when doing so has an expected positive value to them. So-called achievements may have negative as well as positive values. To the extent that an act is punished rather than rewarded, potential achievers will avoid the behavior.

Several studies indicate that nontraditional achievement by women is often unrewarded and sometimes punished. As a result of the perceptions of women's performance as inferior to that of men, it is less likely that women will be equally rewarded for equal performance on competitive masculine tasks. A study by Hagan and Kahn (1975) indicates that, as well, men devalue successful women with whom they are competing and tend to exclude them from further interaction (see also Wyer and Malinowski, 1972). Some researchers have found that women who are interested in nontraditional fields fear that isolation and loneliness will result (Stewart and Winter, 1974), while neutral observers feel that male-dominated professions are not very satisfying to women (Feather, 1975). Such fears may have some basis in reality.

On the other hand, if women were equally rewarded with men, we may fairly ask what their achievement level would be. Recent work indicates that women who are accepted for good performance are more likely both to repeat and to want to repeat their superior performance than are those who are rejected; women who are rejected for a poor performance are more likely to subsequently improve than those who are accepted for it (Fisher, O'Neal, and McDonald, 1974; Jellison, Jackson-White, Bruder, and Martyna, 1975).

Women can achieve, then, but many competent women probably perform below their capabilities simply because they find poor performance relatively more rewarding and sex role appropriate (see also Ireson, 1976; Komarovsky, 1973; Larwood, O'Carroll, and Logan, 1977). The way in which women's performance could be improved is obvious: intelligence and successful achievement must be made as rewarding for women as for men. One mechanism is through a redefinition of sex role so as to exclude any consideration of achievement as appropriate or inappropriate to either sex. If society were to become aware of the real present achievements of many women, this process could occur quite rapidly. In the meantime, it is only the exceptional woman who both recognizes her abilities and chooses to exercise them in nontraditional ways.

Why aren't traditional women's outlets for achievement considered here? Surely a woman who succeeds in homemaking has achieved success analogous to that in a management environment. However achievement motivation concepts are frequently defined in terms of a specific task structure including: observation by others, limited probability of success, financially-relevant outcomes. While the position of executive combines these factors, that of homemaker does not. In terms of personality measurement, the achievement motive thus defined can be readily separated from other motives (such as affiliation and power) which, while important, predict different behaviors.

Assertiveness and Power

The concept of achievement centers on the demonstration productive capacity to others and sometimes in competition with them. An executive or manager with a high desire to achieve would be distinguishable by a strong inclination to tackle projects that mix challenge with a fair probability of success. Although there is little doubt that many managers desire achievement, recent work by McClelland (1975) indicates the importance of an additional dimension, a desire for power, motivating many successful executives. Top executives occupy positions in which they exercise command through other people. As a consequence, we may expect that those who are interested in and capable of obtaining influence over others have a better-than-average probability of dominating their organizations.

There are of course many ways in which people can be influenced. They could be threatened, bribed, or convinced through debate to support someone else's demands. Men and women may prefer different techniques for influence. For example, McClelland's evidence indicates that women are more concerned with their physical appearance and financial freedom as ways of influencing others than are men. Unfortunately, however, too few studies have yet been completed with the few women who have worked their way into top management positions to be certain whether their desire for power or techniques for gaining it differ substantially from those of men. When we shift consideration to women in general, however, there are some definite sex differences in the assertiveness and leadership styles of women and men.

Aggression—The Learning of Assertion

Research concerning interpersonal aggression has frequently found that both boys and men are more physically aggressive than girls and women—at least in Western societies (cf. Maccoby and Jacklin, 1974, pp. 230–233).[2] The usual differences in aggression levels are deceptive, however, since they depend very much on what age group, target, instigation, and mode of expression are being considered. Young children of both sexes are often highly and seemingly randomly aggressive. The early aggression shown by girls is not so predictive of aggression in later life as is that of boys, however (Kagan and Moss, 1962); girls begin to inhibit much of their aggression at an early age. Although children of both sexes learn to aggress, in part, by watching aggressive models, girls are not so likely as boys to freely imitate modeled aggression unless they are first assured that their resulting behavior is socially acceptable (Bandura, 1965; Feshbach and Feshbach, 1972).

Classroom studies have shown that the aggressive interactions of young children are heavily dependent on the rewards or punishments meted to the aggressor (cf. Patterson, Littman and Bricker, 1967). It seems likely that the emergence of assertiveness is similar to that of other social activities: assertion increases in frequency when rewarded and decreases when not rewarded or threatened with punishment. Boys and girls both learn aggressive behaviors, but it is more likely that they will be condoned for boys than for girls. While successful instrumental aggression may have its own rewards, attempts at aggression are more likely after observation of the behavior in use by a parent or friend of the same sex who lends an aura of appropriateness (Levin and Sears, 1956), or after specific approval and reward by others (Bandura, 1965; Hicks, 1965).

Learning from childhood influences later adult behavior. In adulthood, it is considered sufficiently unusual for a woman to strongly assert herself that steps are often not taken to repulse threats from women. In fact, we can generally predict a chain of events like the following. Women make threats (serious ones) less frequently than men. When a woman does begin to assert herself in this manner, she is unlikely to be believed or taken seriously by men. When her aggressive intentions are established beyond a doubt, however, the woman is a double threat; not only is she as aggressive as a man, but she also behaves unpredictably and inappropriately. At this point, others have license both to counteragress to maintain their own positions and to enforce social norms for appropriate behavior against the woman. The double threat is most likely to occur when an assertive woman encounters a man. In contrast, men anticipate appropriate assertiveness from each other; they have developed cue and bargaining strategies to assess and deal with the assertiveness and are unlikely to provoke overreaction from such behavior. In interactions between two women, either can readily justify allowing the other to assert herself.

The work of Hagan and Kahn (1975) supports these contentions—men who are surprised by a woman's assertion of competence (competitively beating their own scores in a laboratory game) appear to be more upset by, and counter-reactive toward, her skill than are either male observers or participating women. Others have found that assertive women are more likely to incur physical aggression from men (Kaleta and Buss, 1973) and that women are similarly willing to protect their positions by making extreme counterattacks when unexpectedly and inappropriately physically attacked by men (Taylor and Epstein, 1967).

Dominance

Physical or verbal assertiveness are often behavioral manifestations of the interest in gaining or expressing power over others. It has also been suggested that some people possess a personality trait related to deliberately manipulative behavior (Machiavellianism) or to attempts at control in social interactions (dominance). Administration of paper and pencil tests to measure these constructs has generally found little or no sex difference among children. However, for adults, men often score somewhat higher than women for both Machiavellianism and dominance. As with intelligence testing, the interpretation of these differences is murky at best and deceptive at worst. If the results can be believed and have operational significance, they still cannot be applied across the entire range of situations. Obvious conditions exist in which a low-dominance woman would attempt to assert control over a man.

An additional limitation of paper and pencil personality tests lies in determining the validity of using similar (or identical) questionnaire items for both sexes. There is as yet no satisfactory way to determine that men and women are not reacting differently on the tests because of their different familiarity with and interest in the question content, rather than because of some underlying personality feature. Put another way, there is no reason to assume that men and women of equal dominance will answer the questions in the same manner; if they did, we would be uncertain of how to interpret the similarity.

One step toward clarification of the meaning of paper and pencil tests is to examine the behavior of those who score differently on them. Since men and women have had quite different experiences and reinforcement histories, we might anticipate considerable differences in the styles used to express themselves. Perhaps the best example is provided by Megargee (1969). Two person teams were assigned to perform a task in which one would act as the leader dictating transcription to the other. The task itself was bogus; the investigator was interested only in which member of the pair would emerge as leader. Pretesting had allowed the division of subjects into high- and low-dominance groups for each sex. The results of the study showed the expected patterns for both male-male and female-female pairs: high dominance individuals made the decision concerning who would be the leader about half the time, and in both male and female pairs 67 percent of the high-dominance individuals agreed to lead their low-dominance partners. When a high-dominance man was paired with a low-dominance woman, both sex role and dominance worked the same way: 88 percent of the high-dominance men appointed themselves as leaders, while only 12 percent of the low-dominance women appointed themselves. In sharp contrast, when high-dominance women were paired with low-dominance men, the women made the decision as to who would be the leader 69 percent of the time—but in 91 percent of their decisions, they told the low-dominance man to lead.

In summary, investigations of aggressiveness, dominance, and related dispositional patterns indicate that women often express less assertiveness than men. As with achievement, these differences can be explained in large part as arising from learned differences in the type of behavior seen as most appropriate and most likely to be rewarded (see also Lakoff, 1973). Studies that balance for sex role, or which in some other way indicate that assertiveness is appropriate or directly rewarded, generally find that women are as assertive as men.

Those who emerge as leaders are likely to be those making an effort to lead. The result of the inappropriateness of assertiveness and its lack of rewards for women is undoubtedly a decrease in the number who try to enter top management. Since those women who have some success are likely to threaten the men with whom they directly compete, an additional barrier to power is imposed near the goal. Men can freely assert themselves in repulsing an "inappropriately grasping'' woman as a normal concomitant of role processes without feeling guilt over discrimination.

Women can manage to assert themselves, then, but the process is probably more difficult for a woman who has accepted the prevailing female role than for a man. As mentioned before, however, assertiveness has its own rewards. Through it, we are able to persuade others to do as we would like . . . a process that most people find rewarding if there are no external sanctions. In order to encourage assertiveness on the part of women, it would seem that circumstances must be arranged in which the potential value of the behavior outweighs its potential social cost. Assertiveness training techniques attempt to do this by allowing women freedom to be aggressive in controlled circumstances that are free of possible reprisal; gradually, they can learn to savor the fruits of their efforts. We can similarly suggest that women are more likely to be aggressive within a system that supports rather than punishes their aggressiveness (cf. Larwood, O'Neal, and Brennan, 1977), such as membership in the military or police. Finally, it should be emphasized that women are more likely to be aggressive when the social costs are de-emphasized; thus they are more likely to be assertive with one another than with a date.

Self-reliance

Self-reliance is often considered a disadvantage to executives in large firms where people must cooperate with one another rather than work independently. In response, some people point out that two heads are not better than one—that they seldom produce as much as two independent persons working separately. The truth lies between these poles. Many projects are too large or too involved to be undertaken by one person; on the other hand, careful coordination is needed to avoid wasteful duplication and to ensure continued progress.

A second argument against total self-reliance asserts that careful questioning of knowledgeable colleagues is useful in making accurate judgments. Others have noted, however, that an individual decision is based on an individual rational judgment; any kind of group decision may be the subject of a variety of objectively irrational group influences. Again, the truth is not clear-cut. Groups and people dependent on others do make decisions that vary in objective risk from those of individuals acting alone; in most cases we lack knowledge as to whether the result is better or worse.

The following section investigates the dependence of men and women and the relationship of dependence to risk taking. Despite the evidence that will be cited, you should keep in mind that the impact of dependence and willingness to undertake risks depends very much on the situation. That is, we must ask whether the risk is worth taking, who the risk taker is dependent on, and how the fact of dependence alters mutual careers and productivity.

Dependence

For some time, psychologists accepted the notion that girls and women are relatively dependent. Efforts at demonstrating that girls rely on others more than do boys, however, have generally failed (cf. Maccoby and Jacklin, 1974, pp. 191–226). Instead, it has been determined that the dependence of young girls tends to predict their dependence in later life (Kagan and Moss, 1962). In contrast, dependent boys are not as likely to show related behaviors as they grow older. The relationship is remarkable in that it constitutes a complete reversal from the findings concerning aggression. The same mechanism seems to be at work concerning both aggression and dependence—only the sexes are reversed.

Although children of both sexes are identically reliant on others, our society accepts reliance in women while asking men to be independent. One consequence is that women are reinforced somewhat for dependent behaviors while men are not. For example, a study by Gruder and Cook (1971) indicated that women who requested and needed assistance would get it, whereas a woman who did not need help would get much less; moderate help was given to a man who requested it irrespective of his need. Other research has indicated that when incompetence is not socially acceptable, or when help is not available, previously dependent or incompetent women solve their problems substantially better than when they could rely on others (cf. Carey, 1958; Hoffman and Maier, 1966).

A related concept to social dependence is that of "field dependence." Field dependence research concerns the degree to which individuals accept cues from their environment in making a judgment (dependence) in place of applying some internal standard (independence). In the original research, experimental subjects attempted to turn a rod until it was (say) perpendicular to the natural horizon. The rod was enclosed by a frame which itself was tilted. Researchers measured the extent to which the tilt of the frame influenced alignment of the rod. Rod and frame tests and related studies have frequently found sex differences indicating greater independence on the part of males than females (cf. Witkin, 1950; Saarni, 1973).

Although this effect may arise in part from the sex difference in average spatial perception noted earlier in this chapter, we have reason to suspect other causes as well. Vaught (1965) noted that, among male college students, those with higher ego strength were generally more independent on the rod and frame test. Women who scored at the feminine end of a sex role inventory and who also had high ego strength were quite dependent. Similar results were obtained among ten- to fifteen-year-old children by Saarni (1973): the most intellectually advanced girls were the most field dependent, while the reverse tended to occur for boys. Far from confirming the incapacity of women to solve the problem at hand, the results suggest that many women deliberately make little effort at a correct solution—and that they may even have preferred an incorrect one.

Why might this occur? The task at hand is mechanical, and is therefore defined as more nearly in the male domain. If the women are less interested and involved than their male counterparts, they might be expected to take the easiest route. The least taxing response to a researcher's imposition is to align the rod with the frame rather than vertically. To the extent that the individual is disinterested in the task, or finds it unfeminine, she predictably completes it "incorrectly."

Similar results have been noted in other studies. For example, try the following test: Imagine that you are holding two jars, one in either hand, and that your arms are outstretched to your sides so that you can see neither jar when facing forward. Each jar is half-filled with water. Next, tilt the jar in your right hand by exactly 45 degrees (half-way over—90 degrees would be on its side). Now, by how many degrees should the jar on your left side be tilted (in the same direction) so that the top surfaces of the water in both jars will be aligned or level with each other? Answer: The same amount (45 degrees)? Less than 45 degrees? Not tilted at all (0 degrees)? Opposite direction?

When you have completed that task, you might like to try another before looking at the correct answer: Imagine that an individual is in the horse-trading business. The horse trader buys a horse for $60 and sells it for $70. Later, the horse trader buys the same horse back for $80 and resells it to someone else for $90. How much money (if any) did the horse trader make overall? Answer: Lost money? Broke even? Made money?

Women take longer than men to solve the water jar problem correctly and are more often wrong (cf. Thomas, Jamison, and Hummel, 1973; Willemsen and Reynolds, 1973). The correct response is, of course, that no tilting of the second jar is necessary. You may use your own judgment of why women are less often correct than men; Thomas et al. maintain that 50 percent of college women do not understand that the surface of still water is horizontal. Unpublished data (personal communication with Jack Maser) indicates however that women do substantially better when the water jar problem is presented to them by another woman rather than by a male researcher.

Similar results occur with respect to the horse-trading problem. Women are more likely than men to respond that the horse trader broke even (that the trader made $10 on each sale but lost $20 when buying the horse back at $20 over its original value). However, the correct response, more often given by men, is that the horse trader made a $20 profit ($10 on each transaction). As before, data indicate that the presence of a female observer eliminates sex differences (Hoffman and Maier, 1966). Women also do as well as men when they are not allowed to respond with the break-even answer (Maier and Burke, 1967)—more will be said about this later.

These studies all indicate that women have the same potential for independence as men, but that when women are in the presence of men, or are otherwise concerned with sex role, they opt for convenient and unthinking dependent responses. Women are aided in this by our social stereotypes that assert that even the barest rudiments of scientific and mathematical knowledge are completely alien to them. While the reinforcement received by women for dependence undoubtedly discourages the development of analytic ability for some women, it should be recognized that no developmental deficit extends to the depths indicated here. The studies cited use tasks that are utterly devoid of sophistication. The results rely more on sex role than on ability.

Together, the research concerning social and field dependence shows that some women—in certain circumstances—rely more on help from others and less on internalized standards for problem solution than do many men. The results are indicative of the social acceptability of, and even preference for, dependence on the part of women. When independent analytic thinking is expected and acceptable, women seem to do as well as men. Nonetheless, dependence, however temporary, reduces the freedom of the dependent. On at least some occasions many women feel pressured to rely on others and to take behavioral and judgmental cues from the environment rather than to remain independent of it. To the degree that they consent, the women lose personal experience with analytic thinking and are later less able to judge the objective requirements of new situations.

Risk Taking

One expected result is that women should judge some activities as more risky than do men. Even for activities of equal difficulty for either sex, it may be that many women have less real experience than most men and have less developed internal standards for handling the activity. With greater experience, the likelihood of success increases and the perceived risk (assuming correct attribution of success) should correspondingly drop. In fact, several studies have indicated some tendency for women to make more conservative decisions than men (cf. Cvetkovich, 1972; Slovic, 1966; Wallach and Wing, 1968). Since those people who feel there is more risk attached are probably less willing to undertake an activity (cf. Kahan, 1975), we can also predict that women behave somewhat more conservatively than men in many situations. Nonetheless, in circumstances with which men and women are equally as familiar, and under conditions encouraging critical thinking, there seems no reason to expect that either sex would accept greater risks.

Women can be self-reliant, then, when circumstances support their independence. Continued independence probably lowers perceived risks and could allow many women to accept additional challenges more boldly. Although some implications of additional self-reliance will be considered in the next section, many are not completely obvious. Nonetheless, having the confidence to handle a variety of situations independently undoubtedly leads to a willingness to become involved in a wider range of activities and to a more flexible repertoire of responses in existing activities. Unfortunately, self-reliance is subject to a certain degree of circularity: exposure to risks in new situations leads to the development of the ability to handle them, while knowledge of one's abilities leads to a willingness to enter new situations. Probably the quickest way out of the circle for dependent adults who would like to develop their abilities is through overexposure. The individual enters situations which he or she does not understand how to handle; once in those situations, the individual takes deliberate responsibility for decisions but fully utilizes the advice of others when necessary (a technique that is probably entirely foreign to those used to being independent). If the individual recognizes that some mistakes are inevitable at first, experience can be quickly built in a new situation that can later be applied successfully to others. Of course, the individual must be willing to accept the initial mistakes and must be supported by others who are reasonably tolerant of them; others who are more self-reliant and confident may be too impatient to support the learner for an extended period of time.

Strategy Patterns

The previous reviews might be taken to indicate that women are less competitive and more cooperative with coworkers than are men. An individual who is interested in achievement, after all, must achieve more than others. Someone who is also purposefully (instrumentally) aggressive might willingly push others aside to accomplish a competitive achievement. A self-reliant person need not be concerned with the opinions of others during this process. It is tempting to combine these factors by identifying cooperation as a "woman's" organizational strategy, and competition as a "man's" preserve. The suggested assignment is greatly oversimplified, however, if not entirely mistaken; research to date has shown that just the opposite relationship occurs. When they do uncover sex differences in strategy, experimental studies frequently find that men are more cooperative than women (cf. Bixenstine, Chambers, and Wilson, 1964; Bixenstine and Wilson, 1963; Marwell and Schmitt, 1975).

The experimental results cannot be challenged, but the extent to which they should be interpreted as indicative of overall competitiveness on the part of women is subject to doubt (Terhune, 1970; Wall, 1976). Researchers have long recognized that most of the situations used to examine strategy are biased toward the use of competition. For example, in one popular type of study (prisoner's dilemma game), people know that their strategy selection may be upset by an uncooperative opponent acting in individual self-interest; the easiest choice is often to compete from the beginning thereby avoiding potential manipulation. Although women sometimes appear more doggedly competitive in this situation, we can alternatively propose that women are less familiar with competition. When they encounter a task strewn with competitive cues, women are uncertain how to behave, and sometimes seem to over-react. Imagine an analog: an individual who seldom sees the ocean visits a cousin living in a seaside cottage; could we conclude from the behavior that would probably follow that people living inland are more fascinated by water than those living along the coast?

The discussion in this section advances the hypothesis that men and women sometimes use different strategies in bargaining interactions. Irrespective of their intent, persons using different strategies often view each other as uncooperative. In actuality, the strategy preference of men is well-adapted to probing the strategy of others, while that of women is not. On learning that their own strategy is not reciprocated, women perceive a high degree of risk and retreat to a "harder" strategy position than that held by men. The result can profoundly alter outcomes in successive bargaining exchanges.

Principles of Exchange

In general, we can label strategy as "competitive" to the extent each participant works toward a personal goal irrespective of the needs or preferences of others. Thus, when two persons bargain with each other competitively, the intent of each is usually to get as much as possible. In contrast, a "cooperative" strategy is one in which all parties agree (although perhaps not explicitly) on a mutual goal. For example, a cooperatively bargaining group might settle on a division of reward that seems "fair" to each participant; no cooperator would thereafter attempt to seize a larger share of the outcome than had been agreed. People may, of course, agree to a competition. In that event, the competition is usually governed by strict rules defining the range of the competition and the method for calculation of each party's rewards for engaging in it.

Questions can still arise between those attempting cooperation as to what is fair. Suppose, for example, that two people enter a business partnership and later decide to divide the profits fairly. One individual might refer to her greater investment of cash at the beginning of the business and ask for a proportionately greater sum of the profits; the other might disagree and point out that she had worked longer hours toward the organization's success. Objectively we might be tempted to mediate the situation by explaining to each the other's equal contribution, but it is possible that even in view of this information one of the participants feels entitled to a greater share of the proceeds. Perhaps one partner feels that work hours are irrelevant, that only the productivity shown for the time is important and that productivity was the same for both participants. Far from trivial, the example illustrates the reasons for the break-up of thousands of partnerships each year.

In short, individuals who believe they are cooperating with each other may come to feel that their partners are actually competing with them if explicit agreement was never reached on the terms of a fair exchange between the two.

When, by chance, both parties reference the same type of exchange, they feel that their partners have been reasonable and cooperative. If, on the other hand, they apply different concepts of exchange, at least one of the partners may feel that the other is taking advantage.

Two types of exchange are in common use. In one, known as "equality" or "parity," all participants divide the proceeds from their interaction equally between them. Irrespective of the amount of effort that each person has invested, or the amount of time taken, each person obtains the same share. There are a number of reasons why people might want to use the equality exchange. They may be unsure of the exact contribution that each person has made to the final outcome. Alternatively, they may feel that each individual has tried to perform as well as possible and that any differences in contribution reflect differences in initial ability and should not be used as the basis for rewards. Differences in outcome also arise from random luck, which (some feel) should not be rewarded. Imagine, for instance, that you and a friend are walking down the street together and that your friend sees two $50 bills blowing across the road. If you agree with equality as a system of exchange, you will expect your friend to give you one of the bills.

If your friend refuses, we can safely say that he or she does not feel that equality should apply in this situation. In explanation, your friend will probably mention that you did not contribute toward finding the money and that you should not expect to share it. A belief that rewards should be made in strict proportion to contribution is termed "equity." Under the equity system, those who work harder are paid more. Other investments that also deserve a higher proportion of any outcome under the equity system are effort, intent, capital investment, time, and status.

At this point, comparatively little research has examined sex differences in exchange norm preference and application. Some facts are available, however. Sex is a status input under the equity system: women, and those holding lower-level or less skilled jobs, represent less important inputs. That is, less is expected from a woman or an employee than from a man or an employer. Jobs performed by a woman or an employee are not expected to be handled as competently as if done by a man or an employer (Pheterson, Kiesler, and Goldberg, 1971)—therefore those trusting to the equity exchange system need not pay as much for a woman's time or product. On the other hand, for a woman to outperform the low expectations of her, she would need to use more time or apply greater effort than would a man (assuming belief in the equity system). In such a case, she should be at least as highly rewarded as a man performing equally well (Taynor and Deaux, 1973).

Before the woman can be equally paid, a perceptual problem must be overcome, however. The low expectations held of the woman are self-fulfilling prophesies, at least perceptually. Subjectivity is usually involved, and employers and coworkers tend to see an expected inferior performance irrespective of its actual merit. Later, when forced to acknowledge the performance by an objective standard, evaluators tend to ascribe it to blind luck because they "know" that the individual was incapable of doing well by any other means. As has already been mentioned, women who expect less ability from themselves than from men are similarly made uncomfortable by superior work. They can most readily escape by agreeing with their employer, refusing to acknowledge their abilities, and performing more poorly the next time.

Some data indicate that men are more likely to subscribe to the standard equity relationship than women. For men, the exchange is self-serving in that it both predicts that they will do well and provides a rationale for larger rewards. Women are in a position where acceptance of the standard equity relationship is identical with acceptance of inferiority. Two alternatives are possible for them. If a woman agrees that equity is an appropriate norm of exchange, she may still modify the norm somewhat by refusing to accept the notion that she is inferior to and of lower status than otherwise similar men. A second alternative is partial abandonment of equity in favor of equality (Larwood, 1974). The application of equality to work situations is made in recognition that many traditional women's jobs do not link pay to individual performance. Sufficient effort is required to hold a job, but additional effort does not bring an increased share of rewards. A secretary, for example, may earn between $150 and $250 per week—but the specific amount often depends only on her getting to work and observing certain minimum standards. Her taking work home or helping weigh decisions for her employer is unlikely to proportionally increase her pay. The same is true for women who keep their home for their families and do not work outside. It is not overstating to note that a wife, so long as she remains wife, can wash the dishes once per week or once per hour with little change in the reward received from her husband. If her husband increased his workload by a similar extent, he would undoubtedly be paid differently (assuming survival after his coronary).

Since they have experienced equity in more work situations, and since they are favored by it, we can expect that men will also apply the equity norm more often than women. Women who are very sure that their abilities are equal to those of men will probably modify equity investment concepts. Women who are less certain, especially those who are unused to being paid equitably, will more frequently use equality. The differential use patterns, we should note, are normally marginal; the circumstances themselves normally suggest the appropriate exchange. The marginalities are of considerable importance, however, when they are spread repeatedly over a career or lifetime.

Differences in exchange preference introduce a variety of possibilities for conflict between otherwise cooperative men and women. So long as both parties agree on the exchange to be applied, there is no difficulty. However, conflict arises when more is expected than is given in investment or when a smaller reward is returned than seems appropriate. In specific, a man applying standard equity underpays and underestimates a woman who is applying a modified form of equity that does not accept sex as an input. Men are not the only culprits, however. A man, applying the modified form of equity in a liberated manner to a secretary who is concerned with the equality exchange, will probably be disappointed. Although the secretary may have great ability, it is doubtful that she would interpret a pay increase as a signal that her way into management is being opened. She would probably not alter her job performance in exchange for the pay hike.

At a different level of analysis, both equity and equality, when accepted as fair by a woman in an interaction with an employer using standard equity, may result in mutual satisfaction. The relationship also results in the woman being paid less than she is capable of getting. She may be undervalued if she subscribes to standard equity and attempts to do her best. She may not be working to her full capacity if she feels she is partly paid according to equality. Her adoption of a modified equity will help only if she can transmit knowledge of her true ability successfully to her employer; otherwise, her use of this system merely leads to misunderstanding.

Bargaining

The differences in exchange preference concerning pay suggest that in an ongoing series of negotiations there may also be differences in the strategies of men and women. Some caution should be applied in labeling strategies as feminine or masculine however, since the strategy used really depends on the situation as perceived by the user. A man may use a strategy that is more often used by women, because he feels his situation merits it. Three negotiation strategies are discussed below.

1. *Withdrawal.* In entering any extended series of negotiations, we constantly weigh the likely gains against potential losses. When the amount at stake seems to exceed any expected gain, we may choose to discontinue the relationship. Although this is true of face-to-face bargaining encounters, it is perhaps even more true of "career bargaining." For example, when it is made apparent to middle-level executives that they cannot expect further advancement within their organization, they generally do not redouble their efforts and invest more years of their lives. Instead, they frequently leave (if they value advancement sufficiently) or develop interests outside the organization to replace striving for advancement within. Two factors are particularly influential in causing some women to withdraw from striving to succeed in management. The expected value of working for advancement declines to the extent that women are discriminated against for promotions or pay. Similarly, a potential loss might be attached by some to promotion when they feel role conflict over working outside their homes or entering management. The precipitating conditions depend on the organization, the ambitions of the individual, and the individual's specific exchange preferences. The

outcome may be apparent discouragement and alienation from the organization.

2. *Coalition formation.* When the situation seems worthwhile risking (or cannot be withdrawn from), it may be to our advantage to join forces with one or more others. For example, if someone else can arrive at a goal ahead of us, we might choose to cooperate with a third party in overcoming the lead of the first. Similarly, competing firms may merge or cooperate temporarily to prevent domination by a larger firm. The likelihood of coalition is increased by the extent that potential coalition members feel threatened by alternative outcomes and can do better by splitting the proceeds from a successful alliance (cf. Komorita and Chertkoff, 1973; Murdoch, 1967). When others feel secure without the aid of a coalition, of course, they have no desire to split their profits.

We can readily predict that those women who feel less sure of themselves and perceive higher risks than men are more likely to enter into coalitions and thus to cooperate among themselves toward some mutual goal. In fact, experimental results confirm that women on the whole are generally more likely than men to enter into alliances with each other, and that in three-person, mixed-sex groups, the two women frequently ally against a single man (Uesugi and Vinacke, 1963; Vinacke, 1959). In the less frequent cases when two men ally against a single woman in three-person groups, the level of competition between the men is still sufficient to keep their separate outcomes lower than hers.

In terms of overall careers, these results indicate that women are probably more likely than men to link their futures to those of others and to see their success or failure as related to that of their group. In identical circumstances, men are more likely to behave independently. Since it is more frequent for organizations to reward and promote individuals than groups, adoption of a coalition strategy by women may sometimes be harmful to their careers. Since coalitions also allow the members to undertake operations that they might not individually be able to handle, however, they may also be advantageous. No research has yet examined the extent to which coalitions help, as opposed to inhibit, the careers of women.

3. *Competition.* Those who choose to compete frequently fall into one of two categories. An *aggressive* competitor could be defined as someone who desires the entire reward and who feels that there is a reasonable chance of successfully attaining it without the need for cooperating with others. On the basis of the discussion above, we can readily conclude that men are more likely than women to be found in this category. Nonetheless, men may project the appearance of aggressive competition without intending to behave in that manner.

A *retaliative* competitor is one who prefers not to compete. Retaliative competition is provoked by the apparent unwillingness of others to join in a coalition or to adhere to the cooperative norms required by a coalition agreement. Rather than arising through vindictiveness, retaliative competition is probably a useful learned response that sometimes has considerable protective value. Retaliation as a strategy signals that the individual is not weak and is willing to fight for a share of any prize. Any struggle requires effort; unless an opponent is entirely confident of winning and highly values the reward, he or she will probably prefer a reduction in the level of competition—cooperative compromise rather than a fight to the finish (cf. Esser and Komorita, 1975).

Some evidence indicates that retaliative competition is more likely from a woman than from a man. As Terhune (1970; also see Wall, 1976) has noted, women are more likely to seek initial cooperation; men seem more likely to probe the strengths of others while avoiding the appearance of weakness by behaving competitively. After initial confrontations, men may quickly decrease their levels of retaliation in response to reciprocal decreases in competition shown by others. Women seem less aware of the cues signalling the intention of reciprocal decreases in competitiveness—especially if the cues closely follow the initial competitive probing. Instead, when the initial cooperation offered by a woman is not reciprocated, she quickly begins to compete and is thereafter highly resistant to compromise.

Such a result can be predicted by the assumption that women are less familiar with bargaining than men and are less self-assured. As a consequence, they cannot afford to take risks. On entering a situation, they are more cautious than men, joining a coalition if possible. When, through lack of communication or lack of reciprocal cooperation and agreement, a coalition seems impossible, women become persistent competitors in self-defense. Of course, those who are not sure of themselves may let their guard drop and begin to reciprocally cooperate earlier than those who are less secure.

The strategy of retaliative competition is helpful both in limiting competitive risk and in prodding others into a cooperative stance. At the same time, its use can present two difficulties. Initially, the strategy may appear to be overly cooperative and can be mistaken by others as an admission of weakness. For example, an aggressive employer negotiating with an employee for future pay might be tempted to first offer the cooperative employee much less than he or she seems to be worth. If the employee were less reasonable at the beginning, the initial offer might be higher.

The second problem concerns the lack of flexibility in the retaliation phase. If agreement is not reached quickly, it may take longer than necessary because of the unwillingness of the retaliator to take continued risks and to display further weakness. A persistent demand by the retaliative competitor for a better deal than the original compromise offer may seem unreasonable and frustrating to other negotiators.

In summary, the strategies we use are suggested by our perceptions of the situation. While men and women often use the same strategies, their experiences—as well as real discrimination—may lead them to interpret the same conditions differently and to apply different exchange and bargaining strategies (cf. Kidder, Bellellirie, and Cohn, 1977). Women are at a disadvantage relative to men when these differences cause them to take a less active part in organizational activities or to settle for less than the maximum they might otherwise bargain for.

The solution to these differences requires that women select their strategies with awareness of the range of possibilities available. Particular alternatives are, of course, only as good as their eventual result—one cannot say that one strategy is always good or should never be used. Nonetheless, two strategy changes can be suggested. First, when a woman finds herself in a situation in which her output is being evaluated by an employer, she can assume that the evaluation is being made in standard equity terms in which she is considered less valuable than a similar man. Some research indicates that exchange terms are readily modified if explicitly agreed on in advance (Larwood, Kavanagh, and Levine, in press). To accomplish this, the woman might agree with the employer on specific physical measures that can be readily made concerning her performance; alternatively, she could discuss with the employer her views concerning her ability and point out the room for unintentional discrimination in subjective measures of employee performance. In either case, she should ask for explicit agreement by the employer and be wary of defensiveness. Bargaining strategies might also be improved somewhat through a partial replacement of the retaliative competition strategy with the bluff used more often by men. Of course, when the woman knows those with whom she is bargaining, there is no need for change. However, when she negotiates with others who have had no experience with her, it would do no harm to bargain for as much as possible at first while remaining sensitive to the possibility for a suitable compromise.

The Culture Trap . . . A summary

This chapter has found that there are differences between men and women in apparent behavior. Women appear to be less achievement-oriented, less assertive, and less self-reliant than men. These psychological differences serve to partly explain differences in the strategies men and women use in management. Women, for example, are sometimes more willing to compromise quickly; they do not as often seek their maximum advantage in each situation.

How real are these differences? In examining the "average" woman, most research studies purport to speak for those who prefer to be housewives along with those who are already corporate executives. The psychological sex differences found are real enough, but they may be misleading in many, or even most, cases. A woman is not necessarily less self-reliant than a man—the statistically average woman is.

The situational nature of these differences is even more deceptive. There are no inborn sex differences that affect managerial behavior or ability. Differences develop later in connection with sex role learning and self-identification. Although our notions of role and self can limit the types of experiences we enjoy and engage in, there seem to be no major differences between the sexes that affect management even at this level. Of course more men than women are experienced with the administration of major organizations; but the abilities leading to these experiences have been equally developed by adults of each sex.

The major sex differences appear in the likelihood that one sex or another will show specific traits in any particular situation. Because achievement, assertiveness, and self-reliance are considered masculine in our society, they are avoided by many women when circumstances emphasize sex role. Moreover, because these traits are less frequently seen in women, many employers conclude that women do not possess them. The processes of role learning, self-identification, and employee evaluation form a self-perpetuating culture trap for many women.

Why can't women manage? In order for large numbers of women to successfully enter management, society (including women themselves) must become aware that no rational reason exists to keep women from management. There is nothing objectively masculine or feminine about management. No talents, abilities, or behaviors are required that women do not already display in other situations.

This chapter has also concluded that average men and women have somewhat different strategy patterns. A male executive might argue from this that he would prefer to have salespeople or contract administrators who are hard bargaining men rather than compromising women. If there were evidence, which there is not, that any one strategy is usually preferable, this argument would still fail. Women who decide to enter management in the late 1970s are violating a still-potent cultural norm. These women are not attempting to be average, but they are concerned with what seems most suitable for them. If they have already risen several ranks in management, they have demonstrated their ability to handle effectively the situations they encounter.

Put another way, the woman who enters management is a specially selected individual; there is no reason to suspect that she will behave in an average or "feminine" way unless that way seems justified. If it turns out that particular behaviors are more useful than others in successful management, she will use them because she desires success. If aggressive competition were an outstandingly useful strategy, both men and women who intend to succeed would learn to use it. In short, we can predict that women who manage behave very much like men who manage—at least in all aspects that are important to organizational success. It is only in activities that are not crucial that feminine management can be expected to differ from the masculine mold. Employing women managers may make some male superiors uncomfortable, but it does not make them less successful.

Notes

1. Both self-concept, examined in detail in an earlier chapter, and many of the behavioral differences noted in this chapter have sometimes been characterized by a broad pair of phenomenological descriptions labeled "agency" and "communion" (Block, 1973; Carlson, 1971; Gutmann, 1965). This differentia-

tion scheme centers on the finding that males and females structure their psychological worlds differently according to their upbringing. Males see themselves as instruments through which they affect others; in order to know and predict the effects, they must aggressively examine their environment, formulate rules concerning it, and experiment with it. In contrast, women see themselves as part of a network of family and friends; while women can alter interpersonal relationships, they are a dependent—more than independent—part of it. Although useful as conceptual tools, these descriptions were felt to be too broad and overly abstract for use here.

2. Technically the term "aggression" indicates actual or potential harm, while "assertion" indicates forwardness. The two terms, together with others such as "dominance," are used here with some degree of interchangability. A successful aggressive businessperson is, in a competitive sense, both assertive and dominant—although the intention may have been otherwise.

References

Amsterdam, B. "Mirror self-image reactions before age two." *Developmental Psychobiology,* 1972, *5,* 297–305.

Atkinson, J. W. "Motivational determinants of risk-taking behavior." *Psychological Review*, 1957, *64*, 359–372.

Bandura, A. "Influence of models' reinforcement contingencies on the acquisition of imitative responses." *Journal of Personality and Social Psychology,* 1965, *1,* 589–595.

———. "Social-learning theory of identificatory processes." In D. A. Goslin (ed.), *Handbook of socialization theory and research.* Chicago: Rand McNally, 1969.

———. *Aggression. A social learning analysis.* Englewood Cliffs, N.J.: Prentice-Hall, 1973.

———, Ross. D., and Ross, S. A. "A comparative test of the status envy, social power, and secondary reinforcement theories of identificatory learning." *Journal of Abnormal and Social Psychology,* 1963, *67,* 601–607.

Bixenstine, V. E., Chambers, N., and Wilson, K. V. "Effects of asymmetry in payoff on behavior in a two-person, non-zero-sum game." *Journal of Conflict Resolution,* 1964, *8,* 151–159.

———, and Wilson, K. V. "Effects of level of cooperative choice by the other players in a Prisoner's Dilemma game: Part II." *Journal of Abnormal and Social Psychology,* 1963, *67,* 139–147.

Block, D. R., and Kolakowski, D. "Further evidence of sex-linked major-gene influence on human spatial visualizing ability." *American Journal of Human Genetics,* 1973, *25,* 1–14.

Block, J. H. "Conceptions of sex role. Some cross-cultural and longitudinal perspectives." *American Psychologist,* 1973, *28,* 512–526.

Carey, G. L. "Sex differences in problem-solving performance as a function of attitude differences." *Journal of Abnormal and Social Psychology,* 1958, *56,* 256–260.

Carlson, R. "Sex differences in ego functioning: Exploratory studies of agency and communion." *Journal of Consulting and Clinical Psychology,* 1971, *37,* 267–277.

Crandall, V. C., Katkovsky, W., and Crandall, V. J. "Children's beliefs in their own control of reinforcements in intellectual-academic achievement situations." *Child Development,* 1965, *36,* 91–109.

Crandall, V. J., Katkovsky, W., and Preston, A. "Motivational and ability determinants of young children's intellectual achievement behaviors." *Child Development,* 1962, *33,* 643–661.

Cvetkovich, G. "Effects of sex on decision policies used for self and decision policies used for other persons." *Psychonomic Science,* 1972, *26,* 319–320.

Deaux, K., White, L., and Farris, E. "Skill versus luck: Field and laboratory studies of male and female performances." *Journal of Personality and Social Psychology,* 1975, *32,* 629–636.

Esser, J. K., and Komorita, S. S. "Reciprocity and concession making in bargaining." *Journal of Personality and Social Psychology,* 1975, *31,* 864–872.

Fauls, L. B., and Smith, W. D. "Sex-role learning of five-year-olds." *Journal of Genetic Psychology,* 1956, *89,* 105–117.

Feather, N. T. "Positive and negative reactions to male and female success and failure in reaction to the perceived status and sex-typed appropriateness of occupations." *Journal of Personality and Social Psychology,* 1975, *31,* 536–548.

————, and Raphelson, A. C. "Fear of success in American and Australian student groups: Motive or sex-role stereotype?" *Journal of Personality,* 1974, *42,* 190–201.

Feshbach, N. & Feshbach, S. "Children's aggression." In W. W. Hartup (ed.), *The Young Child,* vol. 2. Washington, D.C.: National Association for the Education of Young Children, 1972.

Fisher, J. E., O'Neal, E. C., and McDonald, P. J. "Female competitiveness as a function of prior performance outcome, competitor's evaluation and sex of competitors." Paper presented at 1974 meeting of the Midwestern Psychological Association, Chicago, 1974.

Fling, L. B., and Manosevitz, M. "Sex typing in nursery school children's play interests." *Developmental Psychology,* 1972, *7,* 146–152.

Frieze, I. H. "Women's expectations for and causal attributions of success and failure." In M. T. S. Mednick, S. S. Tangri, and L. W. Hoffman (eds.), *Women and achievement. Social and motivational analyses.* Washington, D.C.: Hemisphere Publishing, 1975.

Gallup, G. G., Jr. "Towards an operational definition of self-awareness." Paper presented at 9th International Congress of Anthropological and Ethnological Sciences, 1973.

Gruder, C. L., and Cook, T. D. "Sex, dependency, and helping." *Journal of Personality and Social Psychology,* 1971, *19,* 290–294.

Gutmann, D. L. "Women and the conception of ego strength." *Merrill-Palmer Quarterly,* 1965, *11,* 229–240.

Hagan, R. L., and Kahn, A. "Discrimination against competent women." *Journal of Applied Social Psychology,* 1975, *4,* 362–376.

Heilbrun, A. B., Jr., Kleemeier, C., and Piccola, G. "Developmental and situational correlates of achievement behavior in college females." *Journal of Personality,* 1974, *42,* 420–436.

Hicks, D. J. "Imitation and retention of film-mediated aggressive peer and adult models." *Journal of Personality and Social Psychology,* 1965, *2,* 97–100.

Hoffman, L. R., and Maier, N. R. F. "Social factors influencing problem solving in women." *Journal of Personality and Social Psychology,* 1966, *4,* 382–390.

Horner, M. S. "Femininity and successful achievement: A basic inconsistency." In J. M. Bardwick, E. Douvan, M. S. Horner, and D. Gutmann, *Feminine personality and conflict.* Belmont, Calif.: Brooks/Cole, 1970.

Ireson, C. J. "Effects of sex role socialization on adolescent female achievement." Paper presented at 1976 meeting of the Pacific Sociological Association meeting, San Diego.

Jackaway, R. "Achievement attribution and the low expectation cycle in females." Paper presented at meeting of the American Psychological Association, Chicago, 1975.

Jellison, J. M., Jackson-White, R., Bruder, R. A., and Martyna, W. "Achievement behavior: A situational interpretation." *Sex Roles,* 1975, *1,* 369–384.

Jorgensen, E. C., and Howell, R. J. "Changes in self, ideal-self correlations from ages 8 through 18." *Journal of Social Psychology,* 1969, *79,* 63–67.

Kagan, J., & Moss, H. A. *Birth to maturity.* New York: John Wiley, 1962.

Kahan, J. P. "A subjective probability interpretation of the risky shift." *Journal of Personality and Social Psychology,* 1975, *31,* 997–982.

Kaleta, R. J., and Buss, A. H. "Aggression intensity and femininity of the victim." Paper presented at meeting of the Eastern Psychological Association, 1973.

Katz, P., and Zigler, E. "Self-image disparity: A developmental approach." *Journal of Personality and Social Psychology,* 1967, *5,* 186–195.

Kidder, L. H., Bellellirie, G., and Cohn, E. S. "Secret ambitions and public performances. The effects of anonymity on reward allocations made by men and women." *Journal of Experimental Social Psychology,* 1977, *13,* 70–80.

Kohlberg, L. "A cognitive-developmental analysis of children's sex-role concepts and attitudes." In E. E. Maccoby (ed.), *The development of sex differences.* Stanford, Calif.: Stanford University Press, 1966.

Kohlberg, L. "Stage and sequence: The cognitive-developmental approach to socialization." In D. A. Goslin (ed.), *Handbook of socialization theory and research.* Chicago: Rand McNally, 1969.

Komarovsky, M. "Cultural contradictions and sex roles: The masculine case." *American Journal of Sociology,* 1973, *78,* 873–884.

Komorita, S. S., and Chertkoff, J. M. "A bargaining theory of coalition formation." *Psychological Review,* 1973, *80,* 149–162.

Lakoff, R. "Language and woman's place." *Language in Society,* 1973, *2,* 45–79.

Larwood, L. "The limits of equity: A developmental extension of the Just World Hypothesis to sex roles." (Doctoral dissertation, Tulane University, 1974). *Dissertation Abstracts International,* 1975, *35.* (University Microfilms No. 75-2938).

———, and Blackmore, J. "Sex discrimination in managerial selection: Testing predictions of the vertical dyad linkage model." *Sex Roles,* in press.

———, Kavanagh, M., and Levine, R. "Perceptions of fairness with three alternative economic exchanges." *Academy of Management Journal,* in press.

———, O'Carroll, M., and Logan, J. "Sex role as a mediator of achievement in task performance." *Sex Roles,* 1977, *3,* 109–114.

———, O'Neal, E., and Brennan, P. "Increasing the aggressiveness of women." *Journal of Social Psychology,* 1977, *101,* 97–101.

Levin, H., and Sears, R. R. "Identification with parents as a determinant of doll play aggression." *Child Development,* 1956, *27,* 135–153.

Maccoby, E. E., and Jacklin, C. N. *The psychology of sex differences.* Stanford, Calif.: Stanford University Press, 1974.

Maier, N. R. F., and Burke, R. J. "Response availability as a factor in the problem-solving performance of males and females." *Journal of Personality and Social Psychology,* 1967, *5,* 304–310.

Marwell, G., and Schmitt, D. R. *Cooperation: An experimental analysis.* New York: Academic Press, 1975.

McArthur, L. Z., and Eisen, S. V. "Achievements of male and female storybook characters as determinants of achievement behavior by boys and girls." *Journal of Personality and Social Psychology,* 1976, *33,* 467–473.

McClelland, D. C. *Power. The inner experience.* New York: Irvington Publishers, 1975.

Megargee, E. I. "Influence of sex roles on the manifestation of leadership." *Journal of Applied Psychology,* 1969, *53,* 377–382.

Milton, G. A. "Sex differences in problem solving as a function of role appropriateness of the problem content." *Psychological Reports,* 1959, *5,* 705–708.

Mischel, W. "A social-learning view of sex differences in behavior." In E. E. Maccoby (ed.), *The development of sex differences.* Stanford, Calif.: Stanford University Press, 1966.

Money, J., and Ehrhardt, A. A. *Man and woman. Boy and girl.* Baltimore: Johns Hopkins University Press, 1972.

Moss, H. A. "Sex, age, and state as determinants of mother-infant interaction." *Merrill-Palmer Quarterly,* 1967, *13,* 19–36.

Murdoch, P. "Development of contractual norms in a dyad." *Journal of Personality and Social Psychology,* 1967, *6,* 206–211.

Patterson, G. R., Littman, R. A., and Bricker, W. "Assertive behavior in children: A step toward a theory of aggression." *Monographs of the Society for Research in Child Development,* 1967, *32* (5, 6).

Pedersen, D. M., Shinedling, M. M., and Johnson, D. L. "Effects of sex of examiner and subject on children's quantitative test performance." *Journal of Personality and Social Psychology,* 1968, *10,* 251–254.

Pheterson, G. I., Kiesler, S. B., and Goldberg, P. A. "Evaluation of the performance of women as a function of their sex, achievement, and personal history." *Journal of Personality and Social Psychology*, 1971, *19*, 114–118.

Saarni, C. I. "Piagetian operations and field independence as factors in children's problem-solving performances." *Child Development,* 1973, *44,* 338–345.

Slovic, P. "Risk-taking in children: Age and sex differences." *Child Development,* 1966, *37,* 169–176.

Stein, A. H. "The effects of sex-role standards for achievement and sex-role preference on three determinants of achievement motivation." *Developmental Psychology,* 1971, *4,* 219–231.

———, Pohly, S. R., and Mueller, E. "The influence of masculine, feminine, and neutral tasks on children's achievement behavior, expectancies of success, and attainment values." *Child Development,* 1971, *42,* 195–207.

———, and Smithells, J. "Age and sex differences in children's sex-role standards about achievement." *Developmental Psychology,* 1969, *1,* 252–259.

Stevenson, H. W., Hale, G. A., Hill, K. T., and Moely, B. E. "Determinants of children's preferences for adults." *Child Development,* 1967, *38,* 1–14.

Sternglanz, S. H., and Serbin, L. A. "Sex role stereotyping in children's television programs." *Developmental Psychology,* 1974, *10,* 710–715.

Stewart, A. J., and Winter, D. G. "Self-definition and social definition in women." *Journal of Personality,* 1974, *42,* 238–259.

Taylor, S. P., and Epstein, S. "Aggression as a function of the interaction of the sex of the aggressor and the sex of the victim." *Journal of Personality,* 1967, *35,* 474–486.

Taynor, J., and Deaux, K. "When women are more deserving than men: Equity, attribution, and perceived sex differences." *Journal of Personality and Social Psychology,* 1973, *28,* 360–367.

Terhune, K. W. "The effects of personality in cooperation and conflict." In P. Swingle (ed.), *The structure of conflict.* New York: Academic Press, 1970.

Thomas, H., Jamison, W., and Hummel, D. D. "Observation is insufficient for discovering that the surface of still water is invariably horizontal." *Science,* 1973, *181,* 173–174.

Uesugi, T. K., and Vinacke, W. E. "Strategy in a feminine game." *Sociometry,* 1963, *26,* 75–88.

Vandenberg, S. G. "Primary mental abilities or general intelligence? Evidence from twin studies." In J. M. Thoday and A. S. Parlees (eds.), *Genetic and environmental influences on behavior.* New York: Plenum Press, 1968.

Vaught, G. M. "The relationship of role identification and ego strength to sex differences in the rod-and-frame test." *Journal of Personality,* 1965, *33,* 271–283.

Vinacke, W. E. "Sex roles in a three-person game." *Sociometry,* 1959, *22,* 343–360.

Wall, J. A., Jr. "Effects of success and opposing representative's bargaining orientation on intergroup bargaining." *Journal of Personality and Social Psychology,* 1976, *33,* 55–61.

Wallach, M. A., and Wing, C. W., Jr. "Is risk a value?" *Journal of Personality and Social Psychology,* 1968, *9,* 101–106.

Weiner, B., Nierenberg, R., and Goldstein, M. "Social learning (locus of control) versus attributional (causal stability) interpretations of expectancy of success." *Journal of Personality,* 1976, *44,* 52–68.

———, and Sierad, J. "Misattribution for failure and enhancement of achievement strivings." *Journal of Personality and Social Psychology,* 1975, *31,* 415–421.

Weitzman, L. J., Eifler, D., Hokada, E., and Ross, C. "Sex-role socialization in picture books for preschool children." *American Journal of Sociology,* 1972, *77,* 1125–1150.

Willemsen, E., and Reynolds, B. "Sex differences in adults' judgments of the horizontal." *Developmental Psychology,* 1973, *8,* 309.

Witkin, H. A. "Individual differences in ease of perception of embedded figures." *Journal of Personality,* 1950, *19,* 1–15.

Wittig, M. A. "Sex differences in intellectual functioning: How much of a difference do genes make?" *Sex Roles,* 1976, *2,* 63–74.

Wood, M. M., and Greenfeld, S. T. "Women managers and fear of success: A study in the field." *Sex Roles,* 1976, *2,* 375–387.

Wyer, R. S., Jr., and Malinowski, C. "Effects of sex and achievement level upon individualism and competitiveness in social interaction." *Journal of Experimental Social Psychology,* 1972, *8,* 303–314.

Part III: Means

Earlier chapters have examined the extent of problems facing women in management. Historic, social, and personal antagonisms often prevent women from developing and applying their full range of abilities. The question remains as to how the problems can be avoided.

Of course, there is no easy one-step magic formula. Instead, the reader must first ask whether she really does want to enter management. Chapter 5 discusses some of the advantages and disadvantages of being a manager and may be helpful in judging your own level of commitment.

Chapter 6 assumes that you have decided to enter management—or have already done so. The most important problem facing you is no longer whether, but how, to succeed. Recent legislation that is helpful in alleviating some forms of discrimination is considered; some general strategies are also suggested. Nonetheless, the strategy that is most useful must be tailored to your own specific situation and ambitions. The chapter finishes with a discussion of how you can develop a personal strategy that will comfortably fit your individual needs.

Part II found that many women give the appearance of not wanting to succeed and that others are forced to withdraw from competition before reaching success. Chapter 7 is concerned with ways in which we can influence our society to help future generations of women with the problems we have faced. As they come into effect, some social changes will give women a greater control over their own lives. They may also decrease the need for careful strategies on the part of those who are already moving up in management.

This section departs somewhat from the style used in earlier chapters. The style in Part III is necessarily more speculative and less academic. While some readers may not be overjoyed at the change of pace, it is hoped that none will be horrified. The change is required by the lack, at points, of useful referents to which one can point in establishing that a given strategy is successful. Instead of fact, the discussion is often based in logic, experience, and belief. In a way, this seems appropriate for Part III, since there can be no grand route to success. Instead, there are only individual paths; the development and utilization of individual ability is, after all, what this book is all about.

Part III was written by Laurie Larwood and Marion M. Wood.

5 Success in Management

Not too long ago, a description of women's position in management would have been much simpler than it is now. Women executives were exceptional. A 1973 report by *Fortune* (Robertson, 1973), in which public reports of 1220 of the largest American businesses were examined, showed only 11 women among the 6500 highest-paid officers and directors. Until recently, an executive suite had a "woman's touch" if it was carpeted, contained a live plant, and had reasonably empty ashtrays. The women who gave the office its distinctive appearance acted as "office wife," caring for the plants, advising on decor, and surreptitiously removing expired cigars. Although they also generally worked as secretaries, that need not have been true—all women were expected to behave in a similar approved feminine manner.

Boardrooms and the offices of men of even modest standing were walled off from the secretarial pool. The boardrooms were a refuge where male executives could meet together to openly discuss important matters without risking annoying external influences. Women were at best appointed to guard duty or to run refueling missions for the conferences. A woman participating on an equal basis at such a meeting would have been as out of place as a competitor wearing red pajamas. Exceptions were granted only when the woman was the owner, indispensable, or sufficiently crusty so as to be accepted as "one of the boys."

Social changes taking place in the past decade have made the situation just described less frequent. Conditions in most large organizations today are not as readily stereotyped, if they are not actually less sexually divided. Many women, and perhaps equal numbers of men, have been reached by the Women's Movement. Both the dumping of ashtrays and the coffee brewing are tasks more likely to be undertaken by their beneficiary than they were before. Many organizations are under some governmental pressure to explain why only women have been hired as secretaries and only men as executives. The executive suite is becoming more egalitarian; the change has a long way to go but seems likely to continue— so long as the social pressures for change do not let up.

The rewards for women entering management at this time can be particularly great. Extraordinarily swift advancement is sometimes possible for capable and hard-working women. By moving at an accelerated pace, they find themselves facing new and more important tasks as rapidly at their talents and capacity allow. Within a short period, a few can move from entry level positions to higher positions of real challenge, authority, and pay. The positions at the very top, such as board and policy-making slots, are still closed to women; it seems quite possible, however, that even these will open as more competent women reach the upper levels of management from which they may be selected.

Many women will not have the advantages described above. For some, management will represent a conflict with family interests; others may develop psychological conflicts keeping them from striving to succeed. Many women will, at one time or another, confront male and female executives who are not ideally liberated. Some of these traditionally minded executives will decide against helping women on their way up, while others may actively oppose their climb.

The present chapter briefly describes both the opportunities and problems. The intent is to allow women who are considering a management career to examine the pros and cons involved in the decision. As in the previous chapter, some assertions will be made that do not apply to everyone. You will find it helpful if you question the ideas that seem unusual by asking whether they are meaningful to your personal situation. The final section of this chapter contains a questionnaire for use in your evaluation of a management career.

The Successful Woman Manager: A Profile

Several wide-ranging surveys of women in managerial positions have been made during the past few years (cf. Harlan, 1976; Kavanagh and Halpern, 1977; Keaveny, Jackson, and Fossum, 1976; Litterer, 1976; Robertson, 1973; Wood and Greenfeld, 1976; "100 Top Corporate Women," 1976). Together, these surveys form a composite image that is striking in both similarity and difference with the male executive profile. For the most part, the similarities concern the manner in which women executives relate to their jobs, while the differences center on family life.

Almost all women managers are pleased with their jobs. Across a wide spectrum of position categories, women managers have a higher degree of job satisfaction than nonsupervisory women (Keaveny et al., 1976). In fact, they seem to be as happy with their positions, and to hold the same expectations of them, as male supervisors (Brief and Oliver, 1976). Moreover, women give similar reasons for being satisfied. In general, they enjoy solving problems and consider that the managerial positions give them a better chance to use their talents than do lower positions; they also enjoy the prospect (or reality) of higher pay, prestige, and future advancement. Moreover, they like managing others; as a team or project leader, they have the opportunity to make their voices heard and to creatively contribute their ideas to the success of the organization.

Women managers are at first expected to behave in a feminine manner by showing their subordinates more consideration and less individual initiative than male leaders (Bartol and Butterfield, 1976). It seems possible that there may actually be some differences between male and female leaders on these dimensions. Nonetheless, women managers seem to be equally capable of eliciting long-term performance and satisfaction on the part of their subordinates (Osborn and Vicars, 1976). If some women are not as demanding of their assistants as men might be, they evidentally succeed in motivating them anyway through the development of a more supportive relationship.

Most of the executives studied by the authors and others are happy with having entered management. Like their male counterparts, they find the increased income, prestige, and freedom of self-development refreshing. These women have no interest in early retirement and intend to work, sometimes with time out for their families, for the rest of their productive lives. Moreover, women executives are ambitious and look forward to being advanced to progressively more demanding—and rewarding—positions. In short, the woman executive thoroughly enjoys her success, believes she has made the right decisions, and looks forward to future advancement.

There are some negative elements, of course. One study of women executives found that every one believed she had been discriminated against in one way or another (Litterer, 1976). Discrimination is a fact of life for most working women; while it has led to the disillusionment of some, for most it has merely led to more careful planning. Although men are more likely to obtain higher incomes and better jobs with the same education (Harlan, 1976), the women who become executives are still far better off than the secretaries and blue-collar women beneath them.

Executive positions often make unusual time and social demands; those who expect success can plan on working more than a forty-hour week.[a] In view of the time demands, many women find it useful to hire domestic help in the home. In comparison, the more successful men have wives who do not work outside the home and are therefore available for the social and personal needs of their husbands (Harlan, 1976); regrettably few women executives have husbands willing to take up this type of support role.

Not unexpectedly, the time demands impose a tighter schedule on the personal lives of executive women than of men. Women are less able to relax at the end of the workday than are men (Wood and Greenfeld, 1976). Although marriage does not slow their career advancement, women are only a third as likely as men to be married (Harlan, 1976; Jusenius, 1976; Wood and Greenfeld, 1976). Married women executives are less likely than male executives to have children (Hoffman, 1974), but they spend more time with the children than the men do. Clearly, the executive woman must be willing to commit herself to her work if she is to succeed. This does not mean abandonment of family "duties," how-

[a]As this is written, there seems to be a growing trend toward "job sharing" in which two people (often husband and wife) are hired for one job. This plan gives the sharers a great deal of freedom, time-wise. Nonetheless, job sharing, flex-time (hours set by the worker), and four-day work-weeks are still the exception to the rule.

ever. In most cases, primary responsibility for assuring care of both children and home falls on the woman irrespective of her employment—if she has a family, she must organize her time extremely well. Although difficult, the organization of time needed for these dual roles is possible.

Before leaving this topic, it may be worthwhile to mention two characteristics that are not in the profile of the woman executive—sexual exploitation and frustration of ambition. Sexual harassment, in the form of advances, threats, or appearance-based remarks, is occasionally encountered in many social situations where men and women meet. The work environment is no exception (cf. Nemy, 1975). Although courts have recently upheld a woman's right to be free of sexual harassment on the job, most women feel they might be jeopardizing their positions by openly complaining against abusive coworkers or superiors.

Women managers normally turn sexual advances back in the same quasi-humorous way in which most are offered, without resorting to external help and without accepting them. For example, one study found that almost all women surveyed had experienced advances from male executives, but practically none had ever had an affair with the men in their organizations (Litterer, 1976). Any type of affair would be a distraction emphasizing sex rather than work roles in the office environment. Since traditional sex roles assume women are less able than men, the resulting relationship could be disasterous for a woman's long-term career advancement. We should also note that the direction of potential sexual exploitation is often not clear-cut. Nonetheless, managers of both sexes emphatically (and indelicately) state that "no one sleeps her way to the top."

Women who enter management also avoid the frustrations of having had their ambitions for personal development stifled. A comparison of the lives of working women with those of homemakers shows that the latter project their ambitions onto their children (Hoffman, 1973). At the time of marriage and childbirth, these women may feel more secure and self-assured than those who have opted for a career. Ten to fifteen years later, however, many of the homemakers find they also entertain personal ambitions but feel trapped—that developing a career so late would be futile. In contrast, although their work is demanding, women who enter management are likely to obtain increasing satisfaction from it and are less likely to feel frustrated as their children grow up.

The frustrations of nonworking women are perhaps best summarized in Birnbaum's (1975) study of the differences between professional women's perceptions of their lives in mid-career and those held by homemakers. The study was based on matched samples of college graduates fifteen years after graduation. The professional women had higher self-esteem, felt they were in better mental health, and seemed less likely to be undergoing an "identity crisis."[1] The professional women were also more satisfied with their friendships but felt they lacked relaxation time. Nonworking women said their lives lacked creative challenge, while professional women credited their careers with enhancing self-esteem, excitement, and fulfillment. Finally, homemakers with children were more likely than professional women with children to cite the children as a source of self-fulfillment (though 61 percent did not even mention that their children counted on this dimension) and self-sacrifice and were more negative in reaction to their youngsters starting school. The implications of this and other studies are that children are second-best and short-run alternatives to work in terms of personal satisfaction. Those women who do not work rely on their children, while those who have a choice do not rely on them and seem more satisfied as a result.

The Others in Your Organization

Previous chapters have indicated that women who are credited with success are often considered more intelligent and are better liked than others who seem less successful (Kristal, Sanders, Spence, and Helmreich, 1975; Spence and Helmreich, 1972). On the other hand, it is also true that many men react negatively toward a successful woman, sometimes misattributing her success on a supposedly masculine activity, or socially isolating her (cf. Hagan and Kahn, 1975; Pleck, 1976). Just how can a successful woman expect others to behave? The answer really depends on the apparent abilities of the woman, the potential competition or assistance she renders to others, and her position. Most women report being well-accepted by their colleagues, but their initial rise often encountered resistance not met by young male managers.

Superiors

Like others in our society, superiors tend to make the assumption that women are poorly qualified. That assumption can be crippling to a woman's career if it is allowed to stand, because it limits the experiences open to her. Fortunately, a woman seldom represents a competitive threat to her superiors as a woman; the opposite seems true: the farther the superior is removed in rank from the woman, the more likely he is to respond favorably toward her work and the less likely he is to discriminate (Collins and Ganotis, 1974). Consequently, many women executives credit their success to careful use of every opportunity to demonstrate and develop their abilities.

Women can expect additional support from their superiors if they are perceived as being *more* competent than a male. In fact, women who succeed usually report that at least one of their male superiors has been instrumental in helping them (Laws, 1975; Wood, 1975). The patron sometimes acts by singling the woman out from his other subordinates and progressively schooling her in the most politic responses to be made in the new situations to which he introduces her. The relationship protects the woman from others who might prefer that she not enter the executive ranks. In this way, as the patron moves up in the organization, the woman working with him is also able to advance.

Since the patron expects continued development on the part of his subordinate, the supportive relationship can be extremely helpful. In most cases, however, the woman must be willing to sever the relationship at some point for two reasons. First, rapid advancement may require moving out from under a slow-rising patron. Second, the male patron's support is contingent on his subordinate not jeopardizing his relationship with male colleagues. Agitation for an end to discrimination or for personal advancement does embarrass the patron, however. A woman who permanently attaches herself to one patron may be used as a token gatekeeper, forced by her patron to unconsciously prevent other women from rising (Laws, 1975).

Coworkers

Male associates vying with a woman for a single promotion are the most likely to feel threatened by her possible success. While men also react competitively to the success of male colleagues, it is easier for them to single out a woman as invading their territory, to stamp her behavior as unacceptable, and to feel her success is unfair. Although major confrontations are rare, a competitive woman can raise the "masculine consciousness" of her associates, and it is not unusual for her to be frozen from their group conversations and social gatherings. The men's rationales include a woman's lack of understanding of men, lack of experience, likelihood of being offended, or merely of dampening an otherwise freewheeling discussion.

The informal communications network provides a valuable mechanism for the exchange of ideas and information. The successful woman executive can be distinguished by her ability to move socially between male and female groups (Litterer, 1976). To the extent that she is accepted as an equal in the male-dominated informal social group, her presence defuses sensitivity to sex role differences. As a result, she can share the expertise and assistance of the group rather than having it used against her.

Acceptance requires at least two features. The woman inobtrusively demonstrates her capabilities in order to show that she has something to add to the group and is not being carried by the organization simply because of her sex. In order for anyone to gain mutual trust and support, it also helps to show support of the group by working with the members (especially with informal leaders) in a cooperative manner. Coworkers return the support of those with whom they identify—those with similarities rather than differences. The emphasis in no way compromises femininity, but neither is femininity overstated. For example, the successful woman need not take up cigars and martinis, but she avoids passing judgment on male peers who display male-defined habits. The result is a close and valuable working relationship with male colleagues.

Subordinates

Tradition has it that no one wants to work under a woman boss; presumably women are picky, opinionated, emotional, softheaded, and unpredictable. Earlier chapters have shown that the stereotype is quite wrong, but it is also true that both sexes tend to behave in a less-than-human manner in low-paying, dead-end, boring jobs. The success or frustration of a superior is felt acutely by those below in terms of the acceptance or failure of their own plans. A woman executive who is making progress enables those working beneath her to make similar progress; when she is able to communicate her confidence and success to her subordinates, any reservations they have about working for her disappear.

A woman's relationships with the others in her organization can be summarized as being cordial and normal (Osborn and Vicars, 1976). The others expect more problems from working with women than occur. Perceptive and capable women who exercise a little care seldom have difficulty in avoiding human relations pitfalls. Necessarily, the route to success is rougher for those who are either blind to potential problems or incompetent, but those persons should avoid management irrespective of their sex.

What a Woman Manager Means to the Organization

If the woman executive can be accepted by her colleagues, she should be heartily welcomed by the organization itself. Instead, as we have seen in earlier chapters, she can expect discrimination. One excuse for the discrimination and for the historic distrust of women managers is the supposed low productivity of women. There is no direct evidence that women are less productive than men having similar experiences, training, and company support. Nonetheless, some economists insist that if women were not less productive, a competitive firm would prefer lower-paid women to more expensive men, thereby advancing the women (cf. Polachek, 1976). The economic argument holds only if those who hire and promote women perceive their productivity correctly. The previous chapters have shown that they do not; men are the "standard" against which women must continually prove themselves.

It follows that organizations hiring women are actually (albeit unwittingly) getting more than their money's worth. The productivity of the average woman per dollar in salary is higher than of men in many high-ranked jobs. The differential may be expected to drop out if the pay of women rises toward that received by men. Meanwhile, however, the hiring of women represents a distinct economic advantage to many organizations.

Equally important to the organization, the significant entry of women managers opens a wider range of strategy options for the firm (cf. Wood, 1976). Whether in marketing, personnel, or planning, the introduction of persons having heterogeneous backgrounds results in more "creative" ideas. As the last chapter pointed out, we have no reason to believe that strategies favored by men have overall superiority. Those women who have the business experience to know when to apply a more feminine strategy bring a flexibility to the decision-making process that few men can match. The need for the rich range of new ideas offered by experienced women is especially marked in the negotiation process, when competition is severe, or when dealing specifically with the problems of female personnel and customers.

Strategy changes, one should note, reverberate through other aspects of corporate life. Every firm has a sort of organizational self-image that many employees work toward maintaining. Some firms pride themselves on being hard-driving, while others are paternalistic or conservative. In some cases, the entry of women may change the organizational climate considerably. For example, a woman product manager might prefer a noncompetitive marketing strategy. Consequently, she would position her products to satisfy market segments left untouched by competing products rather than to meet the competition head-on. As the results of decisions like this become widely known, employees who were formerly competitive with one another may come to realize that situations exist in which one person's win does not bring about another's loss.

Do these changes mean that the organization employing women will become somehow feminized? It is not possible to state in advance just what the changes in organizational climate will be, but in many cases nonfunctional, arbitrary relationships and policies will be gradually abandoned in favor of a greater rationality, flexibility, and efficiency. These results seem to be a long distance from the stereotype of either sex, or of management itself, today. What is assured then is that women's entry into management, though requiring a great deal of effort from the women, will result in their personal growth and simultaneously strengthen the organizations in which they work.

What Your Being a Woman Manager Means to Others

In determining appropriate behavior for ourselves, we constantly model on the others we see. If there are no women executives, we must assume that it is slightly scandalous to be both a manager and female. If such people do exist, then we can observe them to decide whether to undertake similar activities in exchange for the same rewards; we can determine how to best avoid the problems they face. In this sense, women who manage, by their very existence and life-style, encourage other women to enter and rise in management. Each of us who enters the field makes it more attractive to others.

The entry of other women also contributes to the success of those who are already managers. The increasing numbers help erase the stereotypes of management as a masculine domain and of managers as assuredly male; employers and coworkers gain the experience they need with women managers to understand that managerial responsibility given to a woman is still in firm hands. Thus the increase can lift the siege mentality of some women already in the field as well as of some men who feel they must protect their organizations through discrimination.

Children are even more subject to modeling influences than adults, because their role concepts are not yet firmly established. As it happens, the daughters of working women are more likely to admire their mothers and choose them as role models than are the daughters of nonworking women (Hoffman, 1973). The normative role that the children of working women learn is one allowing for a greater than usual range and freedom of activity and self-expression.

The daughters of working women are also more likely to approve their mother's employment and to seek employment themselves (Hoffman, 1973). They often develop a stronger desire for achievement and are less likely than those with nonworking mothers to discredit or devalue the abilities of women (Baruch, 1972). In contrast, there seem to be no negative effects of maternal employment on children of either sex—providing the mother feels no guilt over her employment and assuming that young children are reasonably well cared for in their mother's absence.

It need hardly be added that the effects of a woman's employment, especially of her choosing a meaningful job such as management, ripple in other directions as well. As Hoffman has noted, several studies show that the husbands of professional women come to respect and support their accomplishments; these men later help to encourage independence and achievement in their daughters. Thus the woman who chooses to manage serves as an example that helps to break up restrictive social stereotypes, diminishes the likelihood of further discrimination, and allows others—including her own children—to develop and apply their abilities in a meaningful way.

Personal Decision Inventory

The previous sections of this chapter have described some of the characteristics of women managers, their interactions with others, and some of their effects on others. One element has been left out—professional women have flexibility in their life styles. They can decide whether to place emotional investment in job or family. They can also decide how hard to work, where to work, and the type of work they prefer. When a better position opens in another city, they can consider whether to go on the basis of its advantages rather than being tied to one location.[2] Working women also have a personal source of discretionary income that allows the earlier purchase of homes, clothes, and vacations. The counter-restriction, of course, is that professional women who leave the labor force for long periods of time risk losing their professional status through slow attrition and antiquation of their skills. The decision to enter management results in greater flexibility only if it is considered a serious, semipermanent career choice.

The elements discussed in the sections above have a different importance for each of us. Some women may find the goal of a large family overwhelmingly important, while others may be unconcerned with family life. If you are still undecided about whether you should enter management, you may find the following exercise helpful in reaching your decision.

Instructions for the Personal Decision Inventory

The instructions below refer to the columns of Table 5–1. Completion will take from twenty to forty minutes. At the end, you will find some general guidelines for interpreting whether your responses indicate that you probably should, or should not, seriously plan on a managerial career at this time. For the best results, do each column completely before moving to the next step.

Step 1. In column 1, list all the aspects of being a woman manager that you find interesting, important, or upsetting. Some items are listed as examples, but you should cross them out if they are not personally important to you. Try to add at least five items to the list given. This decision scheme will work better if you have more items, but they should not overlap or repeat each other.

Step 2. In column 2, you should place your evaluation of how important each of the items listed in column 1 is to you personally at this time. Evaluations should range from −7 (as stated, it could be extremely harmful) through 0 (don't care) to +7 (extremely good—something liked a lot). In making these evaluations, don't be concerned with how you think your becoming a manager would affect your ratings—you are rating only their subjective importance.

Step 3. In column 3, rate the extent to which you feel that your becoming a manager will affect the dimensions listed in column 1. Evaluations should be made from −7 (will prevent the dimension listed in column 1 from happening) through 0 (will not affect the item) to +7 (will ensure that the item listed will occur). Do not be concerned on this step with how much you like the effect or how important it is to you; rate only the direction of the effect and the strength of the probable influence that your joining management will have.

Table 5-1
Personal Decision Inventory

Dimension (List)	Importance -7 to +7	Influence (Present) -7 to +7	Product	Importance -7 to +7	Influence (Future) -7 to +7	Product
1	2	3	4	5	6	7
1. High Pay						
2. Interesting Coworkers						
3. Committment						
4. Challenging						
5. Interesting Work						
6. Prestige						
7. Leisure Time						
8. Power/Leadership						
9. Close Family Ties						
10. No Responsibilities						
11.						
12.						
13.						
14.						
15.						

SUM _____ divide

SUM _____ divide

Number of Dimensions = _____

Decision Score (Average) = _____ = _____

Step 4. Multiply the numbers in column 2 by those in column 3; be careful to retain the correct sign. Place the products in column 4.

Example: Suppose you feel that pay is an important dimension to you which is likely to be affected by management. This characteristic is entered in column 1. Considering the personal importance of high pay, you might place a +5 in column 2. Next, if you think that your becoming an executive will greatly enhance your likelihood of obtaining high pay, place a +7 in column 3. Next, multiply

$$\text{High pay} \qquad +5 \times +7 = +35$$

Step 5. Use columns 5, 6, and 7 to repeat this process in evaluating your evaluations for the future, perhaps ten to twenty years from now.

Step 6. Obtain averages for columns 4 and 7 by summing each column separately and dividing the sums by the number of dimensions you have listed in column 1.

Interpretation

As you can readily see, the final decision scores (the averages just obtained) can vary from +49 to −49. Higher positive scores indicate that there is a good chance that you will be satisfied by entering management, while higher negative scores (larger numbers with a minus sign) predict a probability of dissatisfaction. The term "probability" is used here because, of course, each number you have entered is your estimate based on the information available to you; the estimate is more likely to be correct as the information available to you grows, as the list of dimensions grows, and as the list of dimensions becomes more representative of those that are actually important.

The best decision scheme to follow at this point would be to repeat this entire process for each of the life alternatives that you think is realistically available to you. For example, you could now list in column 1 all of the important aspects of being a housewife, then of taking a blue-collar position, becoming a mail carrier, etc. For each possibility, you would recalculate your decision score. After comparing the decision scores, you merely choose the activity having the highest value. With this procedure, you may actively dislike all your alternatives, but choose one anyway as being preferrable to starvation or joining the Foreign Legion. The technique is flawed both by the time required and by the fact that it may commit you to undertaking an activity in which you have no real interest.

Success in management, remember, does require long-term effort. Consequently, the interpretation that follows is more useful (though less systematic) for your career choice. In general, you should probably consider management seriously only if your decision score is above 0. A score above 18 (if you considered only five dimensions) or at least above 8 (if you considered as many as fifteen dimensions) shows that there is an excellent chance that you will enjoy the life of an executive. Lower positive scores are less certain and may indicate that your goals are not yet clearly formed. Similarly, negative scores from 0 to −20, although pessimistic, show that you may do well to re-evaluate your goals again at a later time before making a definite committment to seek a career elsewhere. Women with negative scores from −20 to −49 will probably not enjoy a management career.

Two time frames can be compared using these scores. If your decision scores are both about the same, you can interpret them in the straightforward manner suggested above. If the scores differ markedly from one another, you should ask two questions. First, how important is the foreseeable future to you? Although most people are not very interested in planning for a future more than a few years away, more educated people (including managers) usually plan longer in advance. You may wish to give both scores equal weight and average them before making a decision. Second, how knowledgeable is your intuition of your future preferences? Many people change a great deal and should not try to predict their feelings more than a few years ahead. On the other hand, successful entry into management requires a good deal of investment of time and effort; these inputs pay off over a long period of time. After studying these considerations, you may want to weight your decision scores differently.

Try the exercise above. Chances are that your score will indicate that you are ready for developing some personal strategies for managerial success (next chapter). If your score is not that high, you may have learned something of equal importance.

Note

1. Woman managers who are married are restricted somewhat, but not as greatly as those women who have no career. Married professional women in the Birnbaum (1975) study felt that their husbands were quite supportive of their careers. Other studies have reported an increase in the number of men who are willing to change jobs or relocate when a move is necessary to enhance the opportunities open to their wives.

References

Bartol, K. M., and Butterfield, D. A. "Sex effects in evaluating leaders." *Journal of Applied Psychology*, 1976, *61*, 446–454.

Baruch, G. K. "Maternal influences upon college women's attitudes toward women and work." *Developmental Psychology,* 1972, *6,* 32–37.

Birnbaum, J. A. "Life patterns and self-esteem in gifted family-oriented and career-committed women." In M. T. S. Mednick, S. S. Tangri, and L. W. Hoffman (eds.), *Women and achievement.* Washington, D.C.: Hemisphere Publishing, 1975.

Brief, A. P., and Oliver, R. L. "Male-female differences in work attitudes among retail sales managers." *Journal of Applied Psychology,* 1976, *61,* 526–528.

Collins, J. W., and Ganotis, C. G. "Managerial attitudes toward corporate social responsibility." In S. P. Sethi (ed.), *The unstable ground: Corporate social policy in a dynamic society.* Los Angeles: Melville Publishing, 1974.

Hagan, R. L., and Kahn, A. "Discrimination against competent women." *Journal of Applied Social Psychology,* 1975, *4,* 362–376.

Harlan, A. "Psychological coping patterns of male and female managers." Paper presented at a meeting of the Academy of Management, Kansas City, 1976.

Hoffman, L. W. "The professional woman as mother." *Annals of the New York Academy of Sciences,* 1973, *208,* 211–217.

——. "The employment of women, education, and fertility." *Merrill-Palmer Quarterly,* 1974, *20.* Reprinted in M. T. S. Mednick, S. S. Tangri, & L. W. Hoffman (eds.), *Women and Achievement.* Washington, D.C.: Hemisphere Publishing, 1975.

Jusenius, C. L. "Economics." *Signs,* 1976, *2,* 177–189.

Kavanagh, M. J., and Halpern, M. "The impact of job level and sex differences on the relationship between life and job satisfaction." *Academy of Management Journal,* 1977, *20,* 66–73.

Keaveny, T. J., Jackson, J. H., and Fossum, J. A. "Sex differences in job satisfaction." Paper presented at a meeting of the Academy of Management, Kansas City, 1976.

Kristal, J., Sanders, D., Spence, J. T., and Helmreich, R. "Inferences about the femininity of competent women and their implications for likability." *Sex Roles,* 1975, *1,* 33–40.

Laws, J. L. "The psychology of tokenism: An analysis." *Sex Roles,* 1975, *1,* 51–67.

Litterer, J. A. "Life cycle changes of career women: Assessment and adaptation." Paper presented at a meeting of the Academy of Management, Kansas City, 1976.

Nemy, E. "Women begin to speak out against sexual harassment at work." *New York Times,* August 19, 1975, p. 38.

"100 top corporate women." *Business Week,* June 21, 1976, 56–68.

Osborn, R. N., and Vicars, W. M. "Sex stereotypes: An artifact in leader behavior and subordinate satisfaction analysis?" *Academy of Management Journal,* 1976, *19,* 439–449.

Pleck, J. H. "Male threat from female competence." *Journal of Consulting and Clinical Psychology,* 1976, *44,* 608–613.

Polachek, S. W. "Occupational segregation: An alternative hypothesis." *Journal of Contemporary Business,* 1976, *5* (1), 1–12.

Robertson, W. "The ten highest ranked women in big business." *Fortune,* 1973, *87* (4), 80–89.

Spence, J. T., and Helmreich, R. "Who likes competent women? Competence, sex-role congruence of interests, and subject's attitudes toward women as determinants of interpersonal attraction." *Journal of Applied Social Psychology,* 1972, *2,* 197–213.

Wood, M. M. "What does it take for a woman to make it in management?" *Personnel Journal,* 1975 (January), 38–41, 66.

———. "Women in management: How is it working out?" *Advanced Management Journal,* 1976, *41* (Winter).

———, and Greenfeld, S. T. "Women managers and fear of success: A study in the field." *Sex Roles,* 1976, *2,* 375–387.

6

Doing It in Management

How can women enter and rise in management? With all the problems spelled out in earlier chapters, it seems certain that successful careers are rarely launched by women who wait patiently to be noticed and rewarded for their efforts. Similarly, few managerial jobs are earmarked "hire a strong woman," although the call is still heard for a sturdy man of executive timber.

Nonetheless, in terms of shear numbers, more women are participating in management now than in any other time in history. Over five million women are now employed in professional or managerial positions. That number is steadily rising; the levels of skill and experience of professional and managerial women are growing. As a result, the impact of women on business is increasing. It is significant, for example, that *Business Week* and other managerial publications have begun to headline women as well as men.

This activity is a sign that some routes to the top have opened and that women are "making it" in management. In fact, women entering management at this time are the primary beneficiaries of a relaxation of some traditional restrictions against women. Competent, high-achieving, and hard-working women can now make their way up the corporate ladder through imaginative problem solving, resourceful coping with the pressures encountered, and by learning from the men they are now allowed to work with (instead of for).

Probably the most important single factor behind the transformation of increasing numbers of women into managers has been the publicity obtained by the Women's Movement. Few successful women executives identify themselves as radicals, and many even shun the labels pinned to members of the movement. There is no denying, however, that the Women's Movement has had the effect of waking people to the rigidities and injustices of social stereotypes. As one result, more women have begun seeking education for and entrance to fields previously closed to them. In response to the Movement, the government has passed legislation applying legal pressure to help breach some of the barriers organizations had maintained against women. Because of the publicity surrounding court and legislative victories, many women have begun to realize that they are treated as a block; as women begin to function as a politically aware block, individual victories become victories for all women.

Despite the glowing rhetoric, of course, the revolution is still far from complete. Women are not progressing as rapidly in management as in many other activities. More rapid progress requires an understanding of the specific problems we still face, and the construction of individual strategies effective in overcoming

111

those problems. Fortunately, the necessary ingredients for the construction and implementation of workable strategies are readily available.

This chapter summarizes some of the observations made earlier in order to show some of the specific strengths and weaknesses of women as perceived by others. Since the stereotypic qualities are expected of women, they must either take advantage of the qualities or find ways to dismiss them if they are to succeed. How a woman can take advantage depends on the type of organization she is confronted with and on her actual abilities and interests. There is no cut-and-dried strategy for success; rather each person must decide what personal strategy agrees with her best. The final sections of this chapter show how such a strategy can be developed.

A Brief Review

As the last chapters found, there are few meaningful personality differences between men and women who are successful on the job. Women who succeed parallel men in ability, confidence, and desire for authority, status, challenge, and income (cf. Jacklin and Maccoby, 1975; Schwartz, 1976; Wood, 1976). Similarly, there is little question but that women perform as well as men in actual work situations—although women sometimes work differently. Successful women in predominantly male occupations demonstrate motivation, capacity, and administrative and leadership skill comparable to that of their male counterparts (cf. Osborn and Vicars, 1976; Wood, 1976). In addition, most successful women also show a healthy attitude about being female and are at ease in relating to men (Wood, 1975).

One measure of the success of women who are entering management can be seen in the study by Wood (1976) of men who are working with woman executives. On the whole, the men seem to be adjusting by modifying their images of femininity to encompass the activities and traits they observe in the executive women. These men say they are pleasantly surprised with the way the women are adapting to the new relationship. Few, if any, major organizational or personal adjustments are needed. They rate the women very high on emotional control, decision making, and responsiveness to criticism—all areas in which women stereotypically rate poorly. Once the women have had the opportunity to demonstrate their abilities, the men and women both agree that tension, feelings of threat, and other worries quickly disappear. In fact, the male executives who have worked with the women say that their two most important problems are those of finding and motivating additional qualified women to seek advancement and obtaining their acceptance by others in the organization who have not yet had direct contact with them.

If everyone were as welcoming toward women as the men questioned in the Wood (1976) study, women would have no difficulty in entering management.

The finding that the executives in her study felt that others might not accept women indicates that this is not yet true, however. Because of the differences in traditional sex roles, men and women are still expected to behave differently from one another. Because of the expectations, women must arrange to demonstrate their abilities before they can start to be accepted; having done so, they must work to be seen as capable executives rather than as unusual women who have overreached themselves. People with whom the women work must feel sure of their own abilities before they are willing to attribute the success of women to their ability and effort rather than to good fortune or feminine wiles.

When these conditions are not present, the woman executive may not be allowed to succeed; if she is unsuccessful, the atmosphere of the organization may become even more sex-polarized than before (cf. Bass, Krusell, and Alexander, 1971; Bowman, Worthy, and Greyser, 1965; Collins and Ganotis, 1974). If the conditions for success are present, and the woman does demonstrate her ability, she may still be viewed as an exception—an extraordinarily well-qualified person who is not indicative of how well women usually work out. Other women must then go through the same ritual of proving themselves.

Pressing the Legal Limit—One Alternative

Can the situation just described be remedied? How can women obtain equality in management, and how do those who are in management manage their success? One alternative, which we offer hesitatingly for reasons that will become apparent, is the legal solution. We constantly hear through the news media that women are protected by law from discrimination. As a result, some would go so far as to suggest that there is no longer a discrimination problem; the statistical imbalances seen in the first chapter are already well on their way toward correction. Supposedly this is an ideal time for women to enter management, because, at last, they are greeted by incumbents who have repented from past wickedness. The court-ordered need for women has opened positions for all—even the somewhat incompetent.

There is some truth to this view. Some organizations are feeling the heat of federal and state prosecutors and are honestly or grudgingly attempting to put an end to discrimination. After conducting a national survey of 160 representative organizations, the Bureau of National Affairs (Miner, 1976) found that 60 percent of reporting organizations had altered their employee hiring procedures to meet new legal requirements. In the same sample, the proportion of firms admitting women either to supervisory training, management development, or apprenticeship programs rose substantially from 1967. Among those firms maintaining such programs, the number admitting women increased from 53 to 85 percent, 61 to 81 percent and 21 to 54 percent respectively during the period. In the same sample, 24 percent had instituted special training for women or minority workers. The proportion of woman managers in those organizations rose by 3 percent between 1970 and 1975.

These statistics are very encouraging. However, they pale somewhat when seen in perspective. Sixty-three percent of the organizations in the Miner (1976) study admitted having Civil Rights Act violations filed against them. Nationwide, the Equal Employment Opportunity Commission (the major federal agency concerned with discrimination) had a backlog of well over 100,000 civil rights cases—many over three years old, and many uninvestigated. The agency could respond to the backlog by demanding additional personnel to investigate violations and enforce the law. Instead, it reacted by suggesting new procedures aimed at preemptorily disposing of the case backlog (cf. *Spokeswoman,* 1976, no. 4, 5).

The laws concerning discrimination are an important weapon that a woman can use to obtain her rights. Obviously, however, the extent to which she can expect satisfaction is limited. Moreover, in many cases, women who use the laws to obtain their rights risk their careers in the process—even if they win their cases. A full understanding of the laws is necessary in order to recognize the impact of "going to the feds" with our complaints.

In the discussion below, keep in mind that both the laws and their enforcement procedures are subject to change. As this book was being prepared, several changes in enforcement of the laws described here were proposed. These include changes in procedures governing class actions, and changes in affirmative action plan requirements. Most of the changes were held in abeyance for a decision by members of the Carter administration. Readers should also be aware that recent Supreme Court decisions, which have not yet been broadly interpreted, suggest that the proof of discriminatory intent on the part of employers will be increasingly important in the future. A fine description of the caselaw on discrimination is contained in Matthies (1976), while the details of the laws themselves and the preparations needed for filing a complaint appear in Samuels (1975). Remember, however, that there is no substitute for a trusted attorney, and there is no sure thing.

The Laws

Working women have four special types of legal protection. To a large extent, these overlap with each other, and a woman who files an action under any one should consider whether she is also entitled to file under the others as well.

1. The Equal Employment Opportunity Act of 1972 (P.L. 92-261) and Title VII of the Civil Rights Act of 1974 (42 U.S.C. §2000e et. seq.) are the main legal defense against sex discrimination. They prohibit sex and other types of discrimination by nearly all private and many public employers of fifteen or more persons. The law either exempts or has not generally been applied to religious

organizations, some arms of state and local government, and unions. The "civil rights laws" specifically prohibit discrimination in hiring, promotions, layoffs, transfers, salaries, fringe benefits, and training.

A wide number of other related conditions are also covered. For example, the civil rights laws prohibit enforcement by employers of sex-discriminatory state "protective" labor laws. "Protective" labor laws vary by state. They often prohibit employers from requiring women to lift certain weights or to work overtime. In some states, special working conditions are mandatory for women, but not for men. The result is that employers prefer men for protected positions and women are in practice discriminated against. In fact, some states prohibit women from some categories of employment altogether.

In practice, courts have held that when both federal restrictions against discrimination and state protective labor laws cover the same position, all employees (male and female alike) must be equally "benefited" by the protective labor laws. Thus if a state law says that women must be given two rest periods in addition to the lunch break, men must now be given the same rest periods. In response, many states are eliminating their discriminatory protective labor laws.

Civil rights laws also prevent employers from indicating a sex preference in advertising unless one sex or the other cannot do a particular job, from maintaining sex-based seniority practices, or from enforcing discrimination concerning pregnancy (such as by requiring a woman to take a leave of absence while she is still willing and able to work). As well, employers with 100 or more employees are required to file a form each year detailing their employment of women and four minority groups at each of nine levels within the organization.

2. Executive Orders (E.O. 11246, 11375, 11478) prohibit discrimination by any federal contractor or subcontractor with contracts totalling over $10,000 in any twelve-month period; they also forbid discrimination by any federal office or agency. The orders require that covered employers sign a pledge written into federal contracts against discrimination. Contractors with 50 or more employees are required to develop a written "affirmative action" plan for public availability within 120 days following the signing of any contract for $50,000 or more. Contracts of one million dollars or more require a review before they are signed to determine that the organization is in compliance with the affirmative action requirements, and that the plan is up to date. In practice, however, the review is often waived. As this book was written, more lenient cutoffs had been proposed, but their adoption was unlikely.

Revised Order #4 sets out the details required in the affirmative action plans mandated under the Executive Orders. An employer is required to inventory the present employees in each major job classification at each facility; underutilization of women or minorities in any job classification must be explained. "'Underutilization' is defined by having fewer minorities or women in a particular job classification than would reasonably be expected by their availability" (§S60-2.11 Revised Order #4).

Contractors are advised to consider eight factors in determining underutilization:

1. women's employment in the immediate area
2. the percentage of women working in the locale
3. the availability of women with the requisite skill in the locale
4. the availability of women having the skill in the potential recruiting area
5. the availability of women seeking employment in the potential recruiting area
6. the availability of promotable or transferrable women
7. the community's potential for training women
8. the potential for internal training

Employers who find that they are underutilizing women are directed to establish a timetable and goals for redressing the imbalance; they are to employ "every good faith effort" that can reasonably be expected. The establishment of rigid quotas is, however, specifically prohibited as a means for carrying out the affirmative action plan (§60-2.12e).

3. The Equal Pay Act of 1963 (as amended in 1972 and 1974) makes it illegal to pay one sex less than another for substantially equal work. The act applies to the entire pay package including salaries, overtime pay, bonuses, and fringe benefits. The term "substantially equal work" is interpreted loosely such that minor differences in working conditions or job requirements are not sufficient to excuse pay inequities. Employers cannot set up arbitrary job differences such as adding infrequent or avoidable responsibilities to the work of men, or transferring them to a different department or shift, in order to avoid paying men and women equally. However, the act applies only to comparable types of work performed in the same location by a single employer. Hence different organizations may use their own separate pay scales and may pay men and women who have equally high levels of different skills differently from one another. Rational non-sex-based systems for computing pay are unrestricted by the act. Consequently, experience, seniority, or piece-work pay standards are acceptable (assuming that women and minorities have had an equal opportunity to meet these standards). Certain classes of employers are presently exempt from the Equal Pay Act, although it appears that the act will continue to be tightened until it eventually includes everyone. At present, employers with less than $250,000 in sales, or dealing wholly within a single state, small farmers, elected officials, and a few other categories are exempted.

4. State fair employment laws. Most states have some laws concerning sex discrimination—although some expressly require it through their protective labor laws. Legal interpretations generally find that an employee has the maximum benefits available under either state or federal laws when both apply, but the two

codes do not agree. Thus when the state imposes penalties on employers for discrimination that are higher than those imposed by federal regulations, the employee has the benefit of the state laws; if the reverse were true, the employee could obtain the benefits provided under federal law if the employer is subject to that law. Of course, while every private organization is subject to the state laws of those states in which it operates, smaller employers are often not subject to federal regulations.

Complaint and enforcement policy

The Equal Employment Opportunity Commission (EEOC) handles complaints against all employers who are subject to Title VII except federal government offices. Forms and guidance on entering a complaint may be obtained from a district office of the EEOC or by writing to the agency at 1800 G Street, N.W., Washington, D.C. 20506. Timing of the complaints is crucial. Unless the complaint has been filed earlier with a state agency, filing must take place within 180 days of any act of alleged discrimination; if the act is ongoing, such as a failure to promote women, the time limit is 180 days from the most recent occurrence.

A different schedule applies if you have first filed the complaint with your state agency. Filing with your state is generally unnecessary, however, since the EEOC will file the complaint for you if the state has comparable regulations. The state is then given 60 days to respond; if it agrees to consider the case, an additional 300 days may be given the state to take appropriate action.

Most cases (85 percent) are ultimately processed by the EEOC rather than at the state level (Samuels, 1975). The procedure is intricate, protracted, and not very satisfying. Within ten days after the employee files her complaint, the employer is served with the charge. After the state returns the complaint to the EEOC (if this occurs), the agency has 120 days to investigate the charge and to issue a finding as to whether it believes there to be sufficient cause to suspect discrimination. Thereafter, a brief appeal period is followed by attempts at conciliation of the parties by the EEOC.

If the conciliation is unsuccessful, the EEOC may sue the employer or allow the complainant herself to sue. In order to carry out the suit on her own, the employee requires a "notice of right to sue" letter from the EEOC; such a letter can be demanded at any time after 180 days of EEOC jurisdiction. Once the letter has been issued, suit must be filed within ninety days to be valid. This deadline, like the original filing deadline, is crucial: the right to sue is lost if either deadline is allowed to lapse. Women who are intending to sue should contact a lawyer before asking for the right to sue letter (Ross, 1973).

There is no cost to this process if the EEOC takes the case to court itself.

However the time lag can have stretched to several years at that point. Moreover, there is little chance that the EEOC will actually decide to sue the employer (*The Spokeswoman,* 1976, No. 4). While the agency has done so, it usually concentrates on a few large and (some feel) splashy cases such as the AT&T suit (Wallace and Nelson, 1976). If the complainant and the EEOC both feel a case can be made, the faster and better solution is usually to hire an attorney on the basis of fees to be awarded by the court (provided for by Title VII) in the event of success; if possible, the arrangement should specify that the attorney is not to be paid any added sum.

What can be won through this process? Reinstatement, in the event of having been unfairly terminated, is infrequent. Most often the courts or the conciliation process end with the award of back pay (pay that the employee would have had if she were not discriminated against) for the period from two years prior to filing the original claim to the date of the final settlement and a promise to end future discrimination. Technically, the loser can be required to pay reasonable legal and court costs; in practice, plaintiffs in civil liberty cases are rarely required to do so. The agreement to end discrimination may be accompanied by the requirement that the employer institute an affirmative action program (which the EEOC itself does not normally have the power to require of employers).

Employees of the federal government are also covered by Title VII; each government branch is required to establish an affirmative action program. Unfortunately, this program is overseen by the U.S. Civil Service Commission (1900 E Street, N.W., Washington, DC 20415) a bureaucracy with the particularly dismal record of promoting rather than discouraging discrimination (cf. Ross, 1973).

The Equal Pay Act is administered by the Wage and Hour Division of the Department of Labor (Constitution Avenue and 14th Street, N.W., Washington, DC 20210). Complaints should be filed within two years of any instance of discrimination, although a maximum of three years is allowed if the complainant can show that the employer intended to discriminate. While the timing is somewhat uncertain, the Wage and Hour Division investigates the complaints and attempts conciliation fairly rapidly. If the initial efforts fail, the agency may decide to take the employer to court. At any point along the way, the employee has the right to sue individually.

Two years back pay (three if intent is shown) is the most usual outcome of winning an Equal Pay Act suit. If the employee files suit herself, however, she may also be able to obtain added "damages" against the employer equal to the sum of the back pay award. Attorney's fees and court costs are automatically included in the award if the employee herself sues. Women who allow the Wage and Hour Division to enter court on their behalf, however, cannot obtain damages and cannot be certain of reimbursement of any legal costs. The amount of money at stake under the Equal Pay Act can be substantial. Consequently, it is often most advantageous to sue as an individual if good evidence of discrimination is available; this also eliminates unecessary administrative delays.

The potential penalties to employers reach a peak under the Executive Orders. The Office of Federal Contract Compliance (Department of Labor, Washington, DC 20210) and the administrative organizations associated with it can prevent an organization from bidding on future federal contracts and can order payment and work stopped under present contracts. The OFCC can also sue the organization for breach of contract under the affirmative action clause of each contract. Finally, in a new interpretation of its powers, a federal court has recently held that the OFCC can also sue for back pay (cf. *Wall Street Journal,* January 19, 1977). An employee having these ends in mind should file her complaint with the OFCC within 180 days of any instance of discrimination.

The threat of contract loss is normally sufficient to be extremely worrisome to enterprises that are largely dependent on federal money, such as defense contractors or major universities. However, it is also true that the government is extremely dependent on the output of those organizations. As a result, a sort of Mexican standoff has been reached in which public threatening and groaning is followed by little, if any, real bloodletting. In practice, the OFCC almost never takes its enforcement possibilities seriously (Ross, 1973; Samuels, 1975; Seligman, 1973). No contract has yet been cancelled by the agency, nor has any contractor been sued for breach of contract to our knowledge. However some major enterprises have had substantial contract awards and payments held up while they negotiate a settlement satisfactory to the OFCC or its associated agencies.

Portions of the OFCC's authority are farmed out to organizations such as the Department of Defense, which are presumably more familiar with the situations faced by particular types of contractors. The complaints remaining for central processing are usually first passed along to the EEOC for relevant action. In some cases, the OFCC itself examines progress on the enterprise's affirmative action program. Although this involved process seems imposing, until recently there have been no penalties or assessments that could be levied by the OFCC for the benefit of the complaintant. It remains to be determined how vigorously the OFCC will use its new power to seek back pay. The major advantage of complaining to the OFCC, then, lies in the potential for frightening the employer. Although some employers accept the possibility of contract withdrawal as a calculated risk, most would prefer to avoid the threat of economic strangulation.

Some kinks

As an earlier section mentioned, hiring quotas are expressly forbidden in affirmative action plans. Instead, the employer is expected to hire and advance the best qualified applicant—but must be sure that the pool of applicants is not biased in any way. The problem of how an employer can obtain a fair distribution of employees without using a quota system has been dealt with administratively and by the courts at some length. Despite the best efforts of all concerned, the solutions have sometimes been charged with "reverse discrimination." In most cases the charges are groundless and arise from a lack of understanding of the meaning of affirmative action.

The emphasis of affirmative action programs is supposed to be on results— ending discrimination as quickly as is reasonable. The courts have generally held that the employer's good faith efforts in this direction are sufficient. Good faith, of course, becomes progressively more difficult to demonstrate when no progress in implementing the plan is actually made. In rare cases, when good faith has been repeatedly shattered by legal foot-dragging or simple refusal to implement an affirmative action plan, courts and conciliation efforts have imposed quotas and target dates. The best known case of this type is the "Berkeley Plan" (Johnson, 1975; Spears, 1975). In this particular case, thirty-year departmental quotas were hammered out in negotiations between the Department of Health, Education, and Welfare (which oversees the affirmative action programs in universities) and University of California officials.

Among other results, the Berkeley Plan required that 95.71 women and 1.38 blacks be hired. Supposedly, these figures match the availability of blacks and women with the expected needs of the university thirty years into the future. Unfortunately, however, no one can predict the number of blacks and women who *will* be available and have relevant credentials in, say, twenty years. As discrimination ends, the availability should grow. It seems likely that the rigid quotas are as harmful to the long-term interests of women and minorities as they are absurd to the University of California.

Rather than functioning as a source of reverse discrimination, quotas are a last—but sometimes misguided—resort in removing discrimination. The underlying issue in any affirmative action plan is the extent to which women or minorities should be preferred in situations in which they are equally qualified or can readily become so. Revised Order #4 states that minority and female applicants cannot be required to possess higher qualifications than the least-qualified incumbent. However, there is no provision stating that every female or minority candidate meeting the minimum standards must be hired; employers are merely prevented from imposing a cutoff automatically barring their further consideration.

In fact, employers who obey the rule of common sense are unlikely to have any difficulty with any aspects of current law or its interpretations. For example, outright discrimination is legal under Title VII in the event that it is a response to the need for authenticity or genuineness. The group of positions which can legally specify sex as a "bonafide occupational qualification" (BFOQ) is extremely limited, however. Actors and models are the most obvious examples. On the other hand, men have successfully sued for the right to become flight stewards (U.S. airlines previously hired only stewardesses). The court reasoned that men could perform the required services; ability was considered more important than opposing arguments such as passengers' preferences for stewardesses or the weight penalty that stewards might impose on the airlines.

It is an open question as to whether the BFOQ is needed by employers at all. The courts have tended to feel that the underutilization of either sex is allowable in cases of business necessity. Businesses with an uneven distribution of employees of each sex need only demonstrate that the members of one sex are superior in job performance to those of another. In other words, while employers cannot discriminate on the basis of sex itself, they are free to apply pre-employment screening procedures that have the effect of discrimination. Discriminating procedures must be shown to be the most significant and valid means of predicting job effectiveness. On the other hand, the courts have dealt unkindly with employers whose employment tests discriminate but cannot be shown to be related to job success; they are similarly unappreciative of tests that are valid predictors of success on phony job requirements (Matthies, 1976).

As a hypothetical example, a police department might decide that only those over six feet tall can be considered for police training (sex itself is not a BFOQ for police work). Since most women are under six feet tall, the cutoff is obviously discriminatory. However, it would be legal if the police department could demonstrate that those under the limit are unable to perform well, while people are taller often do better. The limit would probably be disallowed by the courts if it were determined that the special task done best by tall people rarely occurs, or occurs only for police cadets entering some specialized activities for which everyone need not be qualified. The height restriction will also be disallowed if some simple alternative can be found to replace it without too much expense. For instance, weight may be a better predictor of success, while the expedient of converting to longer night sticks may eliminate physical limitations entirely. In any event, if a woman cannot do the job, she need not be hired.

The Legal Solution—Is This a Strategy?

Each of the three major federal restrictions on employment discrimination, and most state laws as well, prohibit the employer from harassing personnel who take legal action. The employee cannot be discharged, transferred to more difficult or demeaning work, or harmed in any way other than what would have occurred in the normal course of the job if legal action were not an issue. These guarantees are worthless in most cases, however, since there is no satisfactory means to establish that harassment has occurred (unless it is quite blatant).

A number of subterfuges have developed in an effort to avoid the reactions of employers by protecting the anonymity of the employee as long as possible. In the end, however, the employer is legally entitled to examine the evidence and will inevitably discover who has instituted the legal action. For lower-level employees, this is probably no real difficulty. For those personnel, potential harassment is more than compensated by the amount to be won and the satisfaction of carrying the case through. All else failing, they can probably leave and do equally well with another organization that is unaware of the proceedings still pending against the original employer.

Managerial and professional employees are in a more difficult situation. Positions are more scarce as one approaches the top of an organization. The visibility and importance of top personnel means that there is a good chance that a reputation for being a "trouble maker" will follow the employee. In some industries, the individual may even be blacklisted and unable to find comparable work at all. Those who remain with their employers sometimes find that their jobs have reached a dead-end in which they are no longer privy to the confidential inner workings of their organization. Both of the authors know of women who are currently in this position, and we hesitate to recommend it to anyone who is already experiencing some measure of career success.

Seldom, if ever, is a promotion into higher management won through legal pressure. Although many new opportunities opening for women may be attributed largely to supportive legislation and the willingness of many women to see it enforced, women who aspire to executive rank are still dependent on the changing attitudes of society in general and of their male employers in particular. Not only is bias difficult to prove at upper administrative levels, but even with a clearcut case of discrimination, a woman usually has more to lose than to gain by resorting to a legal solution at a critical point in her career.

Nonetheless, women who seriously consider legal redress, and who handle it carefully, may be quite successful. The appendix to this book contains an article (Thompson, 1975) describing the procedures used and the problems faced by a group of women in instituting a suit against the Chase Manhattan bank. The article provides an excellent insider's view of the psychological and operational requirements for instituting legal action; it should be considered "must" reading before you make a decision to sue.

The Stereotype—Another View

If not the legal strategy, then what? The careful formulation and execution of a personal strategy is much less appealing than a legal suit, because it requires more time and effort to execute. Nonetheless, a personal strategy approach will probably be more rewarding in the long run. The next two sections inventory some of the advantages and disadvantages women commonly encounter in management. Later, this chapter will examine some basic tactics and strategies that apply the advantages and try to avoid the disadvantages. Throughout these discussions, one should recognize that individual situations, abilities, and interests differ. The reader should be on the lookout for important differences and should incorporate them into the development of an individual strategy at the end of this chapter.

If success in management were an accident, we would find equal numbers of women and men at every managerial level. Of course, it is not accidental. Success for a woman requires that a delicate balance be maintained between acceptable role behavior and demonstrated work abilities. As a rule, a high degree of either one alone is unacceptable to those making hiring, advancement, and salary decisions. Just what is expected of a woman then? The role half of the equation suggests that femininity in the terms expressed in Chapter 2 (warmth, expressiveness, incompetence) is considered desirable. The full implications of this expectation become apparent in a survey of the attitudes of 174 male managers by Bass et al. (1971). The survey showed a great deal of consistency regarding role preferences which, unfortunately, are unfavorable toward women in management.

Support of the Family

The executives studied felt that women should support the needs of their husbands. A woman's career was viewed as the cause of suffering on the part of children as well as the family as a whole. Many men asserted that work itself threatens a woman's femininity and makes life more difficult for her husband.

The executives felt that women already have equal rights since they are able to spend their time making themselves appealing for their husbands rather than having to worry about the financial burdens of the family. The men appeared to be jealous over women's dual role and seemed threatened by any potential loss in control over the family.

Personality Factors

The men also felt that women are overly emotional and incapable of dealing with stress. Many felt that women were insufficiently aggressive. They suggested that women lack the dependability of men and summarily stated that they would prefer a male to an equally qualified female job candidate.

Job-related Ability

The managers tended to feel that women are not discriminated against, but are instead paid just what they are worth. Women were viewed as lacking technical skills and quite unable to supervise male subordinates.

Other researchers have found that many people feel women are not seriously concerned with their jobs (*Business Environment Studies,* 1972; *Issues in Indus-trial Society*, 1971) and have a fear of success (Tresemer, 1976; Wood and Green-feld, 1976). Like the attitudes expressed above, these are generally no more true of women than of men—but they are stereotypes with which women must suc-cessfully deal.

Against the negative evaluations, we can also place some which are support ive of women. Each of these is useful in certain situations, although it may not be applicable across the entire range of conditions.

Social Orientation

Women are presumably more socially oriented than men (cf. Broverman et al., 1972), that is, cognizant of and responsive toward the needs of others. In situa-tions calling for a great deal of sensitivity, women are thought to perceive rele-vant interpersonal cues more readily than men. Similarly, women are expected to place others at ease more rapidly than men.

Nonassertiveness

Nonassertiveness can be an advantage despite the match between the male stereotype and the assumed managerial need for aggressiveness. Women presum-ably have the talent for avoiding competitive arousal on the part of others. The women are expected to be poor competitors in their own right and to support rather than to compete with men. While some men feel competitive with women merely because they are present in an organization, most feel less threat from a woman than from a man and welcome them to their department or to interper-sonal negotiations. Thus many women may be able to succeed by entering situa-tions in which men would not be welcomed or would be treated to an adversary relationship. Once her position is secured, of course, the woman may freely compete.

Carefulness

Supposedly women are more concerned with details than are men. Consequently, when a project is nearing completion, it is often turned over to women (aban-doned by men) so that they can iron out the smaller details. Women can use this situation to compile experience on a number of projects that equally junior men would not be allowed to work with. They also have the ability to place their per-sonal stamp on such projects.

The trait of carefulness follows through in other respects. Women keep their appearance neat, their offices spotless, and are ideal secretaries because they enjoy trivia. As this is written, the authors sit amid piles of papers, books, and discarded notes sufficient to make those who rely on stereotypes gasp in shock. Nevertheless, despite their lack of validity, the stereotypic expectations do exist. The trick is to turn them to our advantage, or to at least bend them out of our path, without being deflected from our intended goals.

The Effects of Organizational Climate

Throughout this chapter and others, we have stressed that women should suit their strategy to the particular organization of which they are a member. Each organization works somewhat differently and contains personnel who will react differently toward a rising women executive. It is also true that some general types of firm offer women a better vehicle for reaching the top than others. If you have the opportunity to choose, what types of organization should you prefer?

Larger firms usually have the best-developed affirmative action programs; they are also more likely to have standardized promotion procedures than smaller firms (cf. Donnelly, 1976). On the other hand, women who do not feel the need for the structured support provided by the larger firms will probably do better in the smaller organizations. Because smaller firms are more flexible, they can more easily promote talented people—although perfunctory, garden-variety promotions are less frequent. The visibility of women middle managers to top management is also greater in small organizations; women who are able to work easily with their predominantly male colleagues but who are demonstrably superior to them are more likely to be recognized there. Finally, women have historically been more successful in small firms (cf. Bowman, Worthy, and Greyser, 1965). A woman who is sure of herself might do well to start with a small firm, moving to a large one when she has gained experience and responsibility.

The nature of an organization's business is also important. Since the promotions in most organizations are awarded at irregular intervals and are based on the impressions that others have of the woman, she should probably find a position where she stands out and impressions are readily formed. A woman is more noticeable in a field that employs few women, such as the steel industry, than in one which traditionally has employed large numbers of women, such as retailing. A highly competent, ambitious, and self-assured woman would probably prefer the steel firm (assuming the same level of discrimination in either organization), because her work there is more readily noticed.

Other factors should also be kept in mind when choosing an employer: Many employers have now lost legal battles concerning discrimination. In some cases the loss has sensitized them to the problems facing women, while in others it has merely made them more careful in the ways they use to maintain the status quo. A careful discussion with present members of the organization will usually disclose whether the organization is primarily progressive or status quo.

Fast-growing organizations often have more room for promotion and therefore have employees who are less threatened by the hiring of a woman. Within the organization, slow-growing work groups are more likely to make a woman's adjustment uncomfortable by adopting a "show me" attitude; members of departments offering faster promotions more often merely expect an incoming woman to do her job.

Finally, it seems likely (although we know of no research confirming this assertion) that women are better able to advance in nontraditional firms than in organizations that pride themselves on carrying on traditional practices. Each enterprise, however, presents a unique combination of advantages and disadvantages; women are best served by examining it carefully and determining how the operation will fit their plans, rather than by viewing it stereotypically.

The Management Game—General Tactics

What should a woman executive or executive candidate do if she feels discriminated against? One answer is to complain the "company way"—to her boss, to her boss's boss, and so on until she gets satisfaction and some action is taken (Pendergrass, Kimmel, Joesting, Peterson, and Bush, 1976; Thompson, 1975). That method, unfortunately, can have some noxious side-effects. The complaint testifies that the woman is unable to handle her own problems and suggests that she is willing to be a trouble-maker. In some cases, complaints to persons further up the hierarchy find their way back to the woman's immediate superior with instructions that he solve the problem any way he sees fit (cf. Pellegrino, 1976). His reaction need hardly be detailed here.

A better set of alternatives may be that of becoming an expert at the management game. The "game" in this sense is the ability to capitalize on the situations that are normally encountered in the management process rather than the ability to manage the work. The work itself is important, too, and we do not mean to encourage incompetence. Nonetheless, the management game has standards that are more likely to produce rapid promotion for nearly anyone when they are carried out reasonably well. Some of these standards are discussed below.

Visibility

As mentioned in earlier sections, a woman is better off in a highly visible position except when her achievements are threatening to others or of a relatively poor quality (Comer, 1976). As a matter of fact, quality is often difficult to rate objectively; those who have the nerve to go public with a mediocre quality performance may be thought more capable than they actually are.

The executive can obtain visibility by publicizing herself in the company newsletter or by sending memos concerning her activities to her superiors. Her own reports and those of subordinates always display her name prominently when they are sent to superiors—except when substantial risk is involved. Similarly, she takes visible seating positions at meetings (Donnelly, 1976) tells others her views even if they duplicate those already expressed, and speaks authoritatively. However, she does not take unpopular positions unless she knows that she has the ability to win her point. In a sense, the woman who is highly visible is engaged in advertising; if she has a reasonably good product, some people will want to buy it.

Ability

Although poor performers often succeed, the woman is far better off if she is able to do her job; in any event, she must be able to convince others that she is able to do it (Bowman, Worthy, and Greyser, 1965; Wood, 1975). The proof of ability is not easy for a woman. Others regularly assume that women do not have the talents needed for executive success; this judgment is often difficult to challenge because of the subjective nature of the evaluations and the ease with which a woman's success can be attributed to good fortune rather than to real ability and effort.

Some methods exist for enhancing the demonstration of ability. One method (fully described in the next chapter) is through external validation by having respected people outside the department acclaim the woman or try to hire her away. She should also deliberately seek readily quantifiable indicators of objective performance (Donnelly, 1976), make certain that these indicators do register success, and broadcast that result as widely as possible. A third possibility, discussed later in this chapter as an independent strategy, is for the woman to make herself indispensable as an assistant or apprentice to a powerful senior executive (cf. Laws, 1975)—preferably one who is not loathe to give credit where it is due. Finally, ability may be demonstrated by means of objective prior accomplishments. Each accomplishment, such as a college degree, license, or prior job experience, is a union card entitling the holder to better positions and more security in the future.

Fellowship

We would like to say that "sisterhood" is a good tactic. It is; women can and should help each other. Nonetheless, in the late 1970s, the ability to get along with the men one is probably working with is usually of extreme importance. The two special needs when working with men are to control the likelihood of being treated as a potential affair rather than as a competent business colleague and to obtain information and assistance when desired. Providing differences between attitudes are not overwhelming, increased experience and easy familiarity should operate to increase understanding and trust and to decrease stereotyping. Any increase in fellowship also increases communication flow and inter-reliance such that the woman is enabled to plug into the information grapevine and to call on her male colleagues for assistance. She will, of course, also be called on in return. The last chapter contained some tips on mechanisms to increase fellowship, including reciprocity, spending time together, and avoiding the assertion of major differences.

Acceptance of Opportunities

Since the assumption can be made that discrimination in opportunity occurs, an antidote is to leave no opportunity begging (cf. Comer, 1976). Many executive women interviewed by the senior author have suggested that this is the most important tip they can offer other women on the way up. Women are not stereotypically expected to have the same ambitions for moving ahead as do men; despite this, women will be offered special opportunities from time to time. However, when the woman does not accept the offer quickly, she confirms the previous suspicions and is mentally stamped as unlikely to succeed; the opportunity is not offered again.

Additional opportunities can be obtained through the behavior modification technique of complimenting anyone offering the potential of fellowship, visibility, experience, or promotion. Beyond compliments, the individual must be willing to take up some of the activities offered if she expects the offers to continue. For example, if a woman's colleagues offer her the chance to accompany them to a meeting, and if she perceives this as leading to later opportunities, she should express some degree of interest and either agree to go or provide a believable reason for refusing. Any suggestion that she is simply uninterested will be met by a drop in the frequency of later offers.

One of the greatest problems may be that of learning to recognize real opportunities. They usually expose us to risk, disrupt plans, and take time, making the first reaction one of automatic rejection. Instead, the best immediate response may be to say "yes" if in doubt concerning any reasonable offer. Thereafter, a little reflection will reveal the preferred response; most offers can still be refused at that point if they need to be, but they may not be renewed once refused.

Managerial Behavior

When a woman has determined to become a manager and to be treated as one, she should begin presenting herself as one. This does not mean that she must begin barking orders, but she should give the appearance of someone who would be at ease in the position she hopes to attain. The person being sought for a position is inevitably one who already fills the role, and nonverbal communication (such as dress and manner) is one of the most powerful means of expression in this respect.

Normally, of course, women act and sound like subordinates; traditionally, they have been subordinates. This means that a woman who intends to distinguish herself should take some pains to act and dress differently from the secretaries in her office (Donnelly, 1976). She should also be careful not to end spoken statements with inflections that imply uncertainty and not to act apologetically for the decisions she undertakes in the normal course of business. Similarly, she should not volunteer for highly visible subservient tasks such as taking the notes of a meeting or watering the office plants. If possible, she should obtain an office that commands respect and be certain that its decor suggests business. The senior author knows of a feminist who decorated her office in the flush pink water color paintings of her three-year-old child; her office was thereafter ignored by her male colleagues and she soon left the organization.)

Femininity

Each of the suggestions above runs counter to the feminine role. Women who are seen primarily in sexual terms will seem to be behaving inappropriately as executives, while there is a tendency to misperceive the femininity of women who seem to be efficient executives. As earlier chapters have noted, some people will be offended by inappropriate behavior and are more likely to see that the woman executive is fired or dead-ended than promoted or recognized for it. Sufficient fellowship is a useful means for avoiding this problem.

When fellowship is not possible, the woman has the option of performing either the managerial or the feminine role—whichever is most appropriate at the time. Simultaneously seeming to perform both roles, at least at this point in the development of American society, is likely to be looked at with suspicion by those who expect to find that the woman is somehow less competent or less feminine than she appears. If objective proof of both femininity and managerial competence is available, the woman may seem to be quite superior, but the occasions on which such proof is available would seem to be infrequent (cf. Kristal, Sanders, Spence, and Helmreich, 1975). In the meantime, women are probably best advised to have both roles available for use in differing (but usually not in the same) situations (Wood, 1975).[1]

Office Politics

Every office with more than one occupant has its political intrigues and rumor mills. These are as natural a part of the office as the chairs and desks and are merely a means of coping with the pressures of the situation. No graceful means for staying clear of office politics has yet been invented; staying out means staying ignorant, and even the ignorant are sometimes unsuspecting pawns in someone else's struggle. Nonetheless, women are in a particularly poor position to deal with office politics. They are often unable to capitalize on a successful showdown, because their male support group is of questionable loyalty; worse, choosing the wrong side in a confrontation can lead to loss of respect, demotion, transfer, or termination. As a result, most women would do well to avoid choosing sides and to assert themselves into political conflicts only with extreme caution. Ideally, all factions will be cultivated as information sources, but no faction will see the woman as a member of the enemy camp or as ripe for sacrifice.

Although the tactics listed above are useful across a broad spectrum of situations, the extent to which any of them should be relied on depends on the strategy selected. Some strategies depend almost entirely on visibility, while some others require that each of the other tactics be employed for their success. The safest approach is to see each of the tactics as a tool that can be considered for possible use in an overall strategy; even those that seem less important can make a difference when handled correctly.

General Strategies

Some fairly specific long-term strategies can be formulated using the tactics above, and the unique abilities, interests, and opportunities available to most women. For the purpose of illustration, the discussion below is confined to general strategies, however. We don't advocate that they be closely followed, because they probably do not meet anyone's special requirements. With the four strategies described below held in mind, however, it should be easily possible to build a personal strategy for success.

Strategy A: The Apprentice

In the previous chapter, we noted that successful managers have often apprenticed themselves to a patron for a period of time. The patron is able to give advice and ensure that the apprentice obtains the necessary experience to move up. In the case of women who are apprentices, the patron also runs interference against any opposition she may encounter as a result of her sex. In return, the patron expects the apprentice to serve him or her without potential embarrassment.

Service as an apprentice is virtually required at some points to successfully move up in the organization. In most cases, the particular loyalties of the apprentice-patron relationship slowly shift, depending on the particular needs of the people involved. An apprentice may find that a new patron has the information needed for completion of a particular project; the former patron, while still on good terms with the apprentice, is less necessary as the new relationship forms.

In one version, however, the loyalties remain constant because the relationship appears to be more rewarding than either party could obtain elsewhere. Often, the woman executive is special because she is a woman—that is, she has a particular social or political status that the patron can not easily replace. This may result from her implied consent to function as a gatekeeper or token who is willing to enforce organizational employee selection programs that effectively keep other women from entering the organization (Laws, 1975).

The evolution of the gatekeeping position is quite natural: the woman owes loyalty to the patron at some point. The patron would like to appear liberal by maintaining a woman junior executive subordinate to him or her. However, the patron's own power rests in not upsetting the system through appearing too radical. Because she knows that the patron will be forced to disown unusual behavior, the woman junior executive can solidify her own position by buffering the organization against change, hence by taking part in the recruitment processes that traditionally work against women. With other women frozen out of the organizational structure, the original apprentice becomes a token for whom no replacement is available.

This is not to say that every woman is a token; very few are. But in the apprentice strategy, the woman finds someone to learn from and to help. As the organization is made successively more change-proof, the woman's position is solidified, and she is assured of continuing to advance as rapidly as her patron advances ahead of her.

Aside from the danger this strategy presents to other women who are attempting to enter or survive in the same organization with the gatekeeper, the strategy has some other interesting aspects. First, it calls for use of the feminine role by nurturing the patron and being supported by him or her in turn. Second, if she chooses to stay with a single sponsor (and probably becoming a gatekeeper), the woman's own rise in the organization may be limited rather than enhanced. If the sponsor's advancement is stymied, the apprentice too can go no further. A more satisfactory approach is that of deliberately cultivating apprentice relationships with several people simultaneously. Because less loyalty is owed to any one person, the woman can respond more flexibly to the requirements made by her patrons, and is probably able to move up in the organization more smoothly.

Strategy B: Using the Stereotype

For all practical purposes, it is impossible to behave in complete agreement with the feminine stereotype and still function as a manager. It is still possible to inject large doses of the stereotype into the job, however (cf. Donnelly, 1976; Wood, 1975). In describing the strategy of using the stereotype, we are making the assumption that the woman who applies this strategy is interested in moving up the managerial hierarchy. That is, while she may want to appear as feminine as possible, she also wants to succeed; to that end, she is willing to somewhat alter the impressions others receive of her by seeming feminine or ignoring that role as it suits her.

The ways in which this strategy can be carried out are varied. Each method depends, however, on applying the feminine role to defuse competitive situations and to elicit help from others. When the men with whom a woman is associated in her work begin to feel competitive with her, their normal reaction is to limit the degree of support given her (they also do this with other men). Any support would, of course, help the woman to beat them in the competition.

In this situation, the woman who is using the stereotype may be able to side-step the potential problem. She does this by helping the men without playing obvious favorites and, if possible, by discovering a positive-sum rather than a zero-sum strategy whereby all are better off. If the competition is still active, the woman can usually do better than most of the men because she has not taken a direct part in it but is perceived as a valuable ally. She also obligates the winner to reciprocate her support by helping her in later situations. Her posture is thus completely nonthreatening, taking a middle ground under conditions of corporate infighting. This mechanism provides an ideal way for a woman to select a patron if she desires to move to the apprentice strategy at some later time.

Femininity can be applied in many other ways. For example, it can be appealed to directly to obtain opportunities that might not otherwise be available. Special interest committees can be reminded that they "need" to include a creative, woman's point of view when they consider problems concerning women, hiring policy, negotiating strategy, or marketing strategy. In each instance, a good case can be made that a fresh outlook, especially a woman's viewpoint, can be exceedingly helpful. The woman executive, of course, uses these opportunities to increase her visibility and experience. After awhile, she is automatically asked to participate in all important functions.

We are not considering feminine role behavior as identical to sex itself. The previous chapter noted that office politics and sex do not mix very well. The woman who is using the feminine stereotype will take pains to make herself appealing; she will not allow her appeal to conflict with her image as an executive. To accomplish this feat, she must be able to turn the feminine role off when necessary.

Specifically, of course, she must switch the role off when she intends to be listened to, taken seriously, and evaluated fairly for her work. In each case, elements of flirting, uncritical support of others (she can still support others, but the support is conditioned on their helping her and on the politics of the situation), or nonseriousness should disappear. In their place, the woman should be able to talk about the serious business at hand with ease and in the style that men and women expect of others of their own sex.

One example of this type of strategy is that of a new woman executive who has not yet established a working relationship with some of the men in her department. She might use her femininity to obtain an invitation to lunch with the men the following day. Once there, the role stereotype can be discarded after a short period by talking about work, politics, sports, or any other activity that is not a stereotypic feminine interest (husbands, children, movie actors, and clothing styles are "out"). Only when the ice has been broken, by abandoning the stereotypic portions of the feminine role, will the men she is sitting with begin to relate to her as a colleague rather than as a woman who has invaded their world. If they begin to feel at ease on this level, there is a good chance that the men will include the woman in later discussions concerning business and office politics.

The woman executive also turns off the feminine role when it is her turn to reap the benefits of her work. When her boss praises her work, she self-assuredly takes the credit for it before mentioning the others who have helped her. When there is the possibility of a promotion, she sees to her own interests first rather than supporting coworkers for the position. The rule for taking credit is to be realistic. When the reward is truly out of reach, the woman who grasps for it is perceived as out of line. If there is little likelihood that the woman will be the one chosen for a reward (promotion, citation, salary increase), she is best advised to support others and to thereby build credits for the future. When she has a good chance to obtain them herself, she should enthusiastically promote her cause and cash in on previous credits. Any other action would be seen as reluctance and insecurity; the opportunity might not arise again.

Strategy C: Circumventing the Stereotype

Many people feel that a strategy such as that above is a little too devious to suit them or too difficult to put into practice. Switching from one role to another, as is appropriate for the circumstance, requires a feat of mental dexterity that they find both annoying and upsetting. Of course, a simple alternative is to avoid altogether those situations that might evoke the feminine role and thereby place it in potential conflict with the role of manager. Rather than switching from one set of behaviors to another, the people who circumvent the stereotype try to arrange situations in which consistent (managerial) behavior is called for. They can, of course, still be feminine, but they make no effort to become more so on some occasions and less so on others.

Since she is choosing situations in which her mastery of management is called for, the woman using Strategy C must have competent management skills. When situations arise in which the feminine role alone might be applied by a Strategy B executive, the woman who is circumventing the stereotype still responds in a manner consistent with her managerial role. For example, if a customer attempts to flirt with her, she might quickly thank him and turn the subject to business by asking him a question about the project he is working on. By failing to reciprocate the sex role cues, the expectations that coworkers and others have that she will behave in a feminine way quickly drop out.

The demonstration of competence itself is somewhat simpler for a Strategy C player than it is for the woman who is using the stereotype (Strategy B). There is less expectation of incompetence to be fought against. Although she is not reinforcing expectations of sex role, the woman playing Strategy C will also be given many of the same special opportunities available to someone who is using the stereotype—simply because she is a woman. In order to boost her visibility, she can accept some of the opportunities, but should do so selectively in order to avoid being stereotyped or perceived as grasping. What appears as a natural assertion of femininity to observers of a Strategy B woman may seem to be taking advantage of her sex to others evaluating a Strategy C executive.

For the most part, women who are circumventing the stereotype avoid situations having even the potential for managerial versus sex role conflict. Toward this end, they find positions in which they can assert their independence or leadership ability; dependent positions, which service the needs and depend on the whims of others, are avoided. This type of person often prefers working as the head of a project team or working alone on a smaller project to helping someone on a larger effort. Because she has control over the project, she is able to use the results to gain the visibility and recognition needed for advancement.

Among the requirements for success at this strategy, the woman executive must be willing to act as her own publicist, constantly bringing her success to the attention of those controlling the assignment of new projects. Because she is an independent operator, it is her responsibility alone to make her work appear useful and successful. Although she may work quietly, projects that a Strategy C woman completes will be displayed, become the subject of memos to superiors, and in general will be surrounded with all the ballyhoo for which they could conceivably be due.

Whenever possible, major successes are followed by unmistakable suggestions for promotion, salary increases, and more responsible projects. The woman who circumvents the stereotype cannot afford to be shy. The penalty for the drop in role conflict from that in Strategy B is an increased need for self-reliance. Although competence is more readily demonstrated, incompetence will cut her career short because of the lack of supportive sex role relationships to fall back on.

Strategy D: Shattering the Stereotype

Women who use the first three strategies are readily tolerated in the organization. If successful, they are usually appreciated by their male colleagues and superiors. To a varying extent, they are at peace with the various roles, either operating within them or at least not challenging them. Some women, of course, would prefer to operate as free agents who are entirely unconcerned with role norms. For these persons, a dangerous but sometimes successful strategy is that of direct contravention of the feminine role norms. Necessarily, in the process of breaking the behavior expectations held by other, the woman will seem abrasive to them; consequently, she must seem indispensable in order to retain or improve her position.

Under Strategy A, a woman provides services valued by her patron in order to succeed. In Strategies B and C, she uses outstanding work in combination with social or public relations skills in order to achieve success. In each of the first three strategies, the work must be satisfactory, but the woman need not be hyperefficient, since success is also a function of other factors. Of course, better work almost always solidifies one's hold on the position (see the discussion in the next chapter on hyperefficiency).

In contrast to the delicacies observed in the first three strategies, the intent of the woman who shatters the stereotype is to attract notice through surprising others and to present them with no alternative once she is noticed but to retain and promote her. She understands, but is seemingly oblivious toward, the attempts of others to reimpose their versions of normatively correct behavior. She also recognizes that when the effort to make her conform fails, her employers would normally prefer to dispose of her as too unpredictable and threatening for a responsible executive position. The intention of the Strategy D person who is operating in deliberate disregard of others is to present sufficiently fine work as to make her dismissal impossible.

Ignoring her is equally impossible. Consequently those who evaluate a successful Strategy D person must either change their views concerning the appropriate norms for feminine behavior, agree to treat her as an exception (perhaps "one of the boys"), or move the woman to another department. The first reaction gives the woman a solid footing in the organization that might not otherwise have been available, the second leaves her in peace, while the third gives her mobility and visibility that she may be able to use in advancing up the organizational hierarchy. In any event, the result is certain to be registered quickly.

The manner in which the feminine norms are broken varies from one person to another. The quickest route in the late 1970s may be to proclaim militant feminism. After ensuring that her work is objectively far superior to that which had been required, the executive might announce that she is unwilling to accept any form of discrimination against her in the future and will refuse to go out of her way to satisfy the expectations or mother the egos of the men with whom she works. She might also lodge complaints against being categorized or treated in certain ways associated with sex role. In cultivating this image, she might allow herself the freedom to behave in an entirely uninhibited manner (which we conservatively suggest might include swapping yarns with the men in the office, dressing casually, or coming to work late).

The woman practicing Strategy D is not particularly interested in seeming masculine. However, she must project an image of competence at any cost and should appreciate eyebrow-raising behavior for its publicity value as much as because she prefers the lack of inhibition. Beyond these factors, she freely behaves as she likes and is totally unconcerned with the delicacies of role expectancies and their demands on her mannerisms.

Because of the dangers involved with this strategy, women should avoid it until after they have been hired, fully trained, and evaluated. Even then, women should be cautioned to move slowly into the strategy and to avoid frustrating the others with whom they work. If she projects a competitive image, the Strategy D woman executive should probably try to moderate its impact by maintaining friendly relations with those with whom she is competing. In this way, she is more likely to enjoy their respect than to find them conspiring for her removal.

Considering the danger, it is easy to ask whether the small amount of increased freedom is worth the risk of undertaking Strategy D. It is worth the risk for women who see the uninhibited behaviors as more closely akin to their own self-concept than those dictated by the earlier strategies. There is a second advantage in the possibility of breaking up situations that have long since petrified. The woman is noticed under this strategy; she can no longer be ignored but must be dealt with. The tricky part is to ensure that when she is noticed she will be dealt with in a favorable manner. In the last analysis, the player of Strategy D must have a clear understanding of how her particular employer is likely to react. Strategy D is a little like playing poker—it works incredibly well when you know the other hand.

In all likelihood, you can find elements in each of the strategies above which are appealing. Fortunately, there is no need to choose just one. Instead, these four are only suggestive of a vast number of possibilities which mix elements from each of these and add other factors into the equation as well. Keep in mind the parts of these strategies that seem most suitable then, but remember that they are limited and are intended only for purposes of illustration. The personal strategy that is the most desirable is the one that fits your personality and abilities and provides the greatest possibility for success in the enterprise in which you are working or are likely to begin work. The next section describes the manner in which a personal strategy can be developed.

Devising Your Own Strategy

Quite possibly, the set strategies described above seemed unbelievably rigid, almost sexist parodies of human, responsive management. They are that, of course, but only unintentionally. Anatomy is not destiny, but to escape such a fate a woman must be cognizant of the impressions others have of her and must be willing to make solid short- and long-range plans for her future. If the artificial strategies like those above seem inappropriate or just don't "feel good," then more careful personal planning is needed. The plans may be readjusted as desired, they may plan for alternative contingencies, and they may allow for complete switches when certain goals have been reached—but they must be made.

The last chapter considered the probable outcome of managerial success in some detail; the next chapter examines life goals. What remains is to see how success can be obtained in your organization in a manner that you can feel satisfied with. The two crucial sides that must be considered in designing a personal strategy are yourself—your needs, desires, abilities, and so on—and the organization—what it expects from you. These two sides must be reconciled with one another.

A Tactical Assessment

Several approaches can be taken in the evaluation of the requirements imposed by the organization. One might interview the employer, since that individual is usually responsible for promotion and salary decisions. Unfortunately, however, the employer frequently has no overall plan in mind and operates on the basis of unrecognized subjective criteria. Also, the employer is heavily influenced by the need to maintain a good working environment for all employees; consequently input from coworkers and reactions concerning the group as a whole can and do color decisions. Another possibility is to obtain a job description and to use the statements it contains as approximations of what is expected of the ideal employee. Sadly, this seldom works. Job descriptions are usually tailored to the last incumbent; however they seldom provide the means to evaluate the nature of this individualization (the last person got away with little work because he/she threw memorable parties and was well-liked), making reconstruction of the entire set of requirements difficult. Additionally, most mechanisms for determining the demands of the organization center on one type of job; since the individual would like to move upward in the hierarchy, they are of little value.

There seem to be three techniques that have some potential for success. One is to model one's self after a successful person having the job sought. Aside from the obvious limitations this presents, the concept itself is personally unsatisfying to many people. When it is available, a better alternative is the development of a contract with the individual who is in a position to evaluate and promote to or from a particular managerial slot. Both individuals agree that evaluation will take place after a specified period, and will be done in a particular, hopefully objective, manner. Similarly, the consequences of the evaluation are fixed in advance such that both sides can live with it.

The third approach is based on the tactics discussed earlier in this chapter. The tactics cropped up repeatedly in the discussion of strategies, because they are important determinants of long- as well as short-term success. One of the ways to determine the requirements of the organization is to assess yourself as others see you in respect to the tactics. In other words, visibility is more than a useful tactic; it is also a demand levied on you for success in the organization. The important question to be answered with respect to these tactics is the extent to which others value them and agree that you have employed them successfully. If your employer is unconcerned with them, or feels that you have been unsuccessful in using them, your belief that you have done so is irrelevant. If your present superior and coworkers agree that you have done well, there is a fair chance that your next superior in your present organization will also agree. Since the organization is merely a group of people, if these people feel that you have met the demands imposed on you, you have done so.

In answering the tactical assessment below, try to follow these steps:

Step 1. In columns 1 and 4, estimate how important each factor is to your boss and coworkers in their judgments of you. Don't concern yourself with how successful they may think you are, since that is covered in Step 2. In completing this and the other steps, it is extremely important that you visualize from the point of view of others, rather than describing how you feel about yourself. A way to do this is to imagine that you really are these people observing your actual self from their perspective. Use a scale from $+2$ to -2 with 0 indicating that these people don't think the factor very important; $+2$ indicates that your boss or coworkers feel that the factor is quite important and are pleased by it, while -2 indicates displeasure.

Step 2. In columns 2 and 5, rate how successful your boss and your coworkers think you are on the factor listed. You might use a scale from 0 (not measurable) to $+2$ (very strong). Note that you may be very strong on a factor that is evaluated negatively in columns 1 or 4. This type of evaluation would indicate that you are doing something that they do not care for.

Step 3. Multiply column 1 by column 2 and 4 by 5; place your results in columns 3 and 6. These values you have just obtained give the relative importance of your various attributes for your job as seen by your employer and your coworkers.

The last section in this table is probably the most difficult to answer, because you are rating your success on dimensions that are often hidden from you. When you have finished, you will note that the form has left out many aspects of each tactic. If you feel that some important ones are missing, you might add them now, although the four listed for each category are probably more than sufficient.

In order to simplify your results, you might scratch all items from the form having weights of -1, 0, or $+1$ in columns 1 and 4. Only the most important considerations remain. If some entire tactic categories are now eliminated, that probably means that the people with whom you work do not care about them or

Table 6–1
Tactical Assessment

Factor	Boss			Coworkers		
	Importance 1	Success 2	Value 3	Importance 4	Success 5	Value 6
	−2 to +2	0 to 2		−2 to +2	0 to 2	

Ability

1. To work independently
2. To solve their problems
3. To manage others
4. To find creative solutions

Fellowship

5. Willingness to work with them
6. Emotional support of them
7. Availability for informal discussion
8. Competitiveness

Opportunities

9. Enthusiasm shown
10. Difficulty in moving to new activities
11. Unused capacity
12. Willingness to accept risk

Visibility

13. Receipt of credit
14. Objectively and subjectively successful
15. Familiarity to higher-ups
16. Willingness to broadcast success

Table 6-1 (Continued)
Tactical Assessment

| Factor | Boss | | | Coworkers | | |
	Importance 1	Success 2	Value 3	Importance 4	Success 5	Value 6
	−2 to +2	0 to 2		−2 to +2	0 to 2	

Appearance

17. Adoption of company style
18. Acceptability of administrative style
19. First impressions
20. General familiarity

Sex Role Values

21. Identification of you with traditional sex role values
22. Acceptability of women as managers
23. Ability of men's conversation to continue with a woman present
24. Their willingness to advance a woman to level above your own

that you have given them no reason for concern. Any change in these categories might be self-defeating.

In the categories remaining, it is possible to have high positive values (important and you are doing well) indicative of an already successful application of the tactics, or high negative numbers (important but you are doing poorly) indicative of poor tactics. Numbers close to 0, if positive, are important tactical considerations that you are not making full potential use of; if negative, they indicate a reasonably successful strategy of avoidance that should be adjusted only with some caution. Obviously this tactical assessment can be used to indicate where improvement would be useful in your particular organization and may already suggest some of the means which you can use to do this. In many cases, you were undoubtedly already aware of difficulties but felt unwilling to adjust them. The inventory below may uncover some means to make these changes that you may not have considered before—and may help in improving an already good tactical assessment score.

Someone who is looking for a new job or an advancement can readily apply the assessment technique with only a few changes. Assessments can be made on the basis of experience with a previous employer, with a personnel interviewer, or with the reputation of the organization. Similarly, you can conduct an assessment through the eyes of the supervisor in the position you hope to be promoted to in order to discover the changes that are most likely to lead to promotion.

Your Own Abilities and Interests

Although it is important to know how others rate us, the information is not very useful unless there is something we are able to do about the rating. The problem is probably more obvious when real abilities such as intelligence are considered rather than when social skills (for instance, dressing appropriately for the job) are examined. Anyone can change social skills. The truth of the matter, however, is that any abilities can be changed, some more readily than others; nonetheless, in the long run the changes must fit the individual's personality as well as the requirements of the job.

This exercise is an audit of needs and abilities. The purpose is to determine your job-related strengths and weaknesses, along with your willingness to change, if required. In order to view yourself objectively, please do not let yourself be influenced by what you feel your job calls for, or by any responses to the exercise in the last chapter. This should be a completely independent assessment.

Step 1. In Table 6–2, you should list up to four of the specific abilities and desires that you feel you have now under each of the factors given. For instance, under the "ability to compete," you might want to add "ability to do the job," "ability to determine the requirements of the job," and so on. Abilities that you wish you had should not be listed here, although you may want to make a sepa-

Table 6–2
Self-assessment

Factor	Assessment		
	Importance *1*	*Immediacy* *2*	*Value* *3*
	1 to 5	–5 to +5	
Ability to Compete			
1.			
2.			
3.			
4.			
Unused Abilities			
5.			
6.			
7.			
8.			
Liking for Competition			
9.			
10.			
11.			
12.			
Liking for Independence			
13.			
14.			
15.			
16.			
Desire for Leadership			
17.			
18.			
19.			
20.			
Desire for Fellowship			
21.			
22.			
23.			
24.			
Liking for Feminine Role			
25.			
26.			
27.			
28.			
Ambitions			
29.			
30.			
31.			
32.			

Table 6–2 (Continued)

Factor	Assessment		
	Importance 1	Immediacy 2	Value 3
	1 to 5	–5 to +5	
Need to Prevent Change from Present			
33.			
34.			
35.			
36.			
Other			
37.			
38.			
39.			
40.			

rate list of them. If you need room for more than four items in each category, you can, of course, extend your list.

Step 2. In column 1, score yourself from 1 (the item listed is not very important, or you are only somewhat able to do it) to 5 (very important and/or you have a great deal of ability along this line). If any listed items are totally inconsequential, they may be assigned a 0.

Step 3. Next, rate the extent to which you feel that it is important that this ability be used (or desire be satisfied) as soon as possible. Don't let this immediacy dimension get confused with the general importance dimension considered in Step 2. For example, it is possible to have a strong desire that, nonetheless, can be put off for awhile. The rating scale used might be from −5 (prefer to put this off forever, if possible) through 0 (don't really care) to +5 (this should be satisfied immediately).

Step 4. In column 3, the values are calculated by multiplying together the results in columns 1 and 2.

As before, you can simplify this assessment by striking out items which are inconsequential. In this case, you might eliminate from consideration any items having immediacy scores of from −3 to +3, or final values from −8 to +8. In any event, your final list should probably not contain more than ten items remaining for consideration. These items are the most important to you and cannot easily be put off; they are the ones to build your strategy around. The other items, if you still feel that they are important to you, can be the subject of secondary strategies—those aimed at cleaning up the details after the major problems have been resolved.

Developing the Strategy

The next step is the design of a personal strategy that allows you to obtain satisfaction in the areas designated by the Self-assessment, while observing the constraints imposed by the Tactical Assessment. There is no easy way to do this. Although arduous, the best solution is to concentrate on the remaining Self-assessment items one-by-one.

Step 1. Using the worksheet, describe a series of three or four strategies that you think could probably arrive at a particular self-assessment item. To do this, list a single self-assessment item under the "Factor" heading, and follow with the strategies.

Step 2. Examine the remaining items on the Tactical Assessment form (Table 6–1) and use it to evaluate the strengths and weaknesses of each strategy as you have described it. Weaknesses, of course, have negative values in Table 6–1, while strengths have positive values.

Step 3. Make any changes in your strategy listing that you feel will compensate for some of the problems just found or take advantage of your strengths. Now reevaluate the strengths and weaknesses of the strategies.

Step 4. Rank the strategies as they now are from 4 (best) to 1 (worst, but still acceptable). Your ranking should take into account your willingness to change yourself so as to disarm the problems found in Table 6–1; it should also discount (rank = 0) any strategies that you feel are really unacceptable.

Step 5. Now move on to another factor from Table 6–2. Repeat the evaluation process listed in Steps 1 to 3. However, now list as disadvantages any strategy conflict seen between a Factor 2 strategy and a Factor 1 strategy already developed above. If necessary, you may want to work backward to revise earlier strategies.

Step 6. When you have developed strategies for each of the important factors in the Self-assessment, try writing a policy statement that combines non-conflicting elements from the preferred strategy to obtain each factor. Next, look at the remaining conflicts. These should be resolved if your strategy is to work successfully. Try to decide the extent to which you are willing to change the impressions given to others if the conflicts arise from problems pin-pointed in Table

Table 6–3
Personal Strategy Work Sheet

Factor	Strategies	Problems/Advantages	Rank
1. a.			
b.			
c.			
d.			
2. a.			
b.			
c.			
d.			
3. a.			
b.			
c.			
d.			
4. a.			
b.			
c.			
d.			
5. a.			
b.			
c.			
d.			

6–1. Some compromises may be needed. If you find some of your selected strategies in conflict with one another, but both equally acceptable to you and to your employer and coworkers, you may want to design a role for yourself that combines them.

A second mechanism exists for resolving conflicts. It may be that one strategy can be applied to obtain one set of goals, while a conflicting strategy can be applied at a later time when the first goals have been met and a second goal set remains important. Thus it is possible to switch from one strategy to another (more properly, to design a switching strategy). Because of this potential, Step 1 may be easiest when it considers the factor that seems most important (has the highest value) first. Others can be considered in order of decreasing importance.

In the end, the strategy designed reflects the ambitions of the designer. It would be an oversimplification to state that, after having gone through this procedure, every woman will have a lifetime strategy. At best, these are guidelines that may serve to structure thinking and, possibly, to uncover some new avenues of approach to managerial success. The process, or a similar one, needs to be done repeatedly as new situations are unexpectedly encountered, and as the executive continues to grow.

Putting the Strategy into Action

This chapter began by discussing a strategy of legal action, concluding that it was a dangerous effort. Four general strategies were then described; these were undoubtedly too vague to be applied directly even if they did seem appealing. Finally, the forms in the sections immediately above were presented as a preferred method for determining strategy; but they have the disadvantages of being long, intimidating, and promising little in the way of results.

In fact, most strategies that seem comfortable and promise an acceptable likelihood of success are quite workable. The key requirements for making them work successfully are that the executive think ahead to their long-term consequences and that she preserve the flexibility to change strategies whenever useful. When these requirements are observed, the consequences of a mistake are mercifully small. One strategy can be quickly exchanged for another that is compatible with the first; no more than a little time is ever lost.

The way to begin, then is to examine the situation and one's own ambitions and feelings regarding it. This can be done informally, or with the help of Tables 6–1 and 6–2 above. After that (which is absolutely necessary), a strategy should be developed if possible. If the strategy is not developed, at the very least, the woman executive must be able to assess how she actually does react; whether intentional or accidental, her actual behavior in the managerial situation constitutes a strategy that affects her future success.

Examination of the "strategy-in-use" has a singular advantage. The executive can observe how others react toward her. The reactions have obvious long range consequences that she can compare with her long-term goals. Having done the comparison, the woman is in a position to make such changes in her strategy as seem appropriate to move from where she would be if the current situation continues to where she would prefer to be. The business version of the psychological win—stay, lose—shift strategy states simply: if it works, use it. Rump strategies may be as good as formal ones; first we must see if it works—if so, use it—if not, change it.

One helpful technique in this regard is that of maintaining a management diary. Each evening, the executive jots down in one column the major interactions she has had with others. In a second column, she enters their reactions to her. A third column is used for her thoughts of the long-term consequences of these reactions. Having diagnosed both problems and advantages in her own behavior in this manner, she can tinker with her strategy by making changes in the manner she intends to react in the future.

Any woman who is clever, careful, hard-working, and a little bit lucky can succeed at management. As with men, however, most women will not be as successful as they would like; there simply are not enough organizations or worthwhile executive slots to go around. Management is somewhat like an inverted funnel in which the majority make little progress and stay near the bottom. The distinguishing characteristics of those who rise rapidly through the narrow neck of the funnel are their ability to plan for success—and their willingness to carry out the plan. Success requires patience and care by impatient, ambitious, and realistic women.

Note

1. This advice is mirrored in the Bowman, Worthy, and Greyser (1965) national survey of male and female executives. Eighteen percent of the men and women surveyed felt that good advice included "behave in a business-like fashion, but don't act like a man," while nearly 14 percent said "be aggressive; have confidence and drive; act like a man."

References

Bass, B. M., Krusell, J., and Alexaner, R. A. "Male managers' attitudes toward working women." *American Behavioral Scientist*, 1971, *15*, 221–236.

Bowman, G. W., Worthy, N. B., and Greyser, S. A. "Are women executives people?" *Harvard Business Review*, 1965, *43*.

Broverman,p I. K., Vogel, S. R., Broverman, D. M., Clarkson, F. E., and Rosenkrantz, P. S. "Sex role stereotypes: A current appraisal." *Journal of Social Issues*, 1972, *28*, 59–78.

Collins, J. W., and Ganotis, C. G. "Managerial attitudes toward corporate social responsibility." In S. P. Sethi (ed.), *The unstable ground: Corporate social policy in a dynamic society*. Los Angeles: Melville Publishing Co., 1974.

Comer, N. A. "Job strategies '76." *Mademoiselle*, 1976, *82* (2), 112–115.

Donnelly, C. "Keys to the executive powder room." *Money,* 1976, *5* (8), 28–32.

Jacklin, C. N., and Maccoby, E. E. "Sex differences and their implications for management." In F. E. Gordon and M. H. Strober (eds.), *Bringing women into management*. New York: McGraw-Hill, 1975.

Johnson, S. K. "It's action, but is it affirmative?" *New York Times Magazine,* May 11, 1975, 18–33.

Kristal, J., Sanders, D., Spence, J. T., and Helmreich, R. "Inferences about the femininity of competent women and their implications for likability." *Sex Roles*, 1975, *1*, 33–50.

Laws, J. L. "The psychology of tokenism: An analysis." *Sex Roles,* 1975, *1*, 51–68.

Matthies, M. T. "The developing law on equal employment opportunity." *Journal of Contemporary Business,* 1976, *5* (1), 29–46.

Miner, M. G. *Equal employment opportunity: Programs and results*. Personnel Policies Forum Survey #112. Washington: Bureau of National Affairs, 1976.

Osborn, R. N., and Vicars, W. M. "Sex stereotypes: An artifact in leader behavior and subordinate satisfaction analyses?" *Academy of Management Journal*, 1976, *19*, 439–449.

Pellegrino, V. "Office politics: Running a clean campaign." *Working Woman*, 1976, *1* (1), 38–43.

Pendergrass, V. E., Kimmel, E., Joesting, J., Peterson, J., and Bush, E. "Sex discrimination counseling." *American Psychologist*, 1976, *31*, 36–46.

Pinck, J. B. "What women bring to management or Oh, why can't a woman be more like a man?" *National Association of Banking Women Journal*, 1976, *52* (2).

Ross, S. C. *The rights of women*. New York: Avon Books, 1973.

Samuels, C. *The forgotten five million: Women in public employment*. New York: Women's Action Alliance, 1975.

Schwartz, E. B. "Entrepreneurship: A new female frontier." *Journal of Contemporary Business*, 1976, *5* (1), 47–76.

Seligman, D. "How 'equal opportunity' turned into employment quotas." *Fortune*, 1973 (March). Reprinted in W. C. Hamner & F. L. Schmidt (eds.), *Contemporary problems in personnel*. Chicago: St. Clair Press, 1974.

Spears, L. "Berkeley's action affirmed by HEW; Labor remains." *California Monthly*, 1975 (March), 1, 12.

The Spokeswoman, 1976, *7* (4, 5).

Staff introduction. *Issues in Industrial Society*, 1971, *2*, 2–20.

"Stiffer regulations to attack job bias by U.S. contractors issued by Labor unit." *Wall Street Journal*, 1977 (January 19), 11.

Thompson, J. A. "The women vs. Chase Manhattan. Diary of a discrimination suit." *MBA*, 1975, *9* (11).

Torrey, J. W. "The consequences of equal opportunity for women." *Journal of Contemporary Business*, 1976, *5* (1), 13–28.

Tresemer, D. "Do women fear success?" *Signs*, 1976, *1*, 863–874.

Wallace, P. A., and Nelson, J. E. "Legal processes and strategies of intervention." In P. A. Wallace (ed.), *Equal employment opportunity and the AT&T case*. Cambridge, Mass.: MIT Press, 1976.

"Women & business: Agenda for the seventies." *Business environment studies*. New York: General Electric Co., 1972.

Wood, M. M. "What dies it take for a woman to make it in management?" *Personnel Journal*, 1975 (January).

———. "Women in management: How is it working out?" *Advanced Management Journal*, 1976, *41* (1).

———, and Greenfeld, S. T. "Women managers and fear of success: A study in the field." *Sex Roles*, 1976, *2*, 375–387.

7

Doing It at Large

In the earlier chapters, we have stressed the implications of a large body of research. That research has shown many ways in which equality of real opportunity is still denied to most women. Nonetheless, it has also indicated that pathways for personal success do exist. Women can succeed in management—and are doing so.

The fact remains that success is more elusive for women than for men. In moving up, women executives must be more careful, work harder, and confront conflict situations that do not exist for men. Too many women decide against managerial careers, either because they are unwilling to undertake the degree of effort required for their success, or because they have encountered and accepted the notion that management is impossible, unusual, or somehow inappropriate for a woman. Something is obviously wrong with a system that virtually impresses some men into its managerial ranks while denying the profession to many women.

What can be done? This chapter outlines some strategies for bringing about both social change and managerial success. The strategies all carry some degree of risk and little in the way of assured success. In describing them, it is simplest to start with the consideration of what cannot be done—and why.

In the past few decades, a number of far-reaching governmental programs have aimed toward establishing what some feel is social justice. The difficulties in implementing these plans are now becoming obvious. While some people might be helped by a project, others are frequently hurt or threatened by it, and their natural reaction is to prevent the plan's full implementation. Programs that result in reactions of the powerful against the disadvantaged will usually be blocked, failing to solve the problems they were intended for while wasting time and resources. Many of the governmental programs have aroused such reactions. We should recognize that women, blacks, inner-city residents, industrial workers, and other disadvantaged groups are disadvantaged because they lack a control of the political and economic power apparatus. As a result of the reactions and consequent failure of social programs to deliver as they had promised, the programs have often been entirely discontinued. If disadvantaged groups are to achieve success in the future, they must establish an independent base of power, or have the help—or at least the acquiescence—of groups having power.

Despite our lost innocence concerning governmental support, some things can still be done. Women have, after all, a considerable block of power and influence if we choose to use it. We control our own behavior and heavily influence that of husbands, children, coworkers, and friends. These other people are concerned with programs that may work for or against their best interests. Few people discriminate for shear pleasure; they do so because they are unaware that the "natural order of things" is discriminatory and because they have developed a stake in maintaining that order. In order to bring about change, we must demonstrate that the opening of fair opportunities and expectations is to everyone's advantage, that it cannot be resisted, or that any change carries little threat to those having the ability to successfully resist.

The ultimate result is not substantially different from that which could be achieved if the government merely issued, and subsequently enforced, an executive order or a Supreme Court decree that all *people* are created equal. Use of the government is illusory, however, for enforcement is a political decision. If those controlling the federal government believed that women are or should be equal to men, the order would already have been issued and enforced. State government is no different from federal government in this respect; if it were, the passage of the Equal Rights Amendment would have been a simple administrative matter. In fact, after the 1976 elections, women had only a 9.1 percent representation in state legislatures, and 3 percent in the U.S. Congress; there were no women in the U.S. Senate. We are suggesting that the process of social change must therefore occur first at the level at which women already have an advantage in cohesiveness and strength—the level of the individual and individuals acting in concern rather than the level of government. We are not denying that legal solutions are powerful and can be successful; however legal solutions are not worth waiting for. Somewhere along the way, legislation will be offered to legitimize a fait accompli.

Obtaining and Providing Opportunities

The most straightforward approach to equality is one of the simplest for us to initiate. Other things being equal, we must ourselves avoid discriminating against women and encourage others to do likewise. Carrying this principle to its end means giving women-run businesses our business, giving women workers a chance to improve themselves and to demonstrate their abilities, and ensuring that employers with whom we have contact do not discriminate in any respect. We are not suggesting that women practice reverse discrimination because doing so would be economically (if not ethically) indefensible; politically, it would also radicalize many neutral persons against the women's movement. Nonetheless, it is up to women to see that women have the chance to improve their positions. Providing this chance is more difficult than it appears, however, since the skill and interest mix of women is not presently comparable to that of men, and since comparatively few businesses are owned by women. The sections below describe some programs to either deal with or avoid these problems.

Entrepreneurship and Capital Financing

1. More women should begin their own businesses; these businesses should be financed more often by other women.

One way to assure an end to discrimination is through direct business ownership. Recent research leads us to suspect that businesses owned by women are less likely than those owned by men to discriminate against women (Larwood and Blackmore, in press). Moreover, despite its risks, entrepreneurship provides women the only sure route to the top short of having wealthy parents. Consequently, it is important that more women do start their own businesses.

Some problems seem to stand in our way, however. The first is the feeling that owning one's own business is masculine or inappropriate. It is a fact that in nearly every type of activity there are fewer female than male entrepreneurs. Entrepreneurship, however, is merely another form of management; no unusual talents or activities are required. A second problem is that of expertise: fewer women than men have had experience in running a business. For obvious reasons, this lack of experience is especially acute in manufacturing or technologically based enterprises. Because of the nature of their product, however, these organizations are usually the ones having the best growth potential; they should not be ignored.

Research on entrepreneurship indicates that the motivations of women who start their own businesses closely parallel the motivations of male entrepreneurs (Schwartz, 1976). In general, an independent business owner likes the freedom to make her own schedule, is highly achievement-oriented, and dislikes following the directions of others. The owner of an independent business is no more satisfied with work than any other employee—but may be a person who would not be satisfied as someone else's employee. One of the primary differences between an entrepreneur and an employee is in the time put into the job; entrepreneurs work longer hours (Eden, 1975). Probably the most distinguishing characteristics between the men and the women who own their own firms are in the nature of the firms themselves. Woman-owned firms are concentrated in the retail and service industries and are usually small. Operations owned or run by men are more variable, ranging across the entire commercial spectrum and including nearly all the larger firms (Bureau of the Census, 1976).

Women are also inhibited from starting or enlarging their organizations by a lack of financial backing. Whether obtained through banks, friends, or the stock market, financing requires an act of faith on the part of the lender or investor. Backing an unproven entrepreneur is an exceptionally risky activity for which there are few objective guidelines. The woman entrepreneur faces the added problem of proving her probable financial success to financiers who are already skeptical that anyone of her sex can succeed.

Fortunately, although most bank lending officers and nearly all investment bankers are men, the largest share of American wealth is owned by (usually elderly) women. In many cases the women were not instrumental in acquisition of the wealth—it was inherited or placed in their names as a tax convenience by their husbands. Nonetheless, it is theirs. Older people generally shunt their capital toward stable investments rather than speculative ventures. Since new or small firms are speculations, women's capital moves toward larger, established businesses (cf. *Forbes,* 1973). This is often as it should be, considering the financial needs of the elderly.

The extent to which we perceive a financial opportunity as safe often depends on our personal experience with it and our ability to control it. The elements of control and personal experience can be injected into entrepreneurship financing in a relatively simple way. Rather than attempt bank loans, women starting businesses which they feel will grow should involve other women as "financial angels" from the beginning. Most financial institutions prefer not to control the stock of their clients. In contrast, the women who are acting as financial angels should be offered a direct measure of control: either offered stock or temporary board positions for the duration of major loans. They can gain experience by being brought in at the planning stages of a new enterprise rather than being asked to help only when the need for cash has become critical.

The first step in organizing, then, is to develop an idea and some concrete plans for it. The second step is to find women backers and to add their input to the plans. The third step is to decide on the organization's financial structure in the light of future needs and the apparent willingness of the financial angels to invest in particular types of financial instruments. Thereafter, the entrepreneur seeks firm commitments. Only then should the entrepreneur begin final preparations for operating the business. In every later step, the backers should ideally be given sufficient information to quiet any fears concerning their commitments.

This organizational scheme inverts somewhat the more usual process. In general, male entrepreneurs bring their businesses as far as possible before looking for investors. Their purposes are two-fold: they maintain the greatest amount of equity themselves by having more than just an idea to sell, and they can better ascertain the appropriate financial mixture after the business has had some experience. Their reaction is that financing follows success; ours is that success follows financing. Many women have good ideas; few can find the financial muscle through normal channels to back up their ideas. Since older women have the money, it follows that we can obtain financing by introducing programs that appeal to them.

Semipermanent women's financial institutions can also be readily evolved from this scheme. Formally organized public financial organizations are subject to a wide variety of governmental restrictions, however, and are be required by law to refrain from discriminating in personnel or financial dealings.[a] For these

---

[a]It may seem contradictory to suggest that women's financial institutions should be concerned with avoiding government sanctions against discrimination while recognizing that many male-run institutions are oblivious to the law. We would like to think that the days of instituzionalized discrimination are numbered, however, and we would prefer not to recommend permanent organizations that rely on discrimination.

reasons, women's banks and investment houses, although valuable, are unable to do the entire financial job that women require. A more promising idea is that of informal investment consortiums of women who are interested in financing woman-owned businesses or buying out those run by men.

The consortium could establish a separate corporation or limited partnership to invest in each new opportunity. The purposes of each corporation would be limited to making and overseeing a specific investment. Members of the consortium could vary or limit their individual risks by purchasing the stock in each single-investment corporation in varying amounts; investments to finance other opportunities would require additional single-investment corporations tailored to suit the needs of the consortium members and the requirements of the organization for which the funds are earmarked. When the capital lent to the entrepreneur is repaid, the single-investment corporation could liquidate itself by distributing the capital to its shareholders (the participating consortium members). In the event of the entrepreneur's failure to meet commitments on schedule, the single-investment corporation could readily absorb the debtor organization and operate it directly.

Getting a Job

2. We should make better use of the women's grapevine in getting and giving jobs.

The great majority of women necessarily work in previously established organizations. The first barrier these people must face is that of getting hired— preferrably by a nondiscriminatory employer. Employment agencies, although sometimes helpful, are often a disappointing solution. While both federal and state legislation prohibit discrimination by New York employment agencies, a study of private employment agencies in the state capital (Sadowski, 1974) found that most practice covert discrimination. Frequently encountered techniques included asking different background questions of men than of women, maintaining separate job lists by preferential employee sex, and employing counselors who specialized in the positions stereotypically appropriate for only one sex. Subsequent research by students working with the senior author suggested that the New York state-operated employment service discriminates in a similar manner. There is no reason for women to expect better treatment in other states.

A good agency can be very helpful. Some executive recruitment agencies are now springing up in major cities for the specific purpose of finding talented women for those employers who either do not discriminate or who are honestly attempting to comply with the requirements of their affirmative action programs. Some of these agencies are run by people sensitive to the problems of discrimination. To date, this group of agencies seems to be operating in good faith. Our advice is that women make full use of any agency available—and keep their eyes open and their fingers crossed in the process.

Unless you are contacted by an executive recruiter, the swiftest passage into management is often through direct contact with those who are already there. Rumors concerning job openings and other opportunities move through a network of friends termed the "old boy network." The network can be put to deliberate use. For example, an employer who is looking for a new employee may let others know that a position is open. The people who "know" earliest are those in closest contact with the position—superiors, subordinates, and coworkers.

Others learn of the opening from those directly connected with it. The information is spread by friends in casual conversation, for instance that occurring at a party. As well, some people act as regular links between formal communication networks. Salesmen calling on those who have resigned are likely to carry that information back to their own organizations and pass it into the communications channels there. As the news spreads, the employer quickly obtains a number of job candidate suggestions. Often the candidates themselves visit or call within a matter of days.

Because of the legendary speed with which rumors travel, the better positions are often filled before a formal announcement of their vacancy can appear. We tend to prefer to talk with others who are similar to ourselves. Since few women enjoy management positions, the rumors travel fastest between men, bringing more male than female candidates for the openings.

Through a cooperative effort, we can make the grapevine work as well for women as it does for men. The most important requirement is that women who become aware of a possible position vacancy always tell other women about the opportunity—whether or not those they talk with could be personally interested in the position. As a result of this grapevine, the "old girl network" can be constantly primed to meet the needs of women who are looking for a job or an advancement. At present we often assume that women are not interested in discussing business problems, while men are. In order to operate the grapevine successfully, however, it is vital that every woman be advised of job information as soon as possible, even if she herself has never worked outside her home.

Of course, the old girl network is not yet as smoothly functioning as its masculine competitor. The best interim advice for the job hunter is to deliberately solicit word-of-mouth information from both men and women. The applicant should try to contact people having the closest possible connection with the position desired. In the absence of friends with direct knowledge, the applicant should question any secondary source available. For example, a member of the secretarial pool may know a secretary in the department having the job sought.

An alternative possibility is to blindly contact someone in the organization—preferably a person who is not in a position to do the actual hiring. Since the person questioned is a complete stranger, he or she can be asked candidly about possible openings and the names of others who can supply further information; there is little risk in the questioning process. Of course, friends might recommend the applicant to the person making the hiring decision, while personal recommendations rarely result from a blind phone call. Nonetheless, the blind call technique is far preferred to having no information at all.

Training and Advancement—The Game of Making It the Easy Way.

3. Women should use their experience as leverage in job advancement.

Successful employers constantly seek ways to maximize their benefits while minimizing their costs. One way to do this is to hire and retain the most efficient (productivity per dollar of salary) employees. When employees are extraordinarily efficient in a way in which others are unable to compete, they secure their jobs semipermanently. The employer can afford neither to replace them nor to move them to higher positions; either decision would entail nonrecoverable inefficiencies relative to the alternative of ignoring the hyperefficient employees. Consequently, those who are overly efficient are often left in peace to grow old in their positions. We should add that employees who are fearful of losing their jobs have a tradition of creating the illusion of hyperefficiency; by failing to disclose the techniques they have developed for use in their work, they ensure that their potential replacements would fail.

The need for efficiency dictates that employers also try to match higher cost employees to more important and exacting positions. When high-salaried employees are performing unimportant tasks, an efficiency-minded employer is faced with the choice of moving them up in some manner, or releasing them. One way of moving the employees up is through retraining. In general, high-salaried employees get higher quality and more expensive training, since the cost of training can be justified by the high salary cost and the potential importance of the employees when they are efficient. In a sense, then, the most upwardly employee is one of average efficiency who is already highly paid.

Armed with this knowledge, employees can choose advancement strategies according to their personal requirements. The employee who wants only security can obtain it through hyperefficiency, while the employee who would like to move up can do so through appearing to be able to benefit from training, or from seeming to have unutilized capabilities. An employee can also move up from becoming so expensive to the organization (for example, by demanding salary increases) that he or she must be moved up or terminated. This strategy has an obvious risk barring its use by those who are uncertain of their abilities.

As we mentioned in an earlier chapter, women are sometimes less self-assured in their behavior than are men. Considering that women have a higher unemployment rate than men, this is not surprising. Nonetheless, the difference in self-assurance can lead to alarming results. In order to obtain a job at all, women are more likely than men to accept positions for which they are overqualified. Once there, the woman is likely to increase her hold on a position through hyperefficiency. To some extent, women who compete in traditionally male jobs find hyperefficiency instrumental in establishing their credibility. A second effect, however, is that of slowing their advancement; the hyperefficient woman executive has proven that she deserves her job, but she is too valuable there to risk moving elsewhere. This problem is compounded by an attitude of uncertainty expressed by some women. If asked whether they would like to move or be trained for better positions, they may appear ambivalent. The possibility of an advancement is intriguing, but it is also threatening; even asking for a pay raise presents a certain vulnerability to an employer who may then decide to replace the woman.

An almost entirely risk-free advancement program is available involving a legal and widely practiced form of extortion. First, the player of the leverage game prepares a background resume that looks as good as possible through reasonable exaggeration and obvious understatement. Men have long excelled at this practice. If they worked for three months as a salesman in Nome, Alaska, they were "Sales coordinator of the Northwestern District, 1968"; on the other hand, an office manager in charge of filing and shuffling paper in a one-person outpost might become simply "Manager—Northwestern District." Low-status activities are omitted entirely unless a high-status name can be found for them.

When the resume is finally flawless, the leverage player should place herself on the job market without alerting her present employer. Her purpose in doing so is to locate an alternative position that is different from her present one, more highly paid, and which she would be willing to take if fired. She need not prefer the new employer to her present one. When the leverage player has received a formal written memorandum of an employment offer from a new organization, she is in the position of a gambler who has been dealt three aces. She shows the written memorandum to her present employer and suggests that she would prefer to stay with her present employer but finds the new offer overpoweringly attractive under existing conditions. While avoiding undue threats, she offers her present employer a grace period to consider alternatives before she will "be forced" to make her irrevocable decision to join the new firm.

The employer must decide whether the woman will really make good on her threat if nothing is done. When convinced that she will, the employer can only afford to ignore the leverage player if she is of little real value relative to her demands. In that event, the employee's bluff has been called, and she is obliged to take the new position if she ever expects to be taken seriously. In most cases, the current employer typically responds by giving the employee part or all the additional benefits conferred by the alternative organization. Experienced leverage players will sometimes respond by returning to the prospective new employer and determining whether the stakes can be raised an additional notch for even better benefits. The best players of this game are those who do not care where they work or who have access to a friendly alternative employer to whom they can repeatedly turn over the years for new evidence of their increasing value.

Most employees can readily obtain at least a small raise in pay at their present job in the manner just described. The effect of the outside offer is both to convince the employer that the individual will be lost if nothing is done and to force an upward reevaluation of her potential. Someone else is willing to pay the employee more, so the employer can easily rationalize that she must be worth more than her present salary. Next, however, the employer must adjust to the increased value of the employee. Whereas she may previously have been hyperefficient, she is now inefficient; a solution is retraining and promotion. In this way, the employee obtains new experience, a pay hike, visibility in the firm, and is set to play the leverage game again if avenues for ready advancement become blocked. The game seldom requires a player to make good on the threat to leave but provides the possibility for doing so if the counteroffers are insufficient. We should note that good leverage players (usually men) continually angle for new jobs with the real intention of merely improving their positions with their present employers.

The Discrimination Union—Making It the Hard Way

4. Women in female-dominated professions should require that their employers end discrimination.

For a variety of reasons, most women office workers find jobs within a narrow group of activities including secretarial and bookkeeping work. Individual women often find it nearly impossible to rise within an organization from these fields to management; they have become type-cast and are far too valuable just where they are. On the other hand, women who do enter management find themselves physically and emotionally isolated from other women and have some difficulty in asserting themselves (cf. Jaquette, 1976).

Power is in the eye of the beholder. As long as women perceive themselves as being either inferior or isolated, it is possible for others to ignore them. This is not to say that employers intentionally ignore their women employees; usually employers merely behave in their own best interest. Employers will see to the needs of their employees when, as in program 3, the employees force them to the discovery that their own interest is served by doing so. In the meantime, employers attend to more pressing problems.

The concept of the Discrimination Union (Larwood and Jafek, 1977; Pendergrass, Kimmel, Joesting, Peterson, and Bush, 1976) is based on the collective power of women working together in an organization to force an end to discrimination. Like employers, unions have tended to ignore women and accept their being paid at lower rates (*Issues in Industrial Society,* 1971). In fact, present legislation does not prohibit unions from engaging in some types of sex discrimination (Smith, 1975; see also Polyhemus, 1975). Presumably most unions have developed to serve the needs of male workers with women being an afterthought. Unless the apparatus of existing unions can be taken over by women, working within them merely perpetuates discrimination. The possibilities for unionization are not limited to the interests more common to men, however; women can form a union with the specific purpose of bringing about an end to discrimination. With that accomplished, the Discrimination Union can go on to other goals; in contrast, most traditional unions place the goal of ending discrimination last.

Since a union is a legally defined body, specific regulations should be followed; these can be obtained from the National Labor Relations Board in Washington and other large cities. In brief, we suggest that a group of women (although men need not be excluded) from one office or at one level in a firm meet to decide on a long range antidiscrimination program. The program may involve a number of activities, but should include: the posting of job opportunities for a period before filling them to allow the women's grapevine a fair opportunity to supply candidates, the scrupulous administration of the firm's affirmative action plan (if any), the opening of the advancement system such that any employee in the organization could (with motivation and ability) move from the entry level to the top positions, the open statement of salaries so that discrimination can be readily checked, and an end to discrimination in salaries, hiring, advancement, and training. If Congress allows the U.S. Supreme Court ruling authorizing firms to discriminate against women in health insurance plans to stand, insurance coverage should also be made an issue. The union should also be concerned with the provision of day care, the possible institution of flexible hours or short shifts, and ensuring that the seniority system does not place women at a disadvantage.

After the women agree on a program, they can petition the NLRB to supervise a secret ballot vote of specific categories of employees to determine whether the employer will be required to deal with the new union. (We are assuming that the employer would at first become alarmed by the unionization of white-collar employees. Consequently, he or she would probably not bargain unless required to do so by law and would discharge organizers if feasible. In no event can an employee be legally discharged for union organizing activity. Proving the reason for discharge may be difficult, however, and we suggest that organizing activities be conducted with extreme caution until the NLRB has been petitioned.) The employee categories to be organized can be tailored to the needs of the union, but the vote must be won in order for contract bargaining to be officially recognized and in order to prevent the employer from cashiering (illegally) the organizers. After winning the election, the union members must decide on what they would like to see in their new contract. The program suggested below is only one of the many possible for the Discrimination Union.

First, any part of the long-term program that is of little or no expense to the employer should be demanded as soon as possible in order to keep member enthusiasm behind the union. Thus position vacancies should be posted immediately, and the union should receive a list of the salaries for each of the organization's positions. The positions of greatest interest should include entry level (secretarial, bookkeeping, management trainee) through at least middle management (department heads, division managers). Within the first year, management should be required to state the qualifications for each of these positions including minimum education, experience, and prior organizational positions.

Second, members of the Discrimination Union must recognize that their employer cannot end discrimination immediately. Doing so would require increased pay for a large number of employees and the replacement of many others; the employer could not survive such an extensive transition. Over a longer period, however (possibly ten years), nearly any change can be made successfully. Consequently, the union should plan for long-term changes. The firm's overall employment should be examined to determine the gap between the wages paid to the average man in comparison to the average woman employee. Differences such as level, position held, age, education, and seniority may be accounted for or ignored depending on how strong a program members feel is warranted. The Discrimination Union should develop a program in cooperation with the employer to eliminate any discriminatory wage differential it finds. One method is to require the employer to close the gap between men's and women's wages by 10 percent of the original amount each year. The mechanism by which this is done may be specified in a negotiated contract, but should have some flexibility. In part, it may include higher wage increases for women than those given men; for example, higher percentage wage increases may be granted employees in lower job categories; women in similar job classifications to men may be moved toward equal average pay with them. At the same time, more women may be hired at higher ranks in the organization.

Because most women are found in the lower levels where everyone earns less pay than in the executive levels, the adjustments required of the employer will inevitably run into some major stumbling blocks. For example, the pay of secretaries would ultimately rise as high or higher than that of their male superiors. The employment of women who earned more than men in comparable positions would subject the employer (but not the union) to law suits for reverse discrimination. Moreover, the employer would experience a difficulty in hiring women at top levels in the organization—only a limited number of women are presently available for such positions.[b] Consequently, at the employer's option, a part of the 10 percent discrimination differential could be applied to retraining programs that have as their goal the opening of the advancement ladder to entry-level employees. Should the employer find such training programs difficult to administer, the union itself might be given the funds with the expectation that it would administer them for specific types of training for existing employees. Those women who preferred to remain in their previous positions, of course,

---

[b]Middle- and upper-level management should not be included in the organizing effort. The percentage of women at those levels is low and attempts at organizing the positions would jeopardize both the union election and the positions of women at those levels. Because of the nature of the program suggested, however, higher positions would be favorably affected by the Discrimination Union; it is possible that their unionization might take place at a later time.

could do so, with their retraining funds either used by others or turned back to the organization.

This program, although exceedingly complex, has the advantage of making major changes without impossible demands. Only the women in one organization or even one part of the organization need to be directly involved. Firms will undoubtedly sacrifice some entry-level women's positions as they become more expensive to maintain. Those who remain in the position, however, will have a higher income, while others will finally have the opportunity to advance. The program can be accepted by the employer, because the adjustments are made over an extended period of time. The firm is also assured of a supply of trained and loyal personnel that it might not otherwise find. During the initial bargaining sessions, many firms will undoubtedly assert that they cannot remain competitive while paying the discrimination differential. The purpose of the Discrimination Union is to end the situation in which discrimination is found, however, not to injure the employer. The firm will remain in business, but at the cost of completely overhauling its hiring, salary, and advancement policies to meet its new needs.

Affirmative Action Programs

Although they can be helpful (cf. Wallace and Nelson, 1976), government-run affirmative action programs have largely failed to solve the problem of discrimination. Ample evidence of this breach was recently released by the General Accounting Office. A GAO survey found no important differences between the personnel practices of employers who had entered conciliation agreements with the EEOC and those of employers who had not; similarly, court-ordered compliance cases were rarely monitored to ensure actual compliance (*The Spokeswoman,* 1976).

Despite the relative failure of affirmative action programs, a number of actions can be taken to improve their effectiveness. The Discrimination Union would be able to provide extensive information to the EEOC or OFCCP in the event of an employer's refusal to negotiate. In fact, agreement not to seek government relief during good faith negotiations is undoubtedly a precondition to an employer's willingness to supply the personnel data needed by the Discrimination Union. Additionally, all employees should document every instance of discrimination irrespective of whether they have been personally affected or intend to institute legal proceedings. The documentation can be helpful to other employees and may be used in class action cases. Active complaints concerning the slow disposition of affirmative action cases can be directed toward local politicians as well as toward the affirmative action organizations themselves.

5. Position opening and availability lists should be developed by skill qualification and locale.

An additional type of program is also needed. Current government-mandated affirmative action programs now require that organizations determine the size of the available pool of women and minority candidates for each type of position. Employers having a limited reservoir of affirmative action candidates to choose from are not expected to hire as many from the group. Although the principle of proportionate hiring seems reasonable, it allows employers a large loophole for de facto discrimination. An employer can freely hire anyone after demonstrating that he or she looked for women or minority employees but could find (i.e. hire, advance, or train) none. This may occur when an employer acting in good faith is simply unaware of how to go about hiring affirmative action candidates.

During the past five years, a number of professions (including bankers, economists, and psychologists) have formed women's groups. Part of the focus of these groups is often to collect information from employers concerning job openings of interest to the membership. Depending on the group, job information may be distributed directly to the members and the employer may advertise in a newsletter or receive a list of available candidates. Some groups centrally match openings with candidates.

Although these operations have achieved modest success, they are limited by the delays and inconvenience associated with mail contact and infrequent publishing dates. Both employers and prospective employees are frustrated by the long delays required to make contact through newsletter operation. Hopefully, however, this system will continue to improve in the future by offering greater speed and convenience.

Meanwhile, an alternative operation working on a local or regional basis could be extremely helpful in providing swift contact between the employer and candidate at a minimal cost. A women's regional employment clearing house could provide employers immediately with a list of women member-subscribers, many of whom might already be employed but could consider accepting a better offer. Similarly, the women who subscribed could receive a list of affirmative action employers and the name of a contact within each organization. A telephone service could take position listings from local businesses and make them available to members who drop by; once a month, a memo listing all open positions could be circulated to the subscribers. In this way, the employers would have access to a list helpful in meeting their obligations, and women would be more readily able to discover position openings before they are filled. The dodge that "no affirmative action candidates are available" would be laid to rest.

Changing Ourselves

As Chapter 4 found, the self-concepts of many women prevent them from fully utilizing or enjoying their abilities. Participation in "unfeminine" activities, ranging from management to auto repair and mountain climbing, is avoided.

Women often do not even realize that they have or could readily develop the skills needed for these activities.

The experiences we allow ourselves and our self-concepts are mutually determined and limiting. We can alter either by somehow changing the other factor. For example, if we were to do something today that we have never done before, the ability to perform that activity would become obvious; the self-concept would then change, and we would have a greater range of experience to draw from in future activities.

One barrier to new activities is the feeling of insecurity resulting when we do them. Can we do it? Do we really want to, and will we like it? If the uncertainties carry sufficient weight, we will decide that the behavior is best abandoned and use our decision to validate our present lifestyle. As noted earlier in this chapter, however, insecurity arises from lack of familiarity with the situation and from a lack of training in the ways to handle it. The authors, if approached, would undoubtedly turn down the opportunity to fly a balloon from Los Angeles to Denver. Since we haven't been aboard balloons before, the decision is hardly surprising—however, it may be that flying the unusual contraptions is simple and requires little experience.

6. We should allow ourselves to sample all that we are capable of doing rather than prejudging our abilities and interests on the basis of the feminine role stereotype.

Many women are upset by the suggestion that they might do well to abandon the feminine stereotype. They equate a decrease in stereotypic femininity with the abandonment of feminine virtues and an increase in masculinity. This problem must be solved on an individual basis. However a growing literature (cf. Bem, 1975) suggest that masculinity and femininity are not natural opposites but are highly restrictive artificial positions among a wider set of possibilities. Diminished stereotypic femininity means increased personal freedom, with the individual able to act as she chooses. In fact, some writers (Jaquette, 1976; Torrey, 1976) feel that femininity itself, far from being natural to women, is a set of behaviors evolved by any oppressed group to avoid angering those in authority. People who are not oppressed would not voluntarily choose subservient behaviors; their choice by those who have nominal equality makes continued oppression possible. In this and the next section, we suggest that both women and men should reevaluate themselves and, if useful, change in nonstereotypic directions.

How can self-concept and experience be changed? One method requires only that you take some time each evening to examine the day's events. Decide in advance what types of behaviors don't fit your self-concept as it is now, but would fit if your self-concept were as you would like it to be. Then decide on a second category comprising behaviors that fit your present self-concept, but not your preferred self. Write your activities down in three separate columns each evening. The third column is for those behaviors that are not considered in the first two classifications.

Next, separate the column, listing activities you feel should be a part of your self-concept from the other two; throw the latter away with as much ceremony as you feel up to. The list remaining is of activities you would not normally do—but did! Study it carefully and try to imagine repeating the activities or others like them. You may want to set a time goal for repetition. After awhile, you will see that everyone already performs most of the behaviors they find unusual or stressful; only the strength and context of those behaviors differs from one person to another. We can reinforce these in ourselves merely by recognizing them and feeling pleased when they occur.

The method just outlined requires that you already be doing some level of the behavior desired and relies on subsequent slow change. Deliberate planned change is more difficult but may ultimately produce faster and more significant results. Planned change requires that you fix long-term goals for yourself, and that you actualize them through specific changes in your lifestyle. Because of the need to clarify interests, the program discussed here takes five weeks to develop and a long period thereafter to affect satisfactory changes. Although you could probably complete the information below in a few minutes, don't start unless you have read the instructions for each step and are willing to follow the procedures.

Actually, this program works backward. Everyone sees some behaviors as improper, resulting in their avoiding them. Long-range goals are normally taken less seriously than immediate behaviors and are less likely to be inhibited. Consequently, this program suggests that long-range planning should be undertaken first. Later, intermediate and near-term activities can be planned when it has become obvious that they are necessary.

One final foreword should be given. Since women perceive more risks than men, they may make more conservative plans as well. Few absolute constraints exist on what anyone can do or become; only the odds favoring success are altered by ability and resource differences. This means that most reasonable personal goals can be reached by anyone who is willing to make sufficient well-planned effort. Don't restrain your long-term goals in this exercise unless you already know that you are unwilling to prepare for them.

For Week 1, make a list of the ultimate goals you would most like to reach (for example, world travel, security, respect, running a firm). Don't be timid.

In Week 2, you may continue to fill in the long-term goal section. Concentrate now on two additional lists, however. First, enter the kinds of positions and situations you would like to obtain during the next five years. Then, make up a similar twenty-year list. You may wish to include events such as being finished with school, freedom to make your own time, obtaining a high executive position, and so on.

In Week 3, you may continue as you did before, but concentrate on adding to the twenty-year list those situations that could result in reaching the goals entered on the long-term goal list.

For Week 4, add to the five-year list only those situations that could result in arrival at the twenty-year situations.

The fifth week is reserved for the elimination of unnecessary and ill-fitting items from the lists. First, eliminate any of the long-term goals that now seem relatively unimportant to you. Next, eliminate any items from the five-year list that now seem to conflict with your remaining long-term goals. Now strike any items from the twenty-year list that conflict with either of the other two.

Your combined list should now provide a homogeneous program of steps to reach your goals. If some goals appear to have no five- or twenty-year situational components, they may be less important than you thought; if so, rule them out. Alternatively, you may have felt unwilling to perform the activities needed to arrive at them. You must now decide whether to give up unsupported goals or to plan for the situations needed to arrive at them. Finally, some remaining situation-goal sets may conflict with one another. By careful thought, you should be able to find alternative situations that are consistent with each of your goals.

After you have resolved these difficulties, you are ready to proceed. The next step is that necessary to arrive at the five-year level you have set for yourself. Make your plans carefully such that they are consistent with both the five- and twenty-year situations. This may require that you adjust your schedule somewhat to avoid being dead-ended at the five-year mark. For instance, if education of some type is needed to reach your twenty-year goals, you may be best advised to obtain it before proceeding. When you are satisfied with the plan, you have only to begin; self-concept will follow.

Redefining Masculinity

Like women, men are available in infinite variety. Many individual women who are married and maintain both a career and a family had no difficulty in obtaining a mate who would encourage their careers. We are compelled to consider the need to redefine masculinity for several reasons, however. The first is that few "liberated" husbands are willing to share half of the homemaking and childcare chores as true equality demands of them (Cook, 1975). As a result, husbands continue to have the time to pursue their career interests, while wives continue to support their habit. Women who are are motivated and competent as their husbands cannot succeed equally until this situation is corrected.

Up to this time, the number of women moving into managerial careers is still small. As the number grows, however, and as the success of those women who have entered management becomes evident, the likelihood of finding an understanding mate among the still-limited number of liberated men is diminished accordingly. The problem is equally evident from the employment side: the success of women is more threatening as it becomes inescapable. Men, or our social fabric, will have to change as women succeed.

Whatever the aspirations women feel for themselves, their children should not be constrained by outmoded sex roles. If children consciously choose traditional roles, that of course is their right. However, parents are powerful models influencing the ways children believe they are expected to behave as they grow older. A woman whose husband does not approve of her working is likely to have children who are similarly suspicious of working women. The way out of the circle is to change the views of our husbands, employers, and friends in the direction of encouraging personal freedom and equality for the members of both sexes.

Changes in the masculine stereotype are virtually inevitable. Society constantly changes in response to the pressures acting on it. One of the problems that is painfully evident to many older women at this time is the apparent shorter lifespan of men. A growing body of research indicates that there is little in the male physique to predestine early mortality—but there is something in the male role that makes men strive for goals which are unrealistic or unsatisfying and that may make them feel overburdened by responsibility. Evidentally parts of the male role are exceptionally stressful to many men and result in life-style patterns terminated by early death (Glass, 1976). A realistic appraisal of their abilities and a fair sharing of responsibilities are urgently needed.

7. Married women must expect equality as a condition of their marriage.

The married woman is in an ideal position to influence her husband toward equality in ways beneficial to the lifestyles of both. The first chapters noted that much of our society scorns the man who is unable to support his family single-handedly. Some of the motivation to prove themselves undoubtedly results from men's feeling that their wives concur with this social pressure (many undoubtedly do). Many of these men would attribute a wife's suggestion that they relax to her observation of their weaknesses. Suggestions of the need for equality will generally meet rejection.

Instead, the wife must assert her right to work by working. The wife's taking a job without consulting her husband seems at first to be a distant and strange way for a woman to behave. Before succumbing to this judgment, however, one should recall the number of husbands who ask their wives for permission to work. If the woman's career is to be taken at all seriously, it must be treated as an accepted fact rather than as a temporary aberration or problem to be resolved. The woman similarly should not ask her husband whether he is willing to assume some childcare and homemaking duties—instead she should state that a division of these duties is fair. If there is no response, she should abandon some obviously needed chores that her husband can do equally well. Shopping and transportation of children may be ideal candidates for abandonment, since they are inescapable.

When the husband does indicate some acceptance of this regimen, he should be rewarded in every reasonable manner—but without compromise. Protests can be responded to in a warm but matter-of-fact manner. The woman's career and the husband's health are not debatable questions; equal and non-sex-biased family duties are an assumption of a successful marriage. Husbands who feel that their own careers may be hampered by a loss in status or in discretionary time can be reminded that complete dedication to work is unhealthy; moreover, few who run the competitive race ever had any real chance of reaching the very top. Manhood is hardly proved when the enforced slavery of a wife and premature death are preconditions for success. Instead, husbands should be counseled to enjoy the drop in their responsibility, rather than to try to run sufficiently faster to make up for new family demands. Some more detailed programs appear below.

8. Married women should explore the possibilities for job sharing when they have similar abilities to those of their husbands.

An increasing number of married couples are finding that employers are willing to consider hiring both the wife and husband to share a single job. This system is often worked so that one member of the couple works mornings and the other works afternoons; other possibilities are an alternate day or week schedule. The system obviously requires a good deal of coordination by the couple sharing the job; since the shared job is not as tiring to either member, however, many find themselves eager to spend the added coordination time required.

Putting job-sharing into effect requires three preconditions. Both the husband and wife (two women can also share jobs, of course) must have similar skills and aspirations. If they do not perform in the same manner, problems of inequity are likely to develop at some later time. The employer must be willing to go along with the experiment in the same manner as if only one person held the job. This stipulation is probably more difficult than it sounds, since promotions and pay increases are often based on subjective judgments that are enormously complicated by having to average evaluations of two half-persons. One solution is to ask the employer to state specific objective evaluation criteria in advance. By laying out the psychological contract in full detail, the likelihood of unpleasant surprises can be minimized. Finally, each spouse must be willing to allow the other to share responsibilities. This means that each person must be willing to work with normal job decisions that have been made by the other. Those men who feel that their wives are inferior and must be protected will probably not accept this requirement; for them, job sharing is one of the swiftest routes to an ulcer.

Job sharing has the advantage of producing mutual respect as each spouse learns first-hand the capabilities and problems of the other. The sharers also increase their self-respect as they apply their spare time to explore hidden interests and learn to handle the unique job situation. The experience of employers has often been that two halves add to more than one whole in terms of motivation and performance.

9. Members of both sexes should be free to enter second careers at any time.

Many people assume that it is necessary to decide early in life on a particular career; thereafter, everything is bent toward success. Despite careful planning, however, some people find themselves in a field for which they feel ill-suited or which they no longer enjoy. The discovery is especially devastating to the head of a household, since that person may feel locked into the position by his or her responsibilities. Despite the difficulties, growing numbers are changing their directions and entering new and successful careers late in life; similarly, many professional women do not even enter the workforce until their forties or fifties.

One of the more interesting advantages of encouraging a second career is its potential for restructuring the family relationship. At least for a period during re-education and re-establishment, the man who is changing careers must rely on the earnings of his wife. His reliance not only legitimizes her work, but makes it essential. At the same time much of the seriousness with which men's careers are often invested is deflated; seen in perspective, life can go on without the husband's income. Women can no doubt hasten the growth of this awareness by explaining that they enjoy their work and are in no hurry for the husband's re-entry.

10. Career conflicts should be resolved to the advantage of both the wife and husband.

As President-elect Carter was choosing his cabinet in late 1976, he learned that the first woman he was about to designate for Secretary of the Department of Commerce felt that her husband could not find a satisfactory job in the Washington, D.C. area. It is not for us to prejudge a person who turns down the highest administrative position ever offered (to that time) a woman in the United States. Nonetheless, we can't recall the last instance of a man turning down a cabinet post to protect his marriage or his wife's career.

Too often in the past, women with promising careers have broken them off in the interest of their husbands by either relocating and leaving the job or failing to relocate when their own job required it. Moving, of course, is only one instance of potential career conflicts. Others include the requirement by some employers that a man use his wife as a social hostess, the requirement for travel, the need for different hours or schedules, and the cultivation of different social circles.

There is no ideal way to solve these conflicts (cf. Kosinar, 1974). It is certain, however, that the woman who always gives up her career for that of her husband is a loser in the resolution. A woman's career is as important to her as her husband's career is to him (cf. Levitin & Quinn, 1974). Preferrably the couple will consider the advantages and disadvantages of each "opportunity" either one receives before a conflict arises. Hopefully, one career will be more readily transplanted or less psychologically rewarding than the other. In some cases, both personal self-respect and the marriage can be best preserved if both parties take full advantage of their respective opportunities—even at the cost of temporarily living in different cities.

Making a Beginning

Where do you start? depending on your own experience and situation, you may have found some of the ideas above helpful. In a few minutes, though, you can probably generate a new set that we missed. That is where we think a beginning should be made.

This chapter is built on the concept that we must take over the direction of our resources in order to get what we feel is needed. The resources and the needs are real and readily inventoried. If experience and self-confidence are missing, there is no way of gaining them short of beginning somewhere; they will develop as your program takes shape.

Consider the example of a woman who is perhaps forty-years-old and who decides that she would like to become an entrepreneur but has very little capital, experience, or expertise. Depending on the type of business she is willing to consider, there are considerable resources available for her. For example, the unemployment rate indicates that many good employees are looking for work, thereby forming a pool of untapped talent. An informal survey at the local employment office will reveal what types of skills are available. The woman might decide to offer a service-oriented business based largely on the available labor pool.

To be successful, she must probably run a lower-cost operation than that which released her potential employees. This can be assured in either of two ways: paying less or developing a more efficient operation; a brief investigation will reveal the most suitable path here. To obtain working capital, the woman may consider borrowing from friends, tapping the grapevine for information concerning women with investable capital, or getting a bank or Small Business Administration loan.[c] Simultaneously she can be looking for advance contracts of the sort that will guarantee marketing success; the potential employees can often supply the names of business contacts for this purpose. Finally, if the woman is willing to take in a few partners, it may be possible to enjoy the services of the "unemployed" free for a few trial weeks while they are still covered by unemployment insurance (legal restrictions prevent this in some states). Done correctly, many new businesses can be successfully launched by persons with little technical knowledge on less than $20.

Not everyone wants to be an entrepreneur, of course, and their situation is quite different. The point is, however, that opportunities do exist. We can move into management successfully, and we can change the underlying assumptions our society makes concerning the abilities of women, by ourselves without the need to wait for governmental assistance.

References

Bem, S. L. "Androgyny vs. the tight little lives of fluffy women and chesty men." *Psychology Today,* 1975, *9,* 58–62.

Bureau of the Census. *Women-owned businesses, 1972.* Washington, D.C.: U.S. Government Printing Office, 1976.

---

[c]The Federal Credit Opportunity Act administered by the Federal Trade Commission prohibits discrimination based on sex in the financial activities of banks, finance companies, credit card issuers and retail organizations. Discrimination based on financial considerations is necessarily legal (the economy could not exist without it) and can be based on subjective criteria that may lead to sex discrimination through "the back door." Because it is a lender of last resort, the SBA is probably more likely to be impartial; beware however: SBA loans are not dischargable in bankruptcy.

Cook, A. H. *The working mother.* Ithaca, N.Y.: New York School of Industrial and Labor Relations, Cornell University, 1975.

"The economics of womanpower." *Forbes,* 1973, *111* (7), 56–60.

Eden, D. "Organizational membership vs. self-employment. Another blow to the American dream." *Organizational Behavior and Human Performance,* 1975, *13,* 79–94.

Glass, D. C. "Stress, competition and heart attacks." *Psychology Today,* 1976, *10* (12).

Jaquette, J. S. "Political science." *Signs,* 1976, *2,* 147–164.

Kosinar, P. "How to cope as a two career family." *National Association of Banking Women Journal,* 1974, July–August, 11–14.

Larwood, L., and Blackmore, J. "Sex discrimination in managerial selection: Testing predictions of the vertical dyad linkage model." *Sex Roles,* in press.

———, and Jafek, B. "The discrimination union." Unpublished position paper, 1977.

Levitin, T. E., and Quinn, R. P. "Changes in sex roles and attitudes toward work." Paper presented at 1974 meeting of the American Association for Public Opinion Research, Lake George, NY.

Pendergrass, V. E., Kimmel, E., Joesting, J., Peterson, J., and Bush, E. "Sex discrimination counseling." *American Psychologist,* 1976, *31,* 36–46.

Polyhemus, C. E. "Sex-segregated unions." *Monthly Labor Review,* 1975, *98* (11), 72.

Sadowsky, K. *"But can she type?"* New York Public Interest Research Group study, 1974 (undated).

Schwartz, E. B. "Entrepreneurship: A new female frontier." *Journal of Contemporary Business,* 1976, *5* (1), 47–76.

Smith, A. B., Jr. "The impact on collective bargaining of equal employment opportunity remedies." *Industrial and Labor Relations Review,* 1975, *28,* 376–394.

The Spokeswoman, 1976, 7 (5), 2–3.

Staff introduction. *Issues in Industrial Society,* 1971, *2,* 2–20.

Torrey, J. W. "The consequences of equal opportunity for women." *Journal of Contemporary Business,* 1976, *5* (1), 13–28.

8 Looking Ahead

This book has tried to transmit an image of the situation of working women in general and women in management in particular. As indicated in the first section, if it were seen as a static, one-time-only snapshot, the current situation of women could only be seen as grim. The statistics show little long-term change; it is really too early to statistically measure the importance of women's gains over the past few years.

The second section of this book pointed out that there are several interrelated explanations for the difficulties women have had in entering and rising in management. Discrimination at the time of hiring or of later assessment is only a part of a much larger phenomenon. Most women never reach the point at which outright employment discrimination could affect them. Before then, they have dropped from the labor force, failed to get the education they need, or learned not to take their abilities and interests seriously.

Many of the rigidly institutionalized restrictions on the success of women have disappeared during the past decade. Although generous heaps of bias remain, the fact is that women who can overcome their early socialization experiences can now succeed in management. Success is still not easy, of course. Because of the bias, more is still required of a woman than of a man. But women who have escaped their own cultural heritage—who have faith in themselves and who try—are succeeding! Moreover, a number of techniques are available to increase the ease with which women can rise in management.

Prediction of the future is perhaps best left to the divinely anointed. Nonetheless, we feel that certain important trends have asserted themselves both in the data presented here and in the apparent direction taken by our society. For the most part, these trends are favorable to women who are interested in a managerial career; whether favorable or not, however, they will surely affect us.

Women seem to be making up an increasing proportion of the students in management master's and bachelor's degree programs; this is partly a result of the lucrativeness of expanding these programs in times of dropping college enrollment elsewhere. Nonetheless it will have the long-term effect of increasing the pool of women from which organizations will draw future managers.

Because of the increasing numbers of available women and the threat of government action, more women will be promoted within the managerial ranks. It will take ten to twenty years for the full effect to be felt at the rarified top management levels, but sex discrimination in management will die a slow death.

171

The increasing numbers of women will result in a progressive deterioration in the status of management as a profession. The relationship between status and proportion of women has been felt in other fields, and we suspect that it is easier to change the status attributed to a field than that attributed to an entire sex. Simultaneous with the dropping status, management will become encrusted with regulations and heavily circumscribed; future managers will have a good deal less power over that which they manage. Business will be less competitive.

More casual working patterns will replace sole reliance on the forty-hour–five-day week. Although half-days, flex-time, and job sharing will make life easier for the working mother, the real forces pushing them will be employee preference, improved scheduling flexibility, and the finding that performance often increases.

Many feminists are bemoaning the fact that young women in their late teens and early twenties are taking for granted the measure of equality that was won only a few years back. The women's movement, like many others, can be seen as a succession of waves. Ultimately the women who now assume the advantages recently won will be older and will run into the barriers that have not yet been lifted. Some will be successful, and some will be disappointed or will not care; others will do something about it. It seems likely that the movement will enjoy a resurgence ten to fifteen years in the future that will effectively eliminate any continuing form of legal discrimination. It can be hoped, of course that passage of the Equal Rights Amendment will already have done this.

Socialization patterns will change greatly—as in fact they already are changing. Women who have not been taught to expect discrimination and who expect to work will naturally bring up children who have the same expectancies and who believe in themselves. This generational socialization process will place growing pressure on our society for full equality in the working environment and, probably, in the home environment as well.

At some point, we expect to find that these changes have occurred and that women are equal participants in management. In the meantime, success is already within the reach of those who carefully plan and execute their strategy.

Appendix A: The Women vs. Chase Manhattan: Diary of a Discrimination Suit

The following diary was kept by a journalist who attended the strategy meetings of a group of women planning a sex discrimination suit against their employer, the Chase Manhattan Bank. It details the germination of the suit, from the group's initial strategy meetings in September 1974 through the filing of class-action charges with the Equal Employment Opportunity Commission nearly a year later, in August 1975.

In these charges, the group alleges that the Chase Manhattan Corporation maintains a pattern and practice of discriminating against women in its recruiting, hiring, salary, and benefits policies; in both its recruitment and exit practices for its training programs; and in its internal promotion practices. They also charge that the bank terminated women due solely to their sex and retaliated against people who opposed the practices described in the allegations. Because the EEOC charges were filed "on behalf of persons aggrieved," the identities of the individuals have been disguised. To date, Chase does not know their names. The women in the group range in age from 22 to 45 and represent workers in clerical through lower management job categories. Most are single. All except two graduated from college or hold advanced degrees. Many were educated at Seven Sisters schools or in prestigious graduate programs. The number of women committed to the group at any given time varied. At its peak, the group had 12 women regularly attending meetings. A few—usually middle-aged clerical workers who had worked at Chase for years—came to one meeting and dropped out immediately because they felt the group was too militant; or they weren't willing to spend the requisite time and energy; or felt that it was too late to influence the direction in which the group was headed. Others contributed time, money, and information critical of Chase and thus attained "active supporter" status.

At little more than a year ago, I was made aware of the fact that a group was forming when a friend informed me that she and five other Chase employees had gathered at a luncheon to discuss their mutual employment grievances. I asked if I could observe the group's progress and write an article if and when a suit developed from such discussions. The group assented with the understanding that I would assist occasionally to obtain information for them. I did so twice—once when I interviewed one of the plaintiffs in the Bank of America sex discrimination suit and once when I wrote to the U.S. Treasury Department's Office of Federal Contract Compliance for a copy of Chase's Affirmative Action Plan. (The group already had a copy but wanted one that was obtained through regular channels.)

"The Women vs. Chase Manhattan," Jacqueline A. Thompson. *MBA* 9 (December 1975) no. 11, pp. 19–29. Reprinted by permission.

During the year that I attended meetings, it became apparent that each member of the group had her own conception of my function. Although some accepted me as a disinterested observer, others assumed I was an active sympathizer who would eventually serve as their chief public relations strategist when the suit became known. These differing views surfaced when the women were given copies of this story to review to insure that their identities are sufficiently disguised. Based on their comments, factual, *not* editorial, changes were made.

In toto, the group met 20 times. However, the diary that follows documents only the most important meetings. My italicized remarks, which I added at the end of the year of meetings, are intended to put the meetings in perspective.

September 26, 1974: Tonight was the group's first evening meeting. (For a description of the principal members of the group, turn to the end.) Paranoia runs high. When Eva, my friend and liaison, introduced me and my intentions, there was much uneasy shifting in chairs and the facial expressions of the women in the room told me they were skeptical, but nobody asked me to leave. The main concern seems to be whom do I know and whom will I tell. They are all worried about losing their jobs if the bank discovers their "subversive" activities.

The group is definitely a mixed bag. Eva appears to be most committed to women's rights. I suspect she would file suit immediately if she could round up support. (She helped organize a group at her last employer.) Joan is a close second. Both have the ability to clarify what others in the group say and to force them to stick to the point of the discussion. This group, like those operating on the "participatory-democracy" theory left over from the student rebellions of the 1960s, definitely needs firm control.

Linda's attitude seems to be: "If you women really do something, I'm with you. But this is probably all talk and no action." Valerie is just plain angry and wants revenge and back pay.

Karen strikes me as wide-eyed and naive, like a little girl who is overjoyed to be included in the activities of her older sisters. If the group wants a cheerleader, she's perfect. She keeps saying, "I'm sure we're going to win!" Sarah is the other extreme, a doubting Thomas. She keeps trying to deflate everyone else's zeal, because she believes pleasant smiles and conciliatory words work wonders, while lawsuits embarrass, antagonize, and cost money.

Much of the evening was spent recounting "horror stories." Although none of the group has ever been active in the feminist movement, there were pronounced consciousness-raising aspects a la women's lib to this evening's meeting. Camaraderie filled the room. Whenever someone would relate a small victory, others would applaud with "Right on!" They discussed how to handle prejudiced bosses and insults from male colleagues, such as "Why aren't you home making babies?"

Their initial goal seems to be giving each other moral support and suggestions on how to negotiate their careers through the obstacle course at Chase.

Actually they see it more like a mine field: one wrong move and they've had it.

Dee Albert, a National Organization of Women (NOW) official who later became the group's advisor, characterized the Chase women as "extremely conservative" compared to the radical anti-capitalists at the other end of the women's right spectrum.

She put the group's paranoia in a new, feminist context: "There is a lot more going on here than meets the eye in terms of individual growth and group dynamics. Their paranoia not only reflects the obvious fear of losing their jobs and damaging their careers, but also a fear that somehow this drastic step they are taking will irrevocably alter the way they relate to other people—and, in fact, it will. Such women experience a lot of internal conflict when they finally forsake their traditional feminine role, however tentatively, and start asserting themselves. Lurking in the background is that unmentionable fear that once they become more demanding, men won't like them anymore.

"The group interaction complicates matters further. As rather traditional women, they have to learn to relate to each other differently. Women in groups are accustomed to dealing with each other in a bitchy, quasi-competitive way and they feel a lot of hostility toward any woman who assumes a leadership position because that is contrary to a woman's natural role in our society. But let's be realistic—somebody's got to come on strong in a group like this or no decisions would ever be made.

"Finally, these women have no psychological template for their situation vis-a-vis the bank. After all, how many groups of women ever have to form a unified front in face of real danger? The games men play from childhood on teach them that."

October 14: Joan reported that she had contracted a young lawyer named Deborah Watarz through the New York Council of Law Associates, which coordinates all pro bono work for attorneys in the city. Watarz made two key recommendations: hire counsel and keep diaries. Keep a running log of sexual insults, innuendoes, and discriminatory acts, directed both at themselves and at other women, she urged. Such journals are admissible in court and will be useful when their lawyer wants to subpoena witnesses with corrobating stories.

Early on, the group faced a crucial question: should they seek internal remedies for their grievances or go outside Chase for help? The decided to go outside. They reached this decision primarily because they believed that the bank's officials in charge of affirmative action were determined to rid Chase of boat-rockers, not to see justice done.

Sarah had been a strong advocate of "let's keep this a family matter" until she attended the Chase officers' annual dinner in mid-October. During a question period persided over by the bank's president, Willard C. Butcher, Sarah submitted a question, anonymously, which read: "What should a woman do if she feels she has been discriminated against at Chase?" Butcher answered that she should complain the company way, first by speaking to her boss, and if she got no relief, then to her boss's boss, and on up the chain of command. "If you talk to me and I don't give you any satisfaction, then by all means, you should go see David Rockefeller." The flippant jocularity of his answer made Sarah furious.

October 30: Joan, Linda, and Eva reported on a meeting with Judith Vladeck, a senior attorney in Deborah Watarz's firm, which specializes in labor law. They felt she had had the necessary experience on similar cases and the self-confidence to take on the mighty Chase.

The group agrees that it is important to be represented by an attorney with a solid, establishment image. They plan to interview a number of lawyers and will choose one based on his or her professional qualifications and image—as well as that of the firm, expressed interest in "the cause," and fee. They are wary of young go-getters out to make a name for themselves.

During the next six months, the group met with seven lawyers; an average of four women attended each interview.

November 21: Valerie brought Bonnie, an acquaintance from the Trust Department, tonight. She's ready and willing to sign a complaint attesting to the discriminatory environment at Chase. However, there is, as yet, no decision to file a complaint.

I played a tape of an interview with Kerstin Magary, one of the leaders of the Bank of America suit filed in 1972 and settled in mid-1974. The group listened to the tape and was particularly impressed with Magary's admonition: don't bring suit unless you are ready to spend money and devote time to analyzing mounds of quantitative data.

Margary cautioned that being a plaintiff in a sex discrimination suit is safer than being a known sympathizer. Bank of America kept hands off the complainants but retaliated against prosecution witnesses and other supporters. This touched off a discussion of who was willing "to sign on the dotted line." Three of the group said they would; one more was considering it.

Karen has a librarian friend at an economics research institute who is feeding her copies of newspaper stories about other discrimination suits. Joan has become the unofficial expert on the group's legal options.

Linda was appointed to attend the inaugural meeting of a new coalition called New York Women Employed. Its goal is to attract representatives from secret feminist caucuses within corporations all over the city. It wants to become a pressure group with a legal defense fund.

The group quickly plugged into the amorphous underground of disenchanted female employees that exists in New York City. Such contacts reinforced their commitment to "the cause," gave them leads to other unhappy women at Chase and a chance to exchange ideas on strategy with more experienced feminists.

January 8, 1975: A lot has happened in a month. Linda has contacted Anne, a Chase employee who feels she is oppressed but who is already involved in a discrimination case against her previous employer. Eva invited Renee, a highly overqualified secretary with no love for Chase. The militancy index of the group went up the minute she entered the room. In Renee, Eva has gained both a rival for center stage and a political associate.

Renee's ex-husband is a union organizer, so she became the group's self-appointed tactician. She rapped about what Chase would do if they discovered the existence of the group, which managed to accentuate everybody's paranoia. At her insistence, the group established ground rules for bringing in new members: candidates should be discussed by the group before they are told of its existence.

In fact, Valerie, one of the original members, has dropped out. Although she has given other reasons, members of the group believe she has done so because she was promoted to a line job.

Karen heard a rumor that a group of women in the bank's EDP operations has just filed suit anonymously against Chase. They decide to make contact with the EDP group, if the rumor checks out.

They drop the idea of sending a letter to the Wage and Hour Division of the Federal Labor Department to harass Chase. One of the lawyers they have interviewed advised them that to do so would only "dilute their case." Wage and Hour is oriented to bluecollar complaints.

All the attorneys they've seen lately say the same thing: acquire a friend in the personnel department, where a gold mine of evidence awaits the person who can do some judicious copying. They are starting to realize that contacts in key departments is the name of this game.

February 2: Dee Alpert, a knowledgable organizer from NOW, monopolized this meeting. She gave them a picture of what goes on politically when a government agency decides to investigate a complaint and explained the difference between a macro (statistical analysis of patterns of discrimination) and micro (involving individual cases) investigation. Macro investigations are usually a cop-out because the agency, rather than the individual complainant, merely signs a pattern-and-practice decree with the employer, who promises to cease and desist. It's the proverbial slap on the wrist. When a micro investigation results in a decision in favor of the plaintiff, the employer must make restitution to that individual.

She speculated about the case Chase will mount against them once they get to federal court (she assumes they will eventually end up there). Chase will characterize them as an atypical group of female employees, a rag-tag bunch of malcontents with dubious work records. Their lawyer should counter that Chase puts women to an unfair "test of perfection," i.e., women have to be more perfect than their male counterparts in order to be promoted. Chase knows it has the tactical advantage in terms of prestige and resources and may try waging a war of attrition, one that could be dragged out for years.

Alpert discussed several other cases pending against Chase and agreed to put the group in touch with those plaintiffs. No word on the EDP group yet. Eva finds it gratifying to know that groups who file anonymously remain that way.

The group is concerned about theft of documents. Is it ethical? Alpert has mixed feelings. She said the essential thing is to know what's available whether you steal it or not, so that a lawyer can knowledgeably request the important evidence during the discovery process. She admitted to being a clearinghouse for all sorts of purloined material. People send her documents in plain brown envelopes all the time and she forwards them to the right person.

Sarah introduced Margaret, an older woman with children who was not promoted, because "your husband is supporting you," until she became a widow. A friend of Linda's from J. Walter Thompson advertising also attended the meeting as an observer.

This meeting marked the beginning of a new phase in the development of the suit. The group had gone through many sessions of ventilating their grievances. They were now ready to start taking a hard look at some of the alternatives available to them. During this meeting I detected a subtle shift in emphasis. In discussions of how to file suit, the group began using the word "when" rather than "if." I could feel the collective blood pressure rise about ten points.

March 17: Margaret and Sarah, who don't want to file suit, were both absent tonight, so the activist contingent took over. Renee, who is exercized over the group's lack of structure, stated that if she hadn't had previous organizing experience and didn't know "how hard it is to get everyone's head in the same place," she wouldn't have attended a second meeting. She thinks the problem stems from the fact that the group represents two levels of commitment.

Reading between the lines, I suspect she and Eva want to segregate Margaret and Sarah without alienating them completely.

She had prepared an agenda to decide: (1) whether to adopt a parliamentary procedures; (2) who can vote; (3) what constitutes a majority; (4) how much should be established as a minimum monthly payment. She also had prepared a list of research projects to divide up—for example, track the careers of women employees by comparing titles in old bank telephone books with those in the current book; compare the benefits for women to those available to men; analyze the bank's internal publications and advertising for instances of bias.

At the conclusion of three sometimes acrimonious hours, it was decided that Eva and Bonnie would establish a savings account (not at Chase) and collect $20 a month from six of them. Those who pay can vote, by phone if necessary. A two-thirds majority rules.

Commitment to a monthly contribution was an implicit signal that the group would eventually file suit. Interestingly, the question of whether to sue the Chase Manhattan Bank was never explicitly brought to a vote.

April 23: Tonight's meeting was low-key, heavier on gossip than decision making.

Jane, a former employee who has already instituted a suit against Chase, was present. She would like to get others to join her suit and help defray the costs. The group was dubious about this but agreed to meet with her lawyer, Brenda Feigen Fasteau.

Jane had heard about the group through "a friend of a friend," both male, which highlights an interesting point: the women have been confiding in their male friends at the bank, thereby establishing a network of masculine allies.

Alpert, who had attempted, through a contact at the Justice Department, to have the Chase suit go directly to Justice rather than to the EEOC, sent a message through Anne that her contact had been promoted and was no longer in a position to accept cases. Their petition had been rejected by another official, who explained that since it contained no element of racial discrimination it was not of interest.

Anne also reported that a woman in an extremely sensitive post has started to feed her information and documents. She couldn't divulge her identity so the group dubbed her "Lady X."

After this announcement, the meeting degenerated. The women went around the room updating their horror stories—ostensibly, as at so many past meetings, for the benefit of a newcomer. Karen told an amusing anecdote.

She had had lunch with a friend and employee of a company located in the Chase headquarters building. Karen gave her a rundown of the collective woes of the Chase women. Afterwards, they ran into the chairman himself in the elevator and the friend asked, "David, are you aware how the women in your bank are treated?" "I assume with the utmost respect," he replied. "I think you ought to start concentrating less on respect and more on equal employment opportunity, David," she rejoined. At this point the elevator stopped, and Rockefeller exited.

No decisions were made at this meeting, which was a waste of time. I record it because it is characteristic of many such meetings that served no purpose other than to maintain continuity.

May 12: It was a circus tonight. Four newcomers showed up, which meant another recap of the group's history and legal options and another round-robin testimonial session. Of the novitiates, only Donna, who has a case pending with EEOC but no lawyer, appears committed to taking the group vows, such as they are.

Another woman, Beatrice, is not joining because the group is "too far down the road for me to have any influence," but she was a disruptive force all night. A few of the group's charter members were visibly unhappy about the wasted time tonight, and Linda walked out in disgust.

The tide had finally turned in favor of filing suit, and the group needed progress to maintain momentum—or start waning in numbers. Already the interest and commitment of the core group had begun to ebb and flow according to what took place—or didn't take place—at each meeting.

Sarah, who hadn't wanted to file unless they could put together an airtight case, abandoned this position as "unrealistic." While the reiteration of stories of unjust treatment had alienated some charter members, it reinforced in Sarah the thought that "we're not crazy; Chase is the one at fault." Also, she had been working on the Chase telephone book project and had seen quantitative evidence of the fact that "women advance slower than men."

June 3: The group has interviewed seven attorneys and still likes Judy Vladeck best. They met with her again to clarify her fee, which is negotiable at this point. Vladeck thinks they've got a good case. She's currently handling sex discrimination suits for plaintiffs at the City University of New York and General Electric.

Judy Vladeck is used to working with groups, knows the pitfalls. She will not accept a class-action discrimination suit unless the women meet the following criteria: (1) they must be a cohesive group with an organization structure; (2) they must appoint specific women to act as liaisons between herself and the group for the sake of efficiency; and (3) the women must be willing to assist on legal research. She won't accept a case on a full contingency basis, not only because she can't afford it but because payment signifies commitment.

June 10: The group touched on many issues but came to a firm decision on only one: to hire Vladeck. They discussed a letter from her summarizing a proposed retainer arrangement and outlining how she expects to proceed legally and the cooperation she expects from them.

Also discussed: individual financial pledges; other fund-raising schemes, for instance, soliciting friends and exploring foundation and feminist sources, especially women who have won large settlements in other discrimination cases; the August deadline for filing, to accommodate Renee's six-month grace period from her termination in March; who will sign the charge (five are presently committed); whether to file anonymously; how to handle publicity; and an acronym for the group (they fixed on CESAR—Chase Employees Against Sexism and Racism—until someone realized it is a man's name).

With business completed, they broke open a bottle of Taylor's champagne and toasted to: "Mother Chase, a huge settlement, and Don Perignon when we win!"

In retrospect, the group's evolution breaks down into distinct stages. By this point they have completed the following phases: a) introductory; b) consciousness-raising, gossip and misinformation; c) the correction-of-misinformation—by interviewing lawyers and linking up with NOW advisors; and d) the who-is-really-committed phase—that is, the separation of the signers from the joy riders. They are still to accomplish: e) the hiring-the-attorney phase; f) the point-of-no-return phase, when they actually file suit; and g) the going-public phase, when they hold press conferences and let the unaware world know what they have been up to.

June 18: The entire group met with Judy Vladeck in her office and put her through an hour's grilling on the subject of fees. Sarah finally apologized, "Unfortunately, we're all bankers and used to looking at the cost/benefits of all situations." Vladeck graciously allowed that sex discrimination cases are new and such financial arrangements are still evolving. "Maybe we'll set a formula that will be useful for women in the future." She asked them for a letter stating their understanding of the agreement.

The discussion turned to the procedures for researching the case. Vladeck said the first phase is educational: she wants to take a crash course on the Chase Manhattan Bank and they are to provide her with the appropriate reading material.

June 26: Tonight's session was the roughest yet. Tempers flared, sarcastic remarks were exchanged, and, periodically, people got up and paced the room. Each was trapped by her inability to either compromise or leave.

The subject was money again. Who was willing to contribute what amount for how long? They also attempted to draft a letter to Vladeck. Jane contributed to the confusion. She begged them to have their respective attorneys cooperate to avoid duplication of effort and cut down her costs.

Jane's case was filed with the New York State Division of Human Rights, an agency that Vladeck intends to bypass by obtaining a Waiver of Jurisdiction. In the end, the two cases were combined.

When the wine drinkers finally resorted to coffee to stay awake, they agreed to give up. It was the only unanimous decision all evening.

Alpert points out that women contemplating discrimination suits invariably throw up roadblocks out of fear. Because the Chase women are bankers, their roadblock took a financial form. The financial formula that they finally produced is "enormously elaborate" compared to most.

June 30: The calm after the storm. Everybody was in a quiet, conciliatory mood and they resolved all the questions left open four days earlier.

After a slight rephrasing of the letter, Eva—the group's scribe—was authorized to send it to Vladeck for approval. They elected Renee to formulate the requirements for women who want to join their suit in the future. They are concerned about new participants sharing in the monetary awards without assuming any of the financial burdens. They gave each other an assignment to write down what they, as individuals and a class, hope to gain in the way of remedies. Finally, they discussed what to do if an individual wants to settle for terms that the group finds unacceptable.

They signed a private financial agreement among themselves that a committed voting members to at least $500 per annum for four years, if necessary, except for Renee who is contributing $20 a month until she finds a job; two pledged $1,000. Those who are contributing less money are expected to do extra work on fund-raising.

They estimate that the case will take a minimum of two to three years. Linda said sardonically, "We'll be big about 1980."

July 3: Donna got a letter from EEOC deciding in her favor. EEOC found that Chase discriminated against Donna in its initial written encounter with her and later retaliated against her for protesting that treatment. The next step in her case is to conciliate with Chase, but there is a four-month EEOC backlog for that process.

July 11: The group got a letter from Vladeck formally acknowledging their financial agreement, which is a hybrid contingency-retainer arrangement. From here on, she is their official legal counselor. Bonnie offered to telephone all the other lawyers and inform them.

The group has finally discarded the rationalizations they clung to during the six-month period in which they interviewed attorneys. They were convinced that they were comparison-shopping for quality. Now, they admit that they were bargain-shopping for the best financial deal—a lawyer who would take the case purely on a contingency basis. None offered. The money issue became crucial in their minds because they felt trapped: as professional women, they were too rich for legal aid, but too poor to afford normal attorney's fees.

July 22: The group assembled in Vladeck's office to discuss evidence and strategy.

Vladeck elicited from them examples of discriminatory hiring and recruiting, salaries, promotions, transfers, training, job segregation, termination, and fringe benefits. She was amazed at some of their stories: "I've never run into many of these before. They are so exotic as to be almost unbelievable!"

She explained the mechanics of filing. Each category of discrimination must appear on a separate complaint form. Did they have at least one woman willing to sign each of the seven charges? She pointed out that those who don't have a personal grievance can still sign the employee benefits charge.

Vladeck advised Linda, who is close to a promotion, to wait. "I don't want any martyrs here," she said. "You can sign later. I'd rather have you in a higher-level position."

They discussed "going public." Although Vladeck is filing "on behalf of persons aggrieved," she warned them that she would eventually have to submit their names to EEOC, which has been known to leak such information to employers. In any event, they will have to be identified when the complaint is filed in federal court.

Eva sees two reasons for surfacing: fund-raising and to encourage other women to come forward. It's a sensitive issue and a few aren't sure they ever want their names known. They appointed a public relations committee consisting of Renee, Donna, and Dee Alpert.

The issue of going public highlighted one of the group members' continuing conflicts. They were aware that as individuals they stood to lose more than they could possibly gain from their legal action. But they were forging ahead anyway for the sake of "the cause"—to put right an injustice perpetrated on Chase women. Thus, they were caught between wanting credit for their bravery and good works and seeking shelter from the wrath of Chase.

August 6: Seven of the group—Eva, Renee, Sarah, Bonnie, Joan, Karen, and Mary—convened in Vladeck's office to sign the charges. The scene was solemn and stirring. The rebels had spent long hard months hatching their "revolution." Now they were stepping forward to sign their own symbolic Declaration of Independence.

Sarah said to Eva: "It's been a long germination period, but it looks like your baby has just been born, Eva."

Eva replied: "I hope you'll take some credit for the parentage."

Renee as usual got the last word: "Let's put in for maternity benefits!"

Epilogue: With the charges filed, the recruiting process became easier. The doubts of potential joiners appear to be lessened when the issue is clearcut: to sign or not to sign.

On November 6th Vladeck obtained from EEOC two right-to-sue letters, one for Jane, who had finally left Brenda Feigen Fasteau (over a strategy dispute) to join forces with the group, and one for Donna, whose conciliation with Chase had broken down. To avoid delay, the group is combining its suit with Jane's and Donna's.

"Lady X," who was let go from Chase, apparently in an employee cutback, emerged at a recent meeting of the group. She and two or three other present or former Chase employees plan to join the suit.

Appendix B: The Women: What We Did Right—and Wrong

MBA magazine asked the Chase women to assess their performance in the year-long development of their equal employment suit. The following, written by "Eva" with the collaboration of other group members, tells what the group learned from the experience and presents some suggestions for others contemplating a similar action.

Getting a Group Together

The women attending our initial meeting came from three areas of the bank. One person had mentioned her idea to two friends, each of whom brought two other women. The multiplier effect really works. We also found several people by confiding in trustworthy friends outside the organization and by attending meetings sponsored by feminist groups.

We thought the sheer size of the bank would prevent us from finding additional supporters in different types of jobs and departments. We were wrong.

We initially took turns meeting at each other's homes; now we use our lawyer's offices. This keeps us from drawing attention to ourselves.

Be careful about conversations at work and in public. One groups member was asked in a Chase elevator about the suit's progress by a woman who had not been able to attend several meetings. Another was about to bring a friend up to date over dinner when she realized that three people from the bank were sitting at a nearby table.

Do, however, confide in trustworthy friends. Since they are likely to be objective, they can be good sounding boards and sources of moral support. The need for confidentiality remains a serious matter. A well-meaning friend introduced one of the litigants at a party as someone involved in something interesting—the Chase suit.

We established the following procedure for introducing new people into the group: A member would make initial contact with someone she thought would be sympathetic. She would speak to the candidate only in terms of personal concern, without mentioning the group. If the woman expressed interest, she was discussed by the group. If no one objected, she was told about the group's existence and our aims and was invited to attend the next meeting.

Should your company want to discuss the matter with you, plead ignorance.

"The Women: What We Did Right—and Wrong." Jacqueline Thompson. *MBA* 9 (December 1975) no. 11, pp. 30–32. Reprinted by permission.

185

We decided that any communication would be either through or in the presence of our attorney. You are definitely protected from retaliation once you file charges with the EEOC. If you feel you are being harassed before taking official action, your ability to prove you are part of a planning group may serve to protect you.

We lost valuable time by not getting in touch with the National Organization of Women immediately. But our conversation with one of the women involved in the Bank of America suit was psychologically important. She made us very aware of what would be entailed.

Evidence and Lawyers

Take your diaries seriously. Put down by date everything even remotely related to discrimination, be it sexual innuendo, disparaging comments made about women in general, promises made and not kept, things said that angered you. Start with a personal history of everything that happened to you and people you know since you started working for your present company: salary, title, type of work, differences in how men were treated, and other matters. Create reasons for writing memos confirming indicative discussions you have had. All of the above is admissible evidence. We relied too long on our memories for a record of discriminatory acts. Now some valuable details have been lost.

Start collecting information as soon as possible. In addition to available Chase data—for instance, promotion lists, transfer announcements, and statistical reports—we found articles on other actions, settlements, and EEOC findings very helpful. Company policy manuals and telephone directories are an invaluable source of information. We managed to find copies of phone books going back for four years.

Get a copy of your company's Affirmative Action program. If they are required by law to file one, it is available from the appropriate government agency under the Freedom of Information Act.

When you're searching for a lawyer, interview several people, both men and women. Take your time and don't accept the first offer of service. Remember that this is going to be a long, close association, so be sure you can trust and confide in the person you select. Although we ended up retaining the first individual we spoke to, we spent several months seeing other attorneys as well. It was time well spent since we now feel sure we found the best person available.

Here are some of the things we asked the lawyers we interviewed: What is his or her experience with Title VII cases? Don't be afraid to check someone's track record. Would the lawyer impose a strategy, or would he or she consider your opinion? What is the best way of handling the case? There are many options available: federal vs. state or city agencies, class or individual action, and so forth. How accessible will the attorney be? Does he or she have enough time to satisfactorily handle the case? Is the firm large enough to adequately handle the scope of the case? Will much of the work be delegated to junior staff? Is the person committed to feminism or is he or she more interested in financial gain or publicity?

We also tried to assess the impact of our candidate lawyers' image. Would a radical type alienate the court or come off badly when compared to the company's battery of well-dressed conservatives?

Know from the beginning what the fee structure will be for handling your case. Are you expected to pay a retainer and cover expenses? Is it on a contingency basis? Is so, do you still have to cover expenses? How often will you be billed?

The jargon can be mind-boggling. Make sure you understand all the terminology. Don't leave before you have a clear understanding of what services will be provided at what cost. How clear is the lawyer about explaining things? Is he or she willing to do so? What is expected from you in the way of time and support?

Contact an organization such as the Council of New York Law Associates for a list of firms experienced in Title VII litigation. If such a clearinghouse for free or inexpensive legal services does not exist in your locale, the ACLU or local Legal Services/Aid organization are good alternatives, as is the local chapter of NOW. A nearby law school and university with a women's studies department may be helpful. If all else fails, a firm specializing in labor law could be helpful since there are many similarities between the two fields.

Finances

Be prepared to make a financial commitment. Even if you find a lawyer to take the case on a contingency basis, you will probably still be responsible for covering out-of-pocket expenses. We consider $5,000 per year a realistic treasury.

Start collecting money as soon as possible. It's easier for most people to come up with a small sum regularly than a lump sum. If you don't file charges, it can always be returned. These small amounts add up. If we had contributed $5 per week from the start, our bank account would now be richer by $600.

We appointed two members as co-treasurers. They set up a joint savings account in their names, listing two other women as co-beneficiaries. Make sure that at least one of your treasurers is not shy about asking people for money.

Keep accurate records. Our book has two pages per month. One lists each deposit by date and individual. The other gives a detailed rendering of expenses. We balance the account monthly. In addition, each contributor has a page where the payments are cross-referenced. Don't be afraid to ask friends for money— either in person or by letter. We got a great deal of financial support that way.

Growing Pains

We soon learned that a gradual increase in size allows for easier assimilation of each new member. We almost lost a couple of people because they thought we weren't interested in them as individuals. When a new person comes for the first time, be prepared to postpone other discussions. It's more important to win her confidence first. Take the time to listen to her story and answer her questions. Only then will she be able to contribute to broader issues.

We never really solved the problem of how to reconcile a new person's need to know us as individuals with the absolute necessity to retell individual stories and to describe the group's history. While the repetition was at times exasperating and time-consuming, we felt that handing out a written summary to new members was too impersonal.

Don't be discouraged by people who drop out. They never betrayed us. As your original group expands, encourage all to participate. We had to stop referring to the "core group." The initial members must be prepared to share control.

We decided that any binding decision had to be approved by two-thirds of the voting membership. Although everyone's opinion was always listened to, we limited the right to vote to those who made the minimum financial contribution—$20 per month before we retained our attorney and $500 per year thereafter. Also, those with voting rights had to be Chase employees.

We made exceptions. One person was unemployed; another had large medical bills to pay; a third had to support her children by herself. They retained the right to vote while paying what they could or contributing extra time.

Although we delegated specific responsibility for various projects—for example, research assignments, making appointments with attorneys, information gathering, public relations—we sometimes got slack and these tasks went undone.

At the request of our attorney, we appointed one individual coordinator for a three-month period. We rotated this assignment, which involved being liaison between our lawyer and the rest of the group, scheduling meetings, passing along other information, and so forth.

One of the most important rules was to stay flexible. We felt that our success in staying together through admittedly rough times is attributable to this. Impersonal rules were never considered more important than individual needs. We often deferred to the wishes of one individual. There is always room for compromise. We became very conscious of the need to be tuned into the way we interacted with each other.

We feel that our ability to reach decisions was dependent on several key conditions. We learned the need for diplomacy and tact—and to appreciate the viewpoints of those who held opposing opinions. We also found that we had to back off and start again when we reached an impasse. We tried to reach at least one decision a meeting, even if it was only to set a date for the next meeting.

We didn't force anyone to come to decisions prematurely. If a woman was undecided about joining our suit, no one tried to pressure her. Basically, we accepted people on their own terms. As long as a woman wanted to remain with the group, she was always welcome. Several somen attended meetings for months before they decided to become fully committed to the group's objectives.

Appendix C: The Women: Who They Are and Why They're Suing

The women profiled below form the core of the group of women who have brought suit against the Chase Manhattan Bank. Seven of them signed the charges filed with EEOC. They are listed in the order of their appearance in the diary. Their names and identities have been disguised to preserve their anonymity.

Eva is a 31-year-old Bryn Mawr math major who joined the bank with seven years previous professional experience. Chase offered her a $12,500 starting salary as a lending officer trainee while inexperienced MBAs five years her junior got $17,000.

After graduating from the commercial credit training program at the top of her class, she got a staff rather than line assignment. Repeated efforts to obtain a transfer have been unavailing.

Her articulateness and strong personality made her a leader of the group, which she helped organize. "I feel that if you have an opportunity to do something about a problem and pass it up, you lose the right to complain," she says.

Joan is a 29-year-old Barnard economics major who was recently promoted to branch manager in Queens after seven years with Chase. She bitterly compares her progress with that of a male friend from Rutgers who joined the bank with her. While he was encouraged to enter the more prestigious 18-month commercial lending training program, she was shunted into the two-year community bank program. By 1970, he was an assistant treasurer in the Asia banking group while she was still a non-titled assistant manager in a branch office in Manhattan. Today, he is a vice president working in Japan.

She joined the group because, "on a personal and emotional level, I resent the way I've been treated and I don't want other women to go through the same thing."

Linda is a 29-year-old black alumna of Stanford University, who is still waiting for a job assignment 16 months after graduating from the commercial credit training program. She joined the group because "I'm angry about promises that never materialize and sick of women who sit around and complain but won't do it where it counts."

Valerie is a 27-year-old Brazilian specialist. Armed with a degree in Latin American studies and a master's from Columbia University's School of International Affairs, she joined Chase as an administrative assistant in the Western Hemisphere banking group, after being assured that she would deal directly with

"The Women: Who They Are and Why They're Suing," Jacqueline A. Thompson, *MBA* 9 (December 1975) no. 11, pp. 19–29. Reprinted by permission.

clients and be promoted quickly. Instead, she says, she found herself tracing missing letters of credit and making dinner reservations for officers and South American customers. It took 6 months for her to discover that she was qualified for the commercial credit training program and another 18 months and a number of well-aimed threats to gain admission.

She joined the group while she was awaiting a job assignment. "Chase may try to project a progressive image," she says, "but the people here are deceitful and hypocritical. I have been lied to right down the line, starting with the Chase recruiter."

Karen is a 26-year-old accountant in the corporate financial controls department. A graduate of Hofstra University, she came to the bank via a Big Eight accounting firm. She claims that it took her twice as long to get a title as a male colleague whose previous work experience was shorter and inferior to hers.

On her first day at Chase, she felt she had regressed to the days when she was working her way through college as a part-time secretary. "It was a blow to me after my last job, where I was treated with respect as an equal."

Sarah, a graduate of Ohio State, is a 32-year-old officer in the college placement department who recruits for the credit training program. Although satisfied with her own status at the bank, she sympathizes with her disillusioned coworkers.

"In the beginning, I was convinced we could work from inside rather than go to the courts. I came around when I saw how our individual lobbying efforts got us nowhere except in trouble."

Bonnie is a 25-year-old trust offiicer and the only woman managing a pension portfolio. She attributes her good fortune to her boss's wife, who is an active feminist "and wouldn't let him come home at night if he didn't give women a fair break." Although she doesn't have a personal grievance, she wants to see Chase and every other major corporation change.

Anne is a 30-year-old economist with an MBA in international finance and solid professional experience working in the Far East. She was once vice president of the National Organization of Women's New York chapter and had a discrimination suit pending against her former employer, a Chase client, when the bank hired her.

According to Anne, the bank initially rejected her application for employment because her suit indicated she would make an "undesirable" employee. The female executive recruiter who had acted as intermediary wrote Anne a letter in which she stated the bank's position, a clear violation of Title VII of the 1964 Civil Rights Act. Chase heard about the letter and threatened to sever business relations with the recruiter, who is extremely reputable and well-known, unless she withdrew her statements. She refused and the bank never carried out its threat.

Anne says that Chase felt compelled to hire her but retaliated by assigning her low-level chores. She quit after she was assigned to another economist, who, she felt, treated her like a gal Friday. She is currently chief economist in the overseas branch of a major airline.

Renee, a 28-year-old secretary, is divorced with one child and holds a master's degree in fine arts and credits toward two other advanced degrees. She was hired with the promise of an early promotion. She says that her continued efforts over a three-year period to get that elusive promotion netted her nothing but humiliation, frustration, and a personnel file that marked her as a troublemaker.

She was fired in March '75 because she took "too much time off to care for her sick child," while a male officer in her department was absent three times as often for the same reason and, unlike her, was not required to count it as vacation.

She joined the group because "I hate Chase Manhattan Bank. Look what it's done to me. Chase has negated me as a person with a mind and feelings. It really galls me that outsiders think Chase is a model corporation."

Margaret, a 45-year-old widow with three children, was promoted to stock transfer officer, she says, after 15 years of filing stock certificates and getting coffee for her male superiors, many of whom she trained when they entered the department.

Although she thinks Chase discriminates against women generally, she believes that her laggard career there was her own fault. "I didn't press for a better job all those years when my husband was alive."

Mary is a 22-year-old teller who works in Joan's branch in Queens. She is unsure of her own career plans at the bank, but resents the possibility that there may be few options open to her. She joined the group because she admires Joan and doesn't believe "in having principles unless you are going to live up to them, idealistic as that may sound."

Jane was a personnel counselor (master's in sociology and three years' professional experience) until she was fired, a month after she had informed Chairman David Rockefeller and another Chase official by letter that she had lodged a formal charge with the New York State Division of Human Rights. She maintains that she was denied transfer to a more responsible position, having trained a 63-year-old man with a high school diploma who later became her supervisor.

Although she continued to pursue her own suit, she came to the group's meetings "so I don't feel so alone in my fight."

Donna, a 28-year-old urban affairs major, filed an EEOC charge against Chase in 1973 alleging that her application for employment was ignored due to her sex.

She gave her resume, which uses initials for her first and middle names, to a friend at the bank whose boss sent it on to the personnel department with a note attached indicating Donna's gender. She got no reply, so her friend sent a second resume to the personnel department, this time without a covering note. A comedy of errors ensued. First, Donna received a letter addressed to "Ms" which said there were no jobs available. Shortly thereafter, she got another letter, addressed to 'Mr.," requesting an interview.

A NOW official confronted Chase's affirmative action officer with the discrepancy. He brushed it off as a mere "clerical error." During Donna's nine subsequent interviews, she was told that she was more suited for the community bank training program, than the commercial credit program that she preferred. She was never offered a job.

Beatrice is a CPA in her forties who attended just one meeting. While her degree would seem to have prepared Beatrice for a financial position with the bank, she was in fact an administrative assistant, a glorified title for a secretary, in the trust department.

Her complaint against the bank spanned virtually its entire relationship with her: the hiring, training, promotion, and ultimately firing of Beatrice. She claimed that she put together a program for more efficiently handling paperwork in the department, which her boss then instituted. She was doubly wronged, she claims, by the fact that she never got credit for the program and was fired shortly thereafter. Why? Because, she says, she was a threat to her boss.

Index

About the Authors

Laurie Larwood is a professor of psychology at Claremont Men's College (coeducational) and of business administration at Claremont Graduate School. She obtained the Ph.D. from Tulane University in 1974. Her research and previous publications include investigations of women in working settings, pay systems, and perceptual planning biases. Before returning to academia, she was president of a small manufacturer. She presently serves as an industrial and personnel consultant and is a member of the Los Angeles Advisory Council for the U.S. Small Business Administration. Dr. Larwood is Chairperson of the Status of Women Interest Group of the Academy of Management.

Marion M. Wood is currently a professor of communication at the University of Southern California. In business for over 20 years, her career began at the advertising firm of Batten, Barton, Durstine, and Osborn. Later, she received the Ph.D. at the University of Illinois, and returned to business as a system scientist at Technomics, a research and development firm. Since joining USC, Dr. Wood's research has focused on the achievement motivation of women managers. Her consulting work has included business workshops for women and men, and communication problems arising from changing sex roles in the working environment.